Special Libraries and Information Centers: An Introductory Text

Second Edition

Ellis Mount, Adjunct Research Scholar
School of Library Service
Columbia University

Special Libraries Association
Washington, D.C.

Library of Congress Cataloging-in-Publication Data

Mount, Ellis.
    Special Libraries and Information Centers: an Introductory Text/Ellis Mount. —2nd ed.
        p.   cm.
    Includes bibliographical references and index.
    ISBN 0-87111-354-6
        1. Libraries, Special.   2. Information services.   3. Information science.
4. Library science.   I. Title
        Z675.A2M65   1991
        025.5'276—dc20

Cover photo courtesy of Cargill Information Center, Minneapolis, Minnesota

Preface

Over the years, thousands of graduates of schools of library science and information science have taken positions in special libraries and information centers. Many of them found that completion of a course devoted to the nature of these organizations proved to be an important factor in the degree of success achieved in their work.

The primary purpose of this book is to serve as a textbook for courses dealing with special libraries and information centers; it describes their modes of operation, their collections, their services, their staffing, and their physical facilities. In addition this book should also be helpful to experienced librarians and other information professionals who are contemplating switching their employment to special libraries and information centers from other positions.

This edition has retained the same general outline of chapters used in the first edition, but considerable updating has been made in many chapters, particularly in those areas which have been subject to rapid changes in the period since the first edition was published. One such chapter involves recent developments in information technology. Two new chapters have been added, one devoted to descriptions of actual operations in several typical special libraries and information centers. The other chapter covers the techniques and experiences involved in getting a job in a special library or information center.

An effort has been made to cite references that provide additional information about topics worthy of further study. Where possible, citations were chosen from books and journals that are apt to be relatively accessible to the average student.

This edition has retained a section devoted to descriptions of different types of special libraries and information centers; all such examples are new, as is the description of the planning and floor plans for an outstanding special library. I am indebted to the authors of those sections as listed in the table of contents; their cooperation was most gratifying.

I also am very grateful to Victoria Dawson for reading the entire manuscript and making many helpful suggestions; thanks are also due to numerous others who were called on for advice. Once again I thank members of my family for their support and interest in the project.

Ellis Mount

Contents

A.   Associations as Sponsors

American Association of Advertising Agencies, Inc.
Marsha C. Appel

B.   Not-for-Profit Organizations

Columbia University, Biological Sciences Library
Kathleen Kehoe

The University Club Library
Andrew J. Berner

Whitney Museum Library
May Castleberry

Wisconsin Regional Primate Research Center
Lawrence Jacobsen

C. For-Profit Organizations

AT&T Bell Laboratories Libraries and Information Systems
Center
Joseph A. Canose

Booz, Allen Research Services
Robin Blumenthal and Richard Willner

Chevron Research and Technology Company
Jacqueline J. Desoer

Daiwa Securities America Inc. Reference Library
Susan M. Gormley

Federal National Mortgage Association
Eileen E. Rourke

Jones, Day, Reavis & Pogue
Joan E. Jarosek

Newsweek Editorial Library
Peter Salber and Ted Slate

Royal Bank of Canada Information Resources
Jane I. Dysart

Richard Drezen

Part 1

Special Libraries and Information Centers: An Overview

Chapter 1 describes some of the chief characteristics of special libraries and information centers, including the features distinguishing them from other types of libraries. This chapter presents a brief description of major features, including history, size, and operation.

Chapter 2 expands upon the activities of typical special libraries and information centers. A brief comparison of two kinds of organizations is also included.

The basic nature of information, a subject which needs to be stressed in a book written for information professionals, is covered in Chapter 3, which briefly touches on such topics as the handling, communication, and retrieval of information.

Chapter 1

The Nature of Special Libraries and Information Centers

Not everyone has heard of special libraries or information centers. Of those who have, many of these persons, including some information professionals, would have difficulty defining the words creditably. Yet these organizations play a major role in the world of information activities; they offer challenging, rewarding careers to thousands of people. This chapter will describe the basic features of special libraries and information centers and show how they differ from other libraries and from each other.

Definitions

The literature contains many definitions of special libraries and information centers. Some writers use collection sizes as a means of identification; others choose the relative narrowness of the fields of interest, staff size, or perhaps the traditional emphasis on personalized service. While all of these aspects can be considered as some of the characteristics of special libraries and information centers, many writers on the subject have accepted other means of identification.

Special Libraries. In this book special libraries are defined as those information organizations sponsored by private companies, government agencies, not-for-profit organizations, or professional associations. Subject specialty units in public and academic libraries are usually labeled as special libraries as well. Thus a special library could be sponsored by the ABC Corporation, or by the Department of Labor in a particular state, or by the XYZ Museum of Art, or an association of insurance agents. A business library at a university or the science branch of a large public library could also be called a special library.

Information Centers. It is more difficult to find a widely accepted definition of an information center. Originally information centers were defined as those organizations in which user services invariably involved a deeper understanding of the subject areas of the sponsoring agency than would be the case in the average special library. Inquiries at the traditional information center were apt to be more complex than in a special library. The staff was often called upon to be deeply involved in the interpretation of information, which usually meant a stronger educational background was required than was needed in the average special library.

While little indicates the exact year in which information centers first began to appear, many writers contend that this occurred during World War II, a period in which private scientific and technical laboratories and government agencies began to require more training and a higher level of service from their special libraries. These information agencies, sometimes called information analysis centers, grew in popularity in succeeding years. A simple description of them is that they are special libraries with a very narrow scope, a special sort of special library. For example, a center devoted to the properties and uses of one particular metal would probably be legitimately called an information center if the level of analysis and retrieval also met the standards mentioned above.

Comparison of Special Libraries and Information Centers.   An article by Garvin compares the two types of organizations and perceives their roles as complementary, not competitive.[1] A similar paper by Douville contains a lengthy review of the literature on the subject.[2]

Because of the present-day similarity between goals and operations of special libraries and those of information centers, for the sake of simplicity the term "special library" in this book can be taken to include "information center" unless specific differences exist, in which case it will be made clear which type of organization is being discussed.

Chapter 2 contains a more detailed description of the operation of special libraries and information centers, citing several papers that describe actual examples of several subject areas. For further information, Appendix 1 contains a dozen or more manager-written descriptions of the operations and characteristics of outstanding libraries and centers.

Characteristics

Although many similarities exist among all special libraries located, it is difficult to name, categorically, numerous characteristics that are common to all of them. Therefore the reader should be aware that this chapter seeks to list the features of the "average" special library or information center.

Organizational Names.   Many names for these units are in general use, only some of which are listed below:

Libraries	Information Centers
Business Library	Information Analysis Center
Corporate Library	Information Service
Editorial Library	Library and Information Service
Research Library	Technical Information Service
Technical Library	Technical Information Office

Of course, many more examples could be given. Do not put too much stock in names, however. No matter what they are called, special libraries sometimes have rather misleading names. For this reason one cannot judge the quality of service an organization is getting simply by considering the name of its information unit.

An "information-analysis center" might not in reality come close to providing the types of services associated with that title.

Keep in mind, too, that several special libraries may exist within one setting; you may be aware of only one. For example, a large manufacturing company might have a corporate library in its main headquarters, probably concentrating on business and finance. That same building might also house its legal library. The company might also have several laboratories and factories, each with its own technical library. Some corporations have enough separate libraries and information centers to have formed their own networks that hold occasional meetings and develop cooperative projects.

On the average, however, one library per sponsoring organization is the norm. Such units must be able to supply the needs of a wider group of individuals than is usually the case in multi-library organizations.

Size. The two most common means of describing the sizes of libraries are in terms of the extent of staff and collection size. While these measures are far from adequate for giving a detailed analysis of a given organization, they are relatively easy to use in comparisons.

One of the best sources of information on the size of special-library staffs is the periodic salary survey conducted by the Special Libraries Association (SLA).[3] The survey taken in 1988 showed that out of some 4,100 responses from SLA members in the United States and Canada, 22 percent of the special librarians supervised no one. Approximately 27 percent supervised one or two persons; thus nearly half (49 percent) of the participants supervised two or fewer people. At the "high" end, only 3 percent supervised over 20 people. It is apparent that special libraries have small staffs compared to public or academic libraries, where it is not uncommon to have hundreds of staff members.

Sizes of collections also vary. Special libraries and information centers tend to concentrate on a rather narrow range of subjects. For example, a library sponsored by a bank might have only a few thousand books, but they would be concerned chiefly with banking and finance. Collections in academic and large public libraries might contain tens of thousands of books on business, but the bank library would probably excel in the field of banking. A typical special library also depends heavily on subscriptions to journals; again a special library in a bank may have a better collection of serials on its subjects of greatest interest than large general business collections.

Still another feature of special library collections is reliance on non-book materials, such as newspaper clippings, technical reports, slides, annual company reports, and a host of other materials not commonly present to any extent in general collections. So it is difficult to estimate the worth of special libraries simply by considering only the number of items they contain.

Services Offered. A tradition of most special libraries and information centers is that their staffs routinely provide excellent service to their clients. Staff members live up to the SLA motto ("Putting knowledge to work"). For example, these organizations have an outstanding record in finding hard-to-locate information; they do not give up easily during difficult searches. In some cases staff members may take on assignments that might seem out of scope to a librarian accustomed to other types of libraries. For instance, helping a top executive write a speech is not considered unusual. Thinking of clever ways to obtain information quickly is often a routine process in such organizations. Tradition of staff capabilities may be among the several reasons for this high level of service; these and other points will be discussed more fully in Part III.

Typical staff members of special libraries usually get fully immersed in the activities and goals of the sponsoring organization. New ideas are turned into research projects, often resulting in valuable products or important advancements in a particular field. Such progress results from teamwork between the library and its clients. This absorption of the staff members into the fabric of the sponsoring organization, whether a museum, corporation, or government agency, makes it imperative that prospective employees feel sure they can give wholehearted support to the work and the goals of the organization before accepting work there. For example, someone who is indifferent to the world of art might find employment in an art museum library less than satisfying; such a person would be better off finding a job in an area of personal interest.

Salaries. The SLA salary survey previously mentioned is conducted annually, with greater depth now provided every second year, since the triennial survey was replaced in 1990 by a biennial survey, thus providing in-depth data more frequently.[4] The biennial survey not only shows mean and median salaries for the total population studied but breaks down the figures into several categories, such as time on the job, type of employer, subject area, effects of geography, and number of people supervised. The 1988 survey shows that the mean salary for SLA members more than tripled from 1970 to 1988, representing an increase of 214 percent. During that time the consumer price index increased 201.5 percent. Thus salaries in special libraries are more than keeping up with inflation.

How do salaries in special libraries compare with those in other types of libraries? A salary survey of 1987 library school graduates on their first job after graduation shows that the median salaries paid by special libraries that year were from two to three thousand dollars more than medians in public and academic libraries.[5] On the other hand, school libraries' median salaries exceeded those paid by special libraries by a few hundred dollars.

For many years pay for women staff members averaged less than men's salaries, but the 1987 figures show that average salaries in special libraries were slightly higher for women than for men; it should be noted that special libraries were the only type of library that year in which men's salaries were not higher than women's.

Relations with Top Management. Unlike academic and public libraries, most special libraries exist because the sponsoring organization (a company, a not-for-profit organization, or a government agency) has seen the need for maintaining a special library. No law requires that these groups have a library, whereas public and academic libraries are almost always maintained because some important document requires them—it might be the guidelines of educational accrediting groups, or a state law—that may specify the type of library service to be offered.

Special libraries thus are vulnerable to changes of outlook about library service when different people occupy top management positions or as economic conditions dictate belt-tightening in an organization. Certainly the best protection a special library can have against budget reductions and staff cutbacks is a record of being so valuable to the organization that strong opposition would arise among other employees if such cutbacks were contemplated. More will be found on this topic in Chapter 5.

Duties of Professionals. Many special libraries have only one professional on the staff; many others have no more than two or three. In either case, the background of special librarians should be broad enough to allow them to perform a wide range of duties, from reference work to cataloging to management. The smaller the staff, the more important it is that the professionals be versatile enough to function well in all phases of the work.

In larger special libraries, more specialization is possible, with positions concerned with only one phase of the work, such as translation, or systems design, or bibliographic instruction for clients.

Librarians aren't always the only staff members of special libraries. The number of paraprofessionals and clerical workers varies from one library to the next. Of course, a shortage of such employees usually means the professionals have to perform more of that level of work than is cost-effective—a professional may type a report in an emergency but having to devote many hours a week to it would be a waste of talent.

History and Development

The history of special libraries in the United States can be traced to 1777 if one includes the Army library at the Military Academy, which contained materials on engineering and military technology at that time, according to a paper by Kadec and Watts.[6] Their article, part of a history of science and technology libraries, pointed out that the collection became a formal library in 1812. Other early libraries sponsored by government agencies include that of the Department of State, founded in 1787.

Specialized library units at colleges and universities have a rather indistinct history, but collections on science and engineering topics at these schools had to have existed at least as early as the 1830s, when what is now Rensselaer Polytechnic Institute began offering civil engineering courses. No doubt formal libraries on college campuses were not created until many years later. As for special departments in public libraries, we know that as early as 1826 George Ticknor proposed that various libraries in Boston that were devoted to architecture, medicine, and science be combined to form the Boston Public Library. Thus such libraries existed in the 1820s.[7]

Libraries serving commercial firms appeared later. The study by Kruzas shows that by 1880 approximately a dozen company libraries existed in this country, although a few scattered special libraries had been established before then (such as the New York Chamber of Commerce Library, founded prior to the 1850s, or the Silk Association Library, established in 1872).[8] The growth of special libraries was undoubtedly aided by the formation of the Special Libraries Association in 1909; it began with a handful of members and gradually expanded to its present size of approximately 12,000 members.

Information centers, on the other hand, are relatively new organizations, with the earliest ones formed in the 1940s, primarily created to provide very specialized service to support research and development in government and private laboratories. Over the years the nature of information services has gradually changed; the period in which information centers were quite different from special libraries has changed to the present environment in which the distinctions have become increasingly blurred.

Regardless of labels, the development of information services is a dynamic process, not a static one. The creation of innovative services, including new ways of aiding clients and establishing flexible goals, has resulted from the constant efforts of information professionals to keep abreast of the times.

Number of Special Libraries and Information Centers

Because of the differences of opinion as to what constitutes a special library or information center, it is not surprising that directories and surveys of the numbers of such organizations are not consistent, frequently showing rather large differences of numbers.

The well-known *American Library Directory* for 1988/89 states that there are 9,950 special libraries in the United States and 1,231 in Canada, for a total of 11,181.[9] This "total includes all law, medical, religious, business, and other special libraries regardless of who operates them." On the other hand the *Directory of Special Libraries and Information Centers* in its 12th edition in 1989 reported a total of 18,800; however, this total includes some units outside the United States.[10] Certainly, counting special libraries and information centers is still an inexact science and probably always will be. A related directory to the last-named title is *Subject Directory of Special Libraries and Information Centers*.[11] It enables one to determine the number of organizations dealing with particular subject fields, often an important bit of information.

Types of Information Professionals

A similar topic is that of identifying the information professionals working in various types of units. Many directories have provided brief biographical sketches of such people; these were not limited to any one type of organization. Now there is a directory available which lists all types of information professionals, including those employed in special libraries and information centers. Entitled *Directory of Library & Information Professionals*, it is a useful resource for data on individuals.[12] Yet another valuable tool for identifying special librarians is the annual SLA membership directory, *Who's Who in Special Libraries*.[13] Similarly, the membership list of the American Society for Information Science is also useful.[14]

Those desiring information about special libraries on a global basis are referred to the *World Guide to Special Libraries*, which lists over 35,000 libraries in 160 countries.[15]

Comparison with Public Libraries

Considerable differences exist between special and public libraries. For example, public libraries are supported by taxes and are under legal requirements to serve all sectors of the public. Special libraries are obligated to serve primarily the members or employees of their sponsors. Any service to other people is subject to the policies of the sponsors. Thus, a special library may be restricted to serving outsiders only in unusual circumstances, such as loaning material not available elsewhere in its locality to scholars or to those with major needs. Special librarians, while appreciative of the value of cooperative projects, may be bound by internal policies as to how far they can go in this service area.

Public libraries serve many users, from a few hundred people in a small town to millions in large cities. In most cases only a small percentage of a library's potential patrons ever use it; only a few of these patrons appear regularly. It is thus difficult for staff members to become familiar with the interests and information needs of their patrons. By contrast, special libraries generally serve small groups whose employment status or membership in professional organizations makes them a relatively stable set of library users and whose interests can be more readily learned by the staff.

The smaller numbers served by special libraries make it more feasible for them to provide expensive, tailor-made services, which most tax-supported libraries could not offer, given the many patrons they must legally serve. Another difference is the broad subject scope of public libraries' collections compared to those of special libraries, whose narrow interests and frequent lack of space usually make it necessary for them to collect only in a few key subjects. A public library is obliged to collect widely, aiming at serving all sectors of the public's interests. Even subject-oriented departments in a public library (such as a business section) must collect more widely than special libraries serving a business, such as a bank, an insurance company, or an advertising agency.

Staff positions in public libraries are not immune from occasional stringent staff budget cutbacks, as could be the case with special libraries in certain organizations that find themselves in precarious economic positions. However, both types of libraries provide steady employment in most cases. Special librarians generally earn more than many public librarians; nevertheless, large public libraries offer greater opportunity for internal advancement because of their larger staffs. Large public libraries usually offer liberal vacation policies as well. Special librarians generally must move from one library to another to advance.

Comparison with Academic Libraries

Most college libraries and all university libraries have a potential set of students and faculty users that numbers in the thousands or tens of thousands, a situation quite unlike that in special libraries. Thus, academic libraries have larger budgets, more employees, larger facilities, and bigger collections.

A main difference between the two types of libraries is that academic libraries are primarily established to support education, which usually includes a certain amount of research. While faculty members are free to make certain demands on the library for aid to their research, graduate and undergraduate students cannot ask for the same support since they must do their own work. In special libraries the emphasis is on serving all users to the fullest extent. Special librarians are generally more aware of the research and project activities of their users than the average academic library staff for a variety of reasons.

Academic libraries may be subject to budgetary fluctuations, but will never be eliminated because the requirements of accreditation boards establish certain minimum levels of library service. Special libraries, however, are dependent on the decisions of top management for the extent of funding they receive. Academic libraries generally have more freedom of participation in networks and consortia than special libraries, although this condition is gradually changing.

As in public libraries, the collections of academic libraries are more broad in scope than those of special libraries for essentially the same reasons. As for salaries, job security, vacations, and promotions, the comments made in the previous section on public libraries all generally apply to academic libraries.

Additional Readings

The reader will find a considerable body of literature on special libraries and information centers. Some of the references in the following list, such as those in the "General Summaries" section, provide a collection of papers on many topics of interest.[16,17,18] The list of periodicals in the next section identifies titles highly recommended for regular examination by the reader, namely *Special Libraries* and the two titles published by the American Society for Information Science.[19,20,21]

Appendix 1 contains descriptions of a dozen or so outstanding examples of special libraries and information centers. They give the reader an insight into the nature of actual units that specialize in a variety of subject areas, representing a range of collection and staff sizes.

Appendix 2 consists of a listing of books and periodical articles that delve more deeply into topics than the scope of the individual chapters of this book permits. Appendix 3 consists of an account of the planning of an outstanding corporate special library.

References

Features of Special Libraries and Information Centers

1. Garvin, David. The information analysis center and the library. *Special Libraries*. 62(1): 17-23; 1971 Jan.

    Reviews the services and functions of information analysis centers and compares them to special libraries. Discusses their relationship to each other.

2.   Douville, Judith A. Technical information centers: specialized services to science and technology. *Journal of the American Society for Information Science*. 23(3): 176-184; 1972 May/June.

     Points out the need for cooperation between special libraries and information centers. Cites 75 pertinent articles.

3.   *SLA triennial salary survey 1989*. Washington, DC: Special Libraries Association; 1988. 72 p.

     Provided 78 tables of data for comparisons of salaries in different jobs, various sizes of libraries, and many geographical areas in the United States and Canada.

4.   *Ibid.*

5.   Learmont, Carol L.; Van Houten, Stephen. Placements and salaries 1988: the demand increases. *Library Journal*. 114(17): 37-44; 1989 Oct. 15.

     An annual feature, surveying all ALA-accredited library schools in the U.S. and Canada. Provides many alternative ways of analyzing the data, such as effects of experience, or areas of the U.S. versus Canada.

Historical Information

6.   Kadec, Sarah Thomas; Watts, Carol B. Scientific and technical libraries in the Federal Government: one hundred years of service, *Science & Technology Libraries*. 8(1): 35-49; 1987 Fall.

     One of several articles in the issue, which traces the development of sci-tech libraries over the past 100 years. Other papers covered the history of public, academic, and corporate sci-tech libraries. This one traces developments since 1777.

7.   Piety, Jean; Ward, Evelyn M. Science and technology departments in public libraries: a review of the past century. *Science & Technology Libraries*. 8(1): 17-33; 1987 Fall.

     Traces the development of sci-tech departments in public libraries, starting roughly with the turn of the century in Pittsburgh, Providence, and Newark, to name a few of the earliest examples. The account continues up to the present.

8.   Kruzas, Anthony T. *Business and industrial libraries in the United States: 1820-1940*. New York: Special Libraries Association; 1965. 133 p.

     A valuable source of information about the development of special libraries over a lengthy time period.

Directories

9.   *American Library Directory 1989-90*. 42d ed. New York: Bowker; 1988.

     This annual directory lists all types of libraries in the United States and Canada, arranged by state or province, then by library name. There is a separate index by library name.

10. *Directory of Special Libraries and Information Centers*. 12th ed. Detroit: Gale Research; 1989. 3 vols. plus supplements.

A very useful directory for North American libraries and information centers. Arranged by library name, the directory has separate indexes by geographical area, subjects, and persons listed as staff members. Includes such extras as a list of depository libraries for U.S. documents and for UN documents.

11. *Subject Directory of Special Libraries and Information Centers.* 11th ed. Detroit: Gale Research; 1988. 5 vols. Biennial.

Lists some 17,500 libraries and information centers in the United States and Canada. Arranged by broad category, then by title. Each volume contains its own subject and title indexes. Volumes are divided as follows: Business/Law, Education & Information Science, Health Sciences, Social Sciences & Humanities, Science & Engineering.

12. *Directory of library & information professionals.* Woodbridge, CT: Research Publications; 1988. 2 vols.

Contains sketches on some 43,000 individuals. Arranged by surnames, also by specialty (if any), and by geographical location.

13. *Who's Who in Special Libraries 1990-1991.* Washington, DC: Special Libraries Association; 1990. 298 p.

The official SLA membership directory. It lists some 12,000 members by name, with additional indexes arranged by geographical area, subject interests, local chapter affiliations, and place of employment. An invaluable reference source.

14. *ASIS handbook and directory.* Washington, DC: American Society for Information Science; 1990. 137 p.

Provides an alphabetical listing of ASIS members, along with memberships of the subject interest groups and local chapters.

15. *World guide to special libraries.* 2d ed. New York: Saur; 1989. 1,200 p. Edited by Helga Lengenfelder.

Arranged by broad category, such as humanities or science & technology, then by country and city. Lists over 35,000 libraries. Gives library name, telephone number, number of volumes, and periodical subscriptions, date formed, name of head, etc.

General Summaries

16. Ahrensfeld, Janet L.; Christianson, Elin B.; King, David E. *Special libraries: a guide for management.* 2d ed. rev. Washington, D.C.: Special Libraries Association; 1986. 75 p.

Originally designed to inform members of management about the nature of special libraries, this compact summary of the field has proved to be helpful to students and practitioners as well. It describes the nature of special libraries, their operation, and their value to sponsoring organizations.

17. Christianson, Elin B. Special libraries. In: *ALA world encyclopedia of library and information services.* 2d ed. Chicago: American Library Association; 1986: p. 772-782.

An excellent summary of the nature of special libraries and special librarianship. Well written and informative.

18. Jackson, Eugene B., ed. *Special librarianship: a new reader.* Metuchen, NJ: Scarecrow; 1980. 759 p.

A selection of seventy papers that covers all aspects of special librarianship, including management, marketing and more general information. Includes several papers that have become classics in the field.

Periodicals

19. *Special Libraries*. Washington, DC: Special Libraries Association; 1910-present. Quarterly.

The official SLA journal. It contains papers on pertinent topics, news about the Association, book reviews, and general news items. Invaluable reading for special librarians.

20. *Journal of the American Society for Information Science*. Washington, DC: American Society for Information Science; 1950-present.

The official journal of ASIS, featuring papers and book reviews.

21. *Bulletin of the American Society for Information Science*. Washington, DC: ASIS; 1974-present. Bimonthly.

Contains short articles, news items about ASIS, and capsule reports on various informational activities.

Chapter 2

Typical Special Libraries and Information Centers in Action

In the previous chapter a brief description was given of the characteristics of the average special library and information center. To enlarge upon that chapter, and perhaps provide a better picture of these organizations at work, this chapter presents descriptions of what goes on in several actual special libraries and information centers. They are typical of many other units.

The chapter also expands on a topic touched on in Chapter 1, namely a comparison of special libraries and information centers.

Special Libraries Compared with Information Centers

As mentioned in the previous chapter, it is not easy to differentiate between special libraries and information centers. They are usually both sponsored by the same kinds of organizations, notably for-profit groups or government agencies, with a few professional organizations also represented. They both aim at giving personalized service to their clients, and their collections tend to be rather narrow in scope.

In recent years the distinctions between the two types of organizations have become blurred. Perhaps the level of skill of the average special library has increased and demands upon the staff made more complex. Theoretically, present-day information centers should have the same characteristics and standards as the original group of such organizations to warrant the use of that name, but in actual practice this hasn't always held true.

Some organizations have named their information unit as an information center for little reason; perhaps the term sounded better to certain executives than "special library." So one organization's special library may give the same service as another organization's information center. Some writers, including White, have taken the position that the differences between the two names are so slight that the name used is no longer a matter of great importance.[1] However, other librarians have described in considerable detail how their information centers differ from special libraries. It is clear there are differences of opinion in the literature about the extent to which these two types of information units vary from each other.

A recent survey of some 80 business firms, chosen from a list of the top 500 corporations, revealed some interesting facts.[2] The book, compiled by Brimsek, lists findings in such diverse activities as handling of overhead costs to ways of charging clients for costs, along with data about librarians and their backgrounds. All aspects of library/information center activities are included, ranging from management to collection development. The volume includes the final report of the SLA President's Task Force on the Value of the Information Professional, prepared in 1987. It cites numerous examples of the benefits provided by corporate information services.

The following section contains descriptions of the operation of typical units, which represent modern practices, whether one calls them information centers or special libraries. The section cites one paper which describes information analysis centers, which do stand out as differing from special libraries.

Typical Special Libraries and Information Centers

A paper by Thury describes changes in seven corporate information units which have provided managements with specialized services that the librarians involved felt were not possible in the special libraries maintained in these companies.[3] In one example a special library for an oil company was merged with an information unit that had been established for the public relations department. The merged unit became known as the company information center, with a staff expanded from one professional and three others to six professionals and eight clerical workers. In terms of services, the center enlarged the scope of a daily set of two newsletters, both of which added to newspaper articles the selected clippings from newsletters and wire services, delivered daily to some 3,000 middle and top managers. Other new services included monitoring network and PBS television programs, leading to an analysis of their content.

Thury's article also describes a bank library which began to emphasize current awareness service for employees; it developed a weekly abstracting service that covered 1,600 periodicals as well as a personalized alerting service for managers. For example, a newspaper article about certain developments in the economy would be sent to a vice president in charge of operations and planning; this is done extensively for managers.

In another bank the information center has become heavily involved in training, distributing packages of workbooks and cassettes for learning foreign languages as well as bank-related courses on such topics as analysis of financial statements. The information center was chosen for this role because it was perceived as being knowledgeable about organizing and distributing information. Still others of its training duties involve handling materials for courses offered by the American Institute of Banking. A third bank information center is responsible for coordinating the creation of research reports on particular industries. Its director, now a vice president in the bank, supervises the work of writers and graphics personnel in preparing the special studies.

A paper by Rothschild describes information analysis centers operated by the Department of Defense.[4] All of the twenty-one units she discusses serve scientific and technical agencies involved in such programs as high-temperature materials, reliability analysis, coastal engineering, and soil mechanics. The centers must not only analyze the global outpouring of sci-tech data but must also create new information products. They produce handbooks, manuals, symposium proceedings, and journals, all of which require a staff of engineers and scientists as well as information professionals. Rothschild states that in the Department of Defense the libraries are expected to handle circulation of materials, perform bibliographic searches, and provide other reference services, whereas the information analysis centers are designed "to produce authoritative technical information in their specialized fields."

Activities in two corporate settings are discussed in the paper by Willard and Morrison, who describe a fifty-year-old conventional library (or information center) and a three-year-old one-person library.[5] In both cases the authors found many differences between corporate units and public or academic libraries. Space was more of a concern, resulting in collections trimmed to minimum size, and access to the collections was more simple. Reference service was given in three areas: one was current awareness (keeping clients abreast of new developments in the literature); another was compiling and packaging information as requested; and thirdly, a variety of duties, including the indexing of company-prepared sales literature or reviewing employee-written manuscripts being submitted for outside publication.

They found corporate libraries need to be cost-effective in order to maintain a solid position in their organizations. Salaries were generally higher than the average, in their view, as based on data found in certain annual federal government publications, such as the *Occupational Outlook Handbook*. It is interesting to note the terminology used; in some cases the larger of the two units was referred to in the Willard article as a special library and in other instances in the paper as an information center. It points out the rather fuzzy distinctions that exist when one is describing special libraries versus information centers.

A description of the network of libraries serving the AT&T Laboratories, written by Penniman and Hawkins, indicates the variety of services they provide, such as translating of foreign literature, special databases for internal use, and a variety of current awareness tools aimed at listing recent literature of interest to different departments.[6]

One of the most thorough surveys of corporate special libraries and information centers was conducted under the supervision of James Matarazzo; in it 164 corporate senior managers were queried about their firms' special libraries and information centers.[7] The study showed that these companies valued the services performed, particularly online searching. One finding that should receive more attention is the lack of a consensus as to how these units bring value to the corporations or even on how to measure their value. The role of the libraries in the firms needs to be more clearly defined.

A useful compilation of descriptions of 13 corporate libraries is found in the book edited by Matarazzo.[8] He has edited summaries of a select group of special libraries, including those in business, science, and publishing.

Additional Features of Special Libraries and Information Centers

The preceding section gave some indication of the main activities commonly found in special libraries and information centers. Perhaps a little more attention to other aspects of such units would be appropriate here.

User Services. It should be obvious that special libraries and information centers are called upon for a high level of service to their users. "I can't help you" is not usually an acceptable statement for their staff members to make to clients, many of whose projects depend upon getting the right information, often needed quickly. One of the main ways of filling their needs is to have staff members who thrive on giving such service. It is not everyone's cup of tea to work under such conditions, while others find such demands rewarding and exciting. At the end of the day the staff member should have a real sense of achievement when requests are handled successfully, deriving a definite sense of participation in the goals of the organization served.

Later chapters in this book will discuss some of the unusual services expected, such as editorial assistance or creating of printed products. Many such services are unknown in other types of libraries.

Collections. Some of the accounts of existing units given above gave a clue as to the specialized nature of their collections. Space requirements alone usually are sufficient reason for keeping collections centered on key subjects, the indispensable materials that must be on hand at all times. These organizations have had to rely on other sources for a great deal of their data—public and university libraries; other special libraries; bookstores which can provide current books quickly; document delivery services which can locate even out-of-print as well as current reports and documents on a rush basis; or others sources, such as publishers, who have a good stock of materials right at hand.

A law library, for example, may be asked to locate a technical report for an attorney involved in a court appearance later in the day. A corporate business information center may be expected to locate within hours a clipping from a back issue of a newspaper, even if the center does not retain old issues. These are typical examples of how these units must be able to produce materials on a moment's notice, no matter what the size of their collection may be. Frequently the cost of locating the requested item is of little importance, so critical may be the need for it.

References

1. White, Herbert S. The "quiet revolution": a profession at the crossroads. *Special Libraries.* 80(1): 24-30; 1989 Winter.

    States that the differences between special libraries and information centers are so slight as to make the topic a non-issue now. Points out what he considers more troublesome topics, such as the competitive roles of management information systems, of computer centers, and other organizations for providing good service, or the effects of budget cuts.

2.	Brimsek, Tobi A., comp. *From the top: profiles of U.S. and Canadian corporate libraries and information centers.* Washington, DC: Special Libraries Association; 1989. 315 p.

Consists of the profiles of 40 U.S. and Canadian special libraries and information centers. Examines the background of library managers, the attitude towards reimbursement for costs in the library, facilities, and user services, to mention some of the more prominent topics.

3.	Thury, Eva M. From library to information center: case studies in the evolution of corporate information resources. *Special Libraries.* 79(1): 21-27; 1988 Winter.

Describes the development of information centers in seven businesses, including banks, an oil company, and a publishing company. Shows how new services have been created, based on more or less traditional special library units. The new responsibilities are discussed.

4.	Rothschild, M. Cecilia. Department of Defense Information Analysis Centers. *Special Libraries.* 78(3): 162-169; 1987 Summer.

Describes the services provided by some score of information analysis centers, managed and funded by the DOD, serving scientific and technical units. Duties include collection of data as well as creating new analyses of pertinent information.

5.	Willard, Ann M.; Morrison, Patricia. The dynamic role of the information specialist: two perspectives. *Special Libraries.* 79(4): 271-276; 1988 Fall.

Reviews the services, collections and general features of two corporate information units, one being a special library with five staff members and the other a one-person operation. Gives the flavor of services and responsibilities (plus benefits) in corporate settings as compared with other types of libraries.

6.	Penniman, W. David; Hawkins, Donald T. Library network at AT&T. *Science & Technology Libraries.* 8(2): 3-24; 1987 Winter.

Provides a detailed analysis of the types of services and kinds of materials involved in the library network for the AT&T Laboratories. A number of special current awareness tools are regularly distributed, and special online retrieval systems are in place for locating outside literature as well as internal documents.

7.	Matarazzo, James. *Valuing corporate libraries: a survey of senior managers.* Washington, DC: Special Libraries Association; 1990. 11 p.

A compact summary of a survey of 164 senior managers in corporations regarding their evaluation of their libraries and information centers and the information specialists who run them. The findings showed that the units were relatively small but were highly regarded, particularly for their database searching service. Other services are discussed in the report.

8.	Matarazzo, James M. *Corporate library excellence.* Washington, DC: Special Libraries Association; 1990. 187 p.

Provides descriptions written by the managers of 13 libraries sponsored by corporations. Covers services rendered to users, collections, facilities, budgets, and thoughts on library excellence. Offers good summaries.

Chapter 3

The Nature of Information

Most people now accept that we are living in what has been called The Age of Information. People in all walks of life are seeing the impact of information on traditional careers, on the creation of new careers, on the ways in which businesses and cultural organizations are operated, and on other sectors of society. Fewer and fewer of us work in factories or on farms; the focus has shifted to service industries. The U.S. Department of Labor issued a handbook in 1989 that predicted that by the turn of the century nearly 80 percent of all jobs will be service-related. Of course, information-related jobs are included in this estimate. According to a 1980 survey a conservative count showed 1.6 million information professionals in the United States, not including those working in government agencies.[1] Note the date of this survey; the figure should be even higher now.

Librarianship is most certainly a part of this transformation; we are beginning to realize more fully that handling and retrieving information is really at the heart of what we do as a profession. The forms or media in which information is found have become less important. Thus, it seems appropriate to devote one chapter in this book to a general overview of information. In the following sections we will consider several of information's major aspects, such as its definition, its acquisition, and its transfer from one person or source to another.

Definitions of Information and Information Science

It is not easy to define information, although most of us feel intuitively that we know what it is. A book by Debons et al. defines information as a continuum, ranging from an awareness of a fact or event to a state of evaluation or a synthesis of the pieces of data.[2] The book shows the relationship between information, knowledge, and wisdom; it also provides a good overall view of the nature and the future of information science, topics that are difficult to "get a handle on."

Information science is also a term that is not simple to describe. A book that is recommended for those just getting acquainted with the subject is the work edited by Olgsgaard.[3] It clearly sets forth the theory of information science as well as its application to information retrieval and library operations. Those desiring to read a short history of information science are referred to the article by Herner, who traces its development during the past forty years.[4] A longer history of information science was written by Lilley and Trice.[5]

It should interest the student as well as those with more knowledge of the field; it is carefully done and well documented.

Ways of Handling Information

The process of handling information could be divided into several categories. No two writers would use exactly the same subdivisions, but the overall treatment could be the same, regardless of the terms used. Some of the basic ways of processing information include:

- *Creation.*   The first step in obtaining processible information is the creation of a recorded version that can be worked with and retained. Many agencies are involved in this process; these range from the commercial publisher to the department supervisor preparing an internal memo to politicians recording the day's events in their diaries.
- *Acquisition.*   Before a group or agency can work with a piece of information it must be in the group's possession, whether through purchase, gift, or exchange.
- *Transformation (Packaging).*   In many cases it is necessary to transform the format or media in which a piece of information was originally created. For example, many instances occur when a text is keyed by a clerk who thereby creates both a typed version and a computer file. This enables the data subsequently to be repackaged in many ways. Another example of transformation would be the conversion of computer output into a microform format, such as microfiche pieces.
- *Retrieval.*   It is crucial to be able to locate (or retrieve) information related to specific requests, such as data on particular subjects or items prepared by a particular author at a certain time. This could be accomplished by using resources such as printed indexes or computer files.
- *Analysis.*   Retrieved information must be analyzed to determine its relevance to the question at hand. The original requestor or, in some instances, a member of the library/ information center staff member would carry out this step. The person involved needs a good subject background and the ability to assess accurately the importance of information to a third party.

Information Transfer

The act of meeting the information needs of users incorporates many of the processes previously discussed. Information transfer seems an appropriate term; until reaching the person who needs it, information serves little purpose. Books, journals, films, databases, and any other resource are of little value if not put to use. The time has long passed when librarians could be content merely to amass a large collection of materials without regard to their use by information seekers. Modern information agencies recognize the importance of empha- sizing the intelligent use of their materials. An example of a simple step in the information transfer is attaching a printed routing list to a recent issue of a journal. A more sophisticated example of this principle might be a six months' research project by an information specialist that would lead to a lengthy report on a complex technical project. Both instances involve the same process—putting information into a package useful to potential data users. For further reading on this topic, see the article in which Back summarizes the relationship of information to its users.[6]

Types of Information

Several methods can be used to describe the different kinds of information that exist. One method is to categorize information in terms of whether it is factual or interpretive (and thus less objective).

- *Factual.* Here are some numerical and textual examples; the accuracy of this sort of information is not considered controversial. *Numerical data:* the boiling point of nitric acid, the December 30 closing price of a particular stock, or the number of known symphonies Mozart composed. *Textual data:* the exact wording of a particular business contract between two firms, the text of a recent presidential press conference, or the spelling of the name of a noted scientist.
- *Interpretive.* This information is subject to the opinions and judgments of the data's originators, compilers, or both. Again, we have numerical and textual examples. *Numerical data*: the forecast of the number of bushels of next year's wheat crop, an estimate of the number of business firms that will fail next year, or the estimated sales of next year's model of a particular automobile. *Textual data:* a proposed new method for producing ammonia, an analysis of the effects of federal price controls, or a discussion of the merits of a certain painting.

These are rather obvious examples, clearly defined as to their degree of accuracy or reliability. On the other hand, even so-called factual data are usually not fully acceptable to everyone. For instance, a research chemist may have recently discovered a superior method of measuring boiling points, that would make the values found in conventional handbooks far less accurate than the values found using the new techniques. Or in musicology, scholars may be convinced of the authenticity of a newly found symphonic score attributed to Mozart. As you can see, accuracy and reliability are relative terms; however, the categories discussed above are generally useful ways of considering different types of data, even though the classifications sometimes become ambiguous.

Sources of Information

Another way of examining the nature of information is to consider the various sources from which it comes. Common methods of categorizing data involve its point of origin in relation to the information user. Two common methods of classifying information involve the source. Is it primary or secondary? Verbal or nonverbal?

- *Primary Sources.* This refers to material coming directly from the source. Primary sources are considered particularly authentic and accurate because they are prepared by the originators of the data, *not* by intermediaries who may have inadvertently introduced error into the description. Thus, primary sources are sought when extreme accuracy or currency is required. *Examples*: most periodical articles, technical reports, patents, diaries, correspondence, conference papers, or oral information.
- *Secondary Sources.* These provide a convenient means of locating primary source materials or those that synthesize, clarify, or criticize primary source data. *Examples:* abstracting and indexing services, review materials, handbooks, encyclopedias, bibliographies, dictionaries, or textbooks.

  Note that both primary and secondary sources can appear in a wide range of physical formats, whether printed publications, microfiche, motion pictures, video or audio recordings, slides, and so on. Content, not format, is the determining factor.
- *Verbal Sources.* These are sources that rely on words, symbols of words (such as numbers) or both to impart information. *Printed Examples:* material found in books, journals, patents, or encyclopedias. *Oral Examples:* informal conversations, formal speeches, motion pictures, and video or audio recordings of meetings.
- *Nonverbal Sources.* Here we find images, symbols, or designs (having no direct relationship to words) that communicate a message. *Examples*: paintings, sculpture, music, drawings, maps, or abstract designs.

In everyday practice, information sources often contain a mixture of verbal and nonverbal elements. For example, a book could contain both text and illustrations, a motion picture could present both conversation and visual imagery. Increasing attention is being given to selecting the most appropriate verbal or nonverbal means of imparting information in specific situations.

Informal Means of Communication

Many librarians tend to overlook how much their clientele depend for information on informal communication methods. It is often easiest to turn to a friend or a colleague when one needs a particular bit of information. If this technique fails, searching a published source is usually the next step.

In some cases, the process of seeking information from colleagues has developed into informal networks, with one person recognized as the unofficial leader or center of the network. DeSolla Price[7] has written a useful paper describing the role of such means of communication, often called the invisible college. An application of the process to a particular field appears in the paper by Salasin.[8] He studied the mechanisms for person-to-person communication in the field of rural mental health services; out of more than 1,600 individuals who were included in the study, only 19 received the bulk of the requests for data.

The reason so many people turn to oral communication so frequently is that oral communication is often quicker than written communication. Direct face-to-face conversation, use of the telephone, and attendance at lectures all provide a speedy means of information transfer. It can be more up-to-date than written communication, which almost always involves delays in printing and publishing. Those on familiar terms with recognized authorities in a given field, for instance, often can get detailed, authentic, and current information simply by placing a telephone call.

On the other hand, oral communications may be inaccurate when dealing with complex, detailed matters or with extensive numbers, such as statistical data. It is easy to make mistakes when transmitting or recording this sort of information if one lacks a written record to use as a check. Another disadvantage is the travel cost to a particular conference to meet the source, or the cost of telephone calls to distant experts, who may not always be available. Then, too, most of us are not familiar with all the experts we might need to consult at a given time.

The literature contains many descriptions of the pros and cons of oral communication. Especially interesting is oral history, which consists of interviewing distinguished people or those with unusual backgrounds to record their views of selected topics in their own voices.

In recent years the ready availability of personal computers has led to a new form of informal communication—the use of electronic mail (or E-mail). This consists of using computer and telephone networks through which messages can be sent quickly. It has speeded up communication tremendously, eliminating the infamous "telephone tag" or the mail delay. Some busy administrators and researchers often contact the same person several times a day through E-mail. This is usually a virtual impossibility when using telephones. By contrast, E-mail messages can be read even when both parties are not free at the same time.

Reasons for Gathering Information

People gather information for countless reasons. Some common ones are:

- Obtaining ideas for new projects or for improving an existing project or product.
- Keeping aware of current developments.
- Building competence, whether in a new field or a familiar one.

Those in reader-service units must know as much as possible about user needs; such knowledge is a great help in the selection of suitable materials, the timing of service rendered, and the choice of format for the finished product furnished the requestor.

Clarification of Information Requests

A common experience for those serving at a reference desk is to find that many clients do not accurately state their information needs. What is the problem? An article by Mount points out that some questioners distrust the ability of the reference person to understand the inquiry or even give assistance if the real question were posed; other people may hesitate because of the delicate nature of an inquiry, an understandable cause for feeling uncomfortable telling another person exactly what is wanted.[9]

Availability of Information

Despite the obvious merits of having information freely available to those who seek it, our society has placed several obstacles in the path of those needing data. Some of the major issues are:

- *Costs.* No matter how excellent our public libraries and other agencies serving the general public may be, some publications or data will always be unavailable to inquirers relying on such sources. Items such as expensive periodicals and rare books simply exceed the budgets of many agencies. While unfortunate, it is a fact of life that one cannot overlook. Many projects, such as shared cataloging and interlibrary loans, are relieving this situation somewhat, but some data will always require extra funds to obtain.
- *Controlled Circulation.* Military security and company security are two main controls governing the distribution and availability of certain types of data.
  - a. *Military Security.* Some day all countries may be able to trust one another completely. Until then, some documents and data will be available only to certain people who have a "need to know" the contents of the publications for the performance of their duties. However necessary this may be for national security, this practice inhibits the efforts of those seeking information. In recent years the U.S. has adopted regulations which require regular reviews of classified documents to see if they can be declassified or at least downgraded. Some administrations in Washington have apparently been lax in carrying out such studies.
  - b. *Company Security.* It has been claimed that more documents and reports are restricted through limitations placed by business and industry than through military-security regulations. At any rate, it is necessary for many private companies to take precautionary steps to prevent certain sensitive materials from falling into competitors' hands.

    Mount and Newman wrote a book describing ways to safeguard confidential information, both military and commercial.[10] The work also discusses ways of obtaining government information, primarily through use of the Freedom of Information Act.

    Note: Those interested in ways to protect classified documents in special libraries should see the article by Shores; in it she describes the control system for such materials.[11]
- *Copyright Regulations.* Most countries, including the United States, have long had laws that restrict the type and amount of copying of published works that those not holding the copyright themselves may do. The purpose is simple enough—to protect

the interests of the publishers of the work, its producers, or both from those who would try to avoid buying the item. A new copyright law was enacted in the United States in 1976 after years of congressional haggling over its provisions. It covers modern technologies that were unheard of when the old law was adopted in 1909. One portion of the law of particular concern to libraries and information centers has to do with photocopying practices. While a full explanation is beyond the scope of this book, in general, the law generally allows the making of a single copy of an article or of a portion of a book. Most multiple copying is forbidden.

An article by Nasri provides a review of the entire matter of copyright regulations, from both domestic and international viewpoints; the discussion encompasses material duplication, database handling, and information for nonprint materials.[12] Those wishing a more detailed discussion of the regulations governing fee-based and library copying services are referred to the paper by Heller.[13] For a comprehensive review of copyright practices, the reader would profit from examining the book edited by Weil and Polansky.[14]

Citations of Information Materials

In many instances a library or information center will be expected to provide citations to publications that would interest inquirers. This practice is so common because, in many cases, the inquirer may need only the citation and not the original source, or may wish to postpone examining the original source. Whatever the reason, the inquirer has a right to expect that citations will be prepared in such a way as to clearly identify the cited item without ambiguity and to provide enough data to make the cited material easy to obtain.

Organizations may or may not prescribe the style of bibliographic citations employees are to use. Some people favor the University of Chicago style, while others use standards developed by professional organizations, such as the American Psychological Association. The National Library of Medicine is among the organizations that has its own standard of preparing citations. Thus, several standards are in current use for the preparation of bibliographic citations, although only one of them was voted upon by well-known libraries, professional associations, and information industry members; this standard is the one the American National Standards Institute (ANSI) adopted several years ago.[15] Now under review for eventual updating, the standard is still useful as a guide to follow in preparing citations for both print and nonprint materials. For a summary of the standard and examples of citations see the article by Mount.[16]

Abstracts of Information Materials

It is frequently desirable to prepare summaries or abstracts of given publications or information sources. These descriptions save the user's time by reducing the full item to a few sentences that can be quickly read and evaluated. Providing an abstract greatly helps the inquirer, who may be unsure from examining just the title and other descriptive data included in a citation whether or not a particular publication would be of interest.

There are two generally recognized types of abstracts, named indicative and informative. Informative abstracts are quite detailed in style and clearly summarize the contents of the original item, citing sufficient details to bring out its main points. Indicative abstracts, on the other hand, are less detailed. They provide a minimum of information, normally mentioning only the topics treated by the original without going into detail about them.

Naturally, informative abstracts are more time-consuming to produce and more demanding of the abstractor's skill; they are also immeasurably more helpful to readers than the less detailed indicative type.

One of the ANSI standards concerns the writing of abstracts.[17] It has stood up well over the years unrevised because of the agreement of editors and writers with the provisions it sets forth. For additional explanatory information see the article by Weil.[18]

References

1. *The information professional—survey of an emerging field*. New York: Dekker; 1981. 271 p. Edited by Anthony Debons et al.

    Summarizes the findings of a survey of information professionals made in 1980. Defines their work, occupational titles, areas of employment, organizational placement, and work incentives.

2. Debons, Anthony; Horne, Esther; Cronenweth, Scott. *Information science: an integrated view*. Boston: G. K. Hall; 1988. 172 p.

    A clear, readable book that covers basic concepts of information and information science. Specific topics included are: the information professional, methods in information science, communication technology, and the future of information science.

3. Olsgaard, John N. *Principles and applications of information science for library professionals*. Chicago: American Library Association; 1989. 142 p.

    The book aims at introducing the practicing librarian to some of the basic concepts of information science. Following three chapters on the theory of information science, three more chapters discuss arrangement and retrieval of information. A like number of chapters is devoted to the practice of information science in libraries.

4. Herner, Saul. Brief history of information science. *Journal of the American Society for Information Science*. 35(3): 157-163; 1984 May.

    Traces developments since the publication of Vannevar Bush's classic paper ("As We May Think") in 1945. Includes discussions of studies on bibliographic organization, the role of computers, the significance of international conferences, and sketches of important figures in the field.

5.   Lilley, Dorothy B.; Trice, Ronald W. *A history of information science: 1945-85.* New York: Academic Press; 1989. 181 p.

A clearly written book that presents the history of information science in terms of events, such as library automation, as well as in terms of the accomplishments of a number of outstanding information scientists.

6.   Back, Harry B. What information dissemination studies imply concerning the design of on-line reference retrieval systems. *Journal of the American Society for Information Science.* 23(3): 156-163; 1972 May/June.

Despite its title the paper emphasizes the major aspects of meeting the information needs of clients. Specific topics include identifying users, information gathering, and using such information sources as printed reference tools versus online databases.

7.   DeSolla Price, Derek J. Some remarks on elitism in information and the invisible college phenomenon in science. *Journal of the American Society for Information Science.* 22(2): 74-75; 1971 Mar./Apr.

An early paper describing the nature of informal communication networks among scientists, including the probable size and importance of such systems.

8.   Salasin, John; Cedar, Toby. Person-to-person communication in an applied research services setting. *Journal of the American Society for Information Science.* 36(2): 103-115; 1985 Mar.

Results similar to classical "invisible college" studies were obtained in this study of professionals engaged in rural mental health services. It shows that a few individuals were the central figures to whom the rest of the people in the study turned for information.

9.   Mount, Ellis. Communication barriers and the reference question. *Special Libraries.* 57(8): 575-578; 1966 Oct.

Describes nine possible causes for the failure of clients to disclose their real reason for requesting information in a reference setting. Possible ways to improve such a situation are listed.

10.   Mount, Ellis; Newman, Wilda B. *Top secret/trade secret: accessing and safeguarding restricted information.* New York: Neal-Schuman Publishers; 1985. 214 p.

Discusses methods of safeguarding military and commercial restricted information, including the problems of protecting computer-based systems. Also describes the means of obtaining government information through such methods as provided for by the Freedom of Information Act.

11.   Shores, Patricia M. Classified documents in the corporate library. *Special Libraries.* 79(1): 15-20; 1988 Winter.

Provides a description of a computerized system devised for use in control and safeguarding of classified military documents.

12.   Nasri, William Z. Copyright. In: *ALA world encyclopedia of library and information services.* 2d ed. Chicago: American Library Association; 1986: p. 223-230.

Covers the history of copyright, important legislation, rules on copying, and regulations for nonprint materials. A thorough review of the topic.

13. Heller, James S. Copyright and fee-based copying services. *College & Research Libraries.* 47(1): 28-37; 1986 Jan.

Explains text of the Copyright Act of 1976 and how it has been interpreted by the courts. Includes cases of profit-making copying versus library copying. Well documented.

14. Weil, Ben H.; Polansky, Barbara Friedman, eds. *Modern copyright fundamentals.* Rev. ed. Medford, NJ: Learned Information; 1989. 460 p.

Consists of 75 articles by authoritative authors on all aspects of the U.S. Copyright Statute and its effects on libraries and laypeople. Includes legal and technological issues. A thorough treatment of the subject.

15. *American national standard for bibliographic references, ANSI Z39.29-1977.* New York: American National Standards Institute; 1977. 92 p.

Presents examples and rules for the creation of bibliographic references of all sorts, including those for nonprint as well as print materials.

16. Mount, Ellis. A national standard for bibliographic references. *Journal of the American Society for Information Science.* 28(1): 3-12; 1977 Jan.

Summarizes the provisions of the ANSI standard and shows examples of several types of common citations, covering both print and nonprint materials.

17. *American national standard for writing abstracts, ANSI Z39.14-1979.* New York: American National Standards Institute; 1979. 15 p.

Different kinds of abstracts are described, with examples given for each type.

18. Weil, Ben H. Standards for writing abstracts. *Journal of the American Society for Information Science.* 21(5): 351-357; 1970 Sept./Oct.

Provides explanations of the different types of abstracts and how to write them. Several sample abstracts are included.

Part 2

Management

The success of special libraries and information centers strongly relates to the quality of their management. In light of this fact, Part 2 treats many aspects of management, ranging from general principles to budgeting details, from the creation of job descriptions to marketing techniques.

Chapter 4 presents an overall view of the nature of management, including qualifications, responsibilities, and benefits. Chapter 5 discusses the importance of good relationships with top management, while Chapter 6 covers planning and budgeting. Chapter 7 deals with unit organization and staffing. Chapter 8 covers staff supervision, followed by marketing techniques in Chapter 9. Evaluation of the unit is the topic of Chapter 10, while Chapter 11 analyzes the effects on management of information technology and other modern tools.

Chapter 4

The Role of the Manager

The management of any special library or information center largely determines how well such a unit will provide a high level of service to its sponsoring organization. This is particularly significant because most of these libraries and centers exist because their sponsoring organizations see them as offering essential services. In practically all instances there are few, if any, statutory requirements that these units exist, the only exceptions being special subject sections in academic and public libraries. For the rest of the special library world, the very existence of the library depends to a large extent upon the support it receives from its clients, especially top management. Such support normally comes about because the library or information center plays a significant role in enabling the sponsoring organization to meet its goals.

Most special libraries must play this role using a small staff. As you read earlier, nearly half have three or fewer employees. A small staff may have certain advantages. For instance, the layout of time and money for innovations and experiments may be less than in larger units. Employees of small libraries may also take greater interest in their work because of varied duties. A small staff, though, may mean a heavy managerial workload. Each professional will probably have managerial responsibilities. Those special libraries with several professionals on staff usually divide up managerial activities. Even so, the longer one stays in special libraries the greater the likelihood of becoming a manager, especially if a higher paying position is desired. A special librarian is much more likely to become a manager than will someone working in another type of library, such as a public or academic library, chiefly because of the larger number of professionals in such organizations. Thus the following section has important implications for the future special librarian.

Those wanting an overview of the problems of library management should examine the book by Stueart, which emphasizes basic concepts.[1] Also recommended is the relatively brief summary by Bailey, which is devoted to the role of the special librarian as a manager or supervisor.[2] The book by White includes management techniques, along with other aspects of special librarianship.[3]

The nature of supervising small libraries, including one-person libraries, is covered in the collection of articles entitled *Managing Small Special Libraries*.[4] A more detailed article on the problems and techniques of managing the one-person library is by St. Clair.[5] Although such jobs are common in the world of special libraries, the literature gives this topic little attention, which makes St. Clair's article most welcome.

Additional guidance for would-be managers appears in the article by Kok, who describes six rules to help the new library manager.[6] Emphasis on the need to maintain a businesslike operation in libraries is stressed in the paper by Echelman.[7]

Some people take to management more easily than others, but nothing is so esoteric about being a good manager that only a favored few can succeed in it. Study of the literature and careful attention to one's efforts can go a long way toward reaching this goal.

Managerial Responsibilities

No two books on the topic of management are likely to touch on the same topics; most writers, though, will agree on the following list of managerial duties. Each area of responsibility will be discussed in greater detail in Chapters 6 through 11.

- *Relating to Top Management.* No matter how much they accomplish or are liked, managers must be adept at working with top management and executives. Top management makes decisions about department budgets, approves expansion plans, and sets broad policies governing the organization. Managers unsuccessful in convincing the upper echelons of the worth of the library/information center may later find needed support withheld.
- *Planning.* Managers must be able to decide what the accomplishments of the library/information center should be. The managers must then develop plans for reaching these goals. Planning requires vision, the ability to look ahead. It also requires skill in translating visions into down-to-earth projects and duties.
- *Budgeting.* While there may be organizations in the world with no fiscal constraints, it is very unlikely that the average manager in the United States will ever experience such a situation. Budgeting for an organization requires estimating the fiscal needs for a given time period, working out the details with higher management to obtain their approval, and then operating within the budget. The most ingenious budget one could devise is worthless if managers are unskilled in controlling expenditures.
- *Organizing and Staffing.* One can find innumerable ways to organize a library/information center based on the number and types of employees as well as their interrelationships. How well this is done strongly influences the way the unit operates. To achieve a smoothly running organization, managers must be able to set up the proper framework of jobs and relationships and select suitable employees.
- *Supervising.* Once the structure and staffing of an organization are decided upon, managers must see that the employees know their assignments, carry them out properly, and work together harmoniously. This also means that managers must have abilities and skills to work well with those supervised.
- *Marketing.* A main duty of managers is to promote or advertise the activities of the special library/information center as widely as possible. Success in this area can help to ensure support of top management.

- *Evaluating Operations.* Good managers not only function well in their positions but also regularly evaluate their managerial effectiveness. Learning the reactions of the clientele and of employees served by the library/information center is a wise way to identify potential problems.
- *Using Management Tools.* Over the years several tools have been found to be indispensable to the success of managers. One of these is statistical analysis, which helps managers accurately assess elements being investigated and improves the presentation of data in reports. Systems analysis is another tool, giving managers a means of examining overall system operations. Perhaps the most important management tool is the computer (or similar modern electronic equipment), which helps the manager carry out daily operations. Of course, managers should be able to use all these tools effectively.

As this list shows, being a manager is a formidable responsibility. It also has benefits. However, no one is expected to be a perfect manager the first day, or to learn the skill overnight. But certainly those who study the subject and give it sufficient thought will master the techniques involved more quickly than those who do not. Many librarians enjoy the challenges of being a manager; others do not. What about them? Many organizations, particularly large ones, have jobs for those who do not wish to be managers. Each person must decide which type of position will provide the greatest personal satisfaction.

Qualifications Of Managers

Certainly no two managers are exactly alike in personality, background, and outlook. Even so, certain qualifications always stand out when managers are being selected and hired. The "ideal" managers depicted here don't exist, but a person lacking a number of these qualifications has little chance of succeeding as a manager.

Personal Traits. Ideal managers are reliable and conscientious about their duties. They show good judgment and the ability to learn quickly. Simply put, good managers have common sense! Furthermore, such people get along with coworkers and treat them with courtesy and respect. No matter how brilliant, those who do not enjoy working with people are not likely to be successful managers.

Nothing impedes the effectiveness and success of managers as much as closed-mindedness about new ideas or different ways of doing things. A willingness to give serious consideration to others' suggestions and the ability to think creatively on one's own are indispensable qualities.

Education. Managers should be educated in the basics of the social sciences and the communication arts. Expressing oneself clearly in written and oral form is essential.

In many situations, facility with foreign languages may also be required. In addition, managers sometimes need to have anywhere from an undergraduate major to a graduate degree in a subject specialty appropriate to the interests of the sponsoring organization. While on-the-job training and self-instruction are widely used in most situations, it is simpler and far less time-consuming to take formal courses (if one's situation allows for this sort of program).

Managers usually need a master's degree in library science, information science, or a closely related field. Some jobs call for advanced study beyond the master's level, especially for those lacking instruction in certain topics or wanting to keep abreast of new developments. This sort of educational requirement continues throughout one's career. Opportunities abound for continuing education, such as courses given by library associations, library schools, information networks or consortia, and commercial sponsors.

Experience. Many entry-level positions in small libraries or information centers involve being in charge of the entire unit. Taking such a position immediately after completing one's formal education means being thrown into the front lines with little chance to get practical experience. Yet many people succeed at this challenge. Most managerial posts, however, are open only to those who have already had some appropriate experience, particularly at a supervisory level. As much as five years of experience may be sought in applicants for certain high-level positions. Having set forth the qualifications of the ideal manager, keep in mind that life does not always follow the ideal pattern. One hears of inexperienced, untrained people who somehow convince employers of their ability and are hired for jobs for which they have few qualifications. True ability will eventually show, and well-qualified people should expect to find rewarding positions from which they might advance to even higher ones. In view of the relatively small staffs in special libraries and information centers, it is often necessary to leave one sponsor and go to a larger, more complex library or information center offering advancement. On the other hand, promotion up the ladder within one organization happens frequently, particularly when levels of professional positions exist.

Benefits For Managers

Lest the reader believe that only responsibilities and demands make up the experience of being a manager, we will now consider the special benefits and privileges available to most managers. The extent to and manner in which managers are rewarded vary greatly from one organization to another, but some benefits are common to most.

As one might expect, managers usually make higher salaries than non-managers. The SLA salary surveys, which indicate the effects of type of positions held on the pay received, show higher salaries are *generally* paid to those with supervisory experience.[8] The highest salaries in the profession are paid to managers, often in proportion to the number and type of people supervised. Managers in some positions in private business frequently receive annual bonuses, the size varying according to the state of the employer's finances. Private sponsors will sometimes also reward librarians with the option to buy stock at special prices, or may actually give valued employees company stock.

Managers are frequently allowed to include enough money in their budgets for all expenses involved in attending one or more professional meetings per year. If full coverage is not allowed, many librarians must pay only registration fees, for example. Quite often *only* the manager receives expense money of this sort; sometimes a certain amount gets budgeted for other professional library employees.

Besides travel money managers may also have impressive job titles. In some special libraries or information centers the titles often sound substantial. Examples include: Director of Information Services, Manager of Information Services, Manager of Technical Information, and Director of Library Services. The managers of some special libraries occasionally get promoted to vice presidents, having a title such as Vice President and Manager of Information Services. An article by Kok and Strable describing such situations points out that this practice is usually confined to libraries in the field of advertising, marketing, and banking.[9] Such promotions do not always mean an improvement in salary or responsibilities, but the higher status indicated by the title generally encourages the person promoted. Titles per se don't always make a tremendous difference; a prestigious job title, though, often indicates strong support by top management for libraries and information centers.

The manager usually receives a better office than those not on that level. Like job titles, a handsome office, attractive furniture, and a carpet on the floor are not the end goals of managers; they do indicate top management's backing, however.

The benefits of managerial status may involve people as well as job titles and a nice office. Many managers have a secretary to handle correspondence, filing, and other routine matters. In very small libraries a clerk may perform such duties.

Managers often can participate in meetings and workshops that are restricted to those on the middle management level. Through these avenues managers gain a better awareness of the goals and activities of the sponsoring organization, which in turn enables them to better serve the organization.

Management's role involves significant challenges while providing numerous rewards, special benefits, and personal satisfaction. Consider these factors if you are considering becoming the manager of a special library/information center. A recent issue of *Special Libraries* provides a useful summary of the main points of this chapter.[10]

References

1. Stueart, Robert D.; Moran, Barbara. *Library management*. 3d ed. Littleton, CO: Libraries Unlimited; 1987. 376 p.

A basic text on the subject. Includes chapters on supervising, organizing, and planning. Includes examples applicable to library situations.

2. Bailey, Martha J. *The special librarian as a supervisor or middle manager*. 2d ed. Washington, DC: Special Libraries Association; 1986. 176 p.

Reviews the literature on the subject and analyzes the responsibilities, the education, and work experience needed for managerial positions.

3. White, Herbert S. *Managing the special library: strategies for success within the larger organization*. White Plains, NY: Knowledge Industry Publications; 1984. 152 p.

Despite its title, covers all aspects of special librarianship. The work emphasizes the nature and problems of management. Includes chapters on technical and user services.

4. *Managing small special libraries*. Washington, DC: Special Libraries Association; 1988. 166 p.

Consists of a collection of articles from SLA publications that deal with managing a small unit, including one-person libraries. Topics range from automation to preparing job descriptions to planning for preservation projects.

5. St. Clair, Guy. The one-person library: an essay on essentials revisited. *Special Libraries*. 78(4): 263-270; 1987 Fall.

Describes the special problems inherent in managing a one-person library. Discusses the role of continuing education, the qualifications for success, and the variety of duties involved.

6. Kok, John. "Now that I'm in charge, what do I do?": six rules about running a special library for the new library manager. *Special Libraries*. 71(12): 523-528; 1980 Dec.

Topics include selecting staff members, learning the needs of users, maintaining good relations with top executives, and promotion of library services.

7. Echelman, Shirley. Libraries are businesses too. *Special Libraries*. 65(10/11): 409-414; 1974 Oct./Nov.

Points out the need for attention to businesslike handling of finances, collection development, personnel matters, and marketing of services. The need for keeping adequate statistics is explained.

8. *SLA triennial salary survey 1988*. Washington, DC: Special Libraries Association; 1989. 72 p.

Provides salary data for more than 4,000 SLA members in the United States and Canada. Relates salaries to such factors as location, staff size, subject area, and number of people supervised.

9. Kok, John; Strable, Edward G. Moving up: librarians who have become officers of their organizations. *Special Libraries*. 71(1): 5-12; 1980 Jan.

Reviews examples of promotions of special librarians to positions such as vice presidents of organizations. Describes situations where such advancements have taken place.

10. Library management issue. *Special Libraries*. 8(2): 90-137; 1990 Spring.

The issue is almost entirely devoted to articles dealing with aspects of management. They range from a discussion of how leadership can be learned to the types of power available to information professionals to strategies for success as a manager.

Chapter 5

Relating to Top Management

The financial status and overall well being of most special libraries and information centers depend heavily upon the perceptions of top management. Key executives' high regard for these departments helps ensure reasonable budgets and the continuing existence of the units. If, on the other hand, top executives find little to praise in the service given, the facility will gain few supporters in those circles. The libraries and information centers may find themselves either curtailed in size or funds, or, in the worst case, abandoned, with the responsibilities for the service they once gave assigned to another department. As you can imagine, managers of information units need to know how to achieve a high level of in-house appreciation and respect. They must serve users well.

If experienced professionals had to pick the major factor governing the success and stability of these units, they would probably name the level of service given to clients. Successful managers who make sure that the service their units provide stays at a high level usually retain the support of top management, even in times of tight budgets. The author knows of organizations where the library service is so good that a literal storm of protests would arise from all levels of the organization if the library or information center's funding were to be drastically cut or the size of the staff reduced. Unlike some academic or public libraries, where the main mark of success is the size of the collection or the number of items borrowed, in special libraries and information centers such measures of activity have little real significance to top management. But a library that saves the time of highly paid employees or that provides information in anticipation of requests occupies a far stronger position than one that relies on collection size or circulation figures for support.

This is not to downplay the importance of maintaining as strong a collection as possible nor the achievement of higher and higher circulation figures; they do indicate certain strengths that have merit. In the eyes of key organization executives, however, they just aren't the major measures of the library's success. An article by Spindler presents the viewpoint of a corporate executive as to what management expects from its library—he lists both adequate collections and prompt service as key elements in what is expected.[1]

Another way of defining the ideal relationship between a library manager and top management is in terms of communication between them. Good communication patterns enhance the library's position. An article by Ceppos, a consultant who surveyed two corporate libraries, reinforces this point.[2] She ends the paper with this statement: "What is most evident from these case studies is that the success of the technical information program is heavily dependent upon communication between the library managers and their respective corporate superiors within the parameters of the corporate culture."

As you probably surmise, a high level of support among top executives does not absolutely guarantee continued success. Many factors may put budgetary matters in a state where costs absolutely have to be cut. Besides the usual ups and downs of economic cycles, other elements may alter business conditions. A rash of corporate mergers and takeovers in recent years, for example, has alone caused many information services to be cut or, in some cases, eliminated; merged companies seek ways to reduce debts, sometimes huge ones, that may result from takeovers or leveraged buyout situations. Company A and company B may each have had excellent library service before a merger, but afterwards, cost reduction measures may cause library cutbacks, or elimination of some information units through consolidations. Cutbacks in staff size are frequently called "downsizing" in an effort to present the situation as euphemistically as possible. Whether employees get "downsized," "let go," or "fired," they lose their jobs, although some organizations have more generous severance pay or special bonuses than others.

We do not mean to present too gloomy a picture of the security of positions in special libraries or information centers. Many such units have never had a cutback in their history and enjoy strong support in good times or bad, but it would be a disservice to the reader to omit this aspect. An article by Bauer lists ways to gain top management support so as to avoid getting into financial and political difficulties.[3] His paper also discusses the need for cultivating awareness of client needs and for publicizing library services so that clients know what the library can do for them.

Organizational Goals

A special library or information center must adopt clearly stated long-range goals directly related to those of the sponsoring organization. A top executive could understandably question the value of supporting an information service whose aims were largely unrelated to the overall goals of its sponsor.

The various ways to publicize goals within an organization depend largely upon the customs and traditions of each group. Company manuals and looseleaf notebooks may be used for recording the duties and functions of each unit. The special library/information center should prepare a statement of its goals and send it to selected representatives of its user groups for comments before submitting it to top management. The manager's supervisor would probably be the appropriate person to send the statement to top management personnel. Even if only certain managerial levels see the document, it should be effective. Should someone question the unit's role, having the document ready would benefit the manager.

Try not to think of a goal as an esoteric, terribly difficult statement to prepare. Common sense can often dictate most of its content. A typical goals statement might resemble the following:

It shall be the goal of the XYZ Company Library to meet the information needs of all employees. A suitable collection shall be maintained, containing a reasonable number of books, journals, documents, films, and other materials to meet the needs of the unit's clientele. Alternate sources for other materials shall be available. The Library will respond quickly and efficiently to all requests for information, and, when feasible, anticipate the needs of users. Modern technologies shall provide users with maximum service.

Certainly, no two managers would prepare the same goals statement. But however it is worded, the goals must emphasize meeting the information needs of the clientele, rather than some scholarly, obscure reason for existence. The manager's supervisor must fully agree with the statement, since he or she would probably be the logical person to introduce or defend the document to top management.

Performance

A library manager must provide management with solid proof of the contribution the library makes towards helping the organization reach its goals. The more specifically one can document this contribution the better. A popular way involves periodically evaluating the library's operation, whether by interviews or questionnaires. More information on these topics appears in Chapter 10.

Another measure of the library's contribution is the number of hours it saves its clients. An article by Kramer states: "The major advantage of an information function is that it can find answers for the inquirer more rapidly than he [or she] could himself."[4] His paper provides examples of this process, based on actual events in a corporate library. A special way of converting the amount of time saved to dollar values is given in the paper by Zachert.[5] She stresses the merits of calculating the all-important return of investment since this figure definitely interests top management.

The special librarian should give good service to all levels of the organization's employees. One should keep in mind, though, that senior management people probably deal with matters strongly related to the organization's success. So while the goal involves providing excellent service to all requestors, the highest echelon executives must receive a very high priority. Their hourly earning rate makes a saving of their time and effort a most important benefit to the organization. However library managers may face some difficult decisions if conflicts arise over meeting the needs of a high–level executive versus those of lesser status; conceivably the non-executive may have the more important needs. The fortunate manager would greatly appreciate a supervisor's moral support should repercussions arise later.

Businesslike Management

Top management has a right to expect its managers to run their departments in a businesslike manner. This means the manager must be knowledgeable about good management practices, such as skill in planning, adeptness at preparing budgets, and good supervisory practices.

Library schools have not always recognized the need to train their graduates in library management, but this is gradually changing as curricula give greater emphasis to administration and management. For example, courses in statistics, systems analysis, and library automation appear increasingly in school catalogs, and courses in special librarianship invariable now give more stress to managerial topics.

Those needing to learn more about the techniques or vocabulary of professional managers may find someone in the organization willing to take the time to aid them. In addition, abundant literature exists on the subject. The article by Echelman cited in the previous chapter stresses the need for the library manager to become aware of the terminology and practices of modern business.[6]

Organizational Placement

The special library may be found in many places in the overall structure of an organization; some locations are preferable to others. It is seldom, if ever, up to the managers of these units to decide where the unit should be placed in the organization; however occasions may arise when the manager can exert some influence on the matter.

Several alternatives have been used for placing the library in the organization's structure. These range from having the manager of the unit report directly to the chief executive or head of the organization, to making the manager one of several groups (such as the typing pool, the motor pool, or even a company cafeteria) reporting to the office manager. In between these two extremes one finds many variations, such as having the manager report to the Vice President for Research or to the Vice President for Administration. White has written a thought-provoking paper about the advantages and disadvantages of different placements of the library on the organizational chart.[7] Certainly, other factors affect the well-being of a library. These include the personality or degree of interest in the work of the library that characterizes the supervisor of the library manager. Some maintain that a supervisor of the library manager who is enthusiastic about the library is preferable to an executive on a higher level who has a lukewarm attitude toward it. Despite the pros and cons of different levels to which a manager might report, most experts see the need for top-level support as essential.

Knowledge of Current Practices

In certain organizations, particularly businesses, the surest way to obtain an extra staff member or to get funds for new equipment involves references to competitors. Say a librarian tells a supervisor that the rival ABC Company Library has installed a new time-saving automatic widget machine. Some top-management people find it difficult to deny one of their own managers a request that the competition has already granted its library. Other sponsoring organizations have no incentive to keep up with the competition; for such groups the logic and validity of the request assure importance. The manager will soon learn the usefulness of quoting facts about competing organizations.

Regardless of management's stance toward libraries in competing organizations, much can be said for managers who keep aware of what their colleagues are doing. This practice keeps one abreast of the times and may lead to needed improvements in some cases.

References

1. Spindler, Donald C. Management looks at the corporate library. *Special Libraries*. 73(4): 251-253; 1982 October.

   An executive describes what corporate management expects from its library. He lists knowledge of company activities, rapid response to inquiries, and fiscal responsibility as some key requirements.

2. Ceppos, Karen Feingold. Corporate climate and its effect on information management. *Special Libraries*. 73(4): 238-244; 1982 October.

   Reports on surveys of operations in two corporate libraries. In each case the managers performed well in meeting company needs, partly because of good communication with top management.

3. Bauer, Charles K. Managing management. *Special Libraries*. 71(4): 204-216; 1980 Apr.

   Shows the importance of meeting the needs of employees, of anticipating needs, and/or promoting the library cleverly and effectively.

4. Kramer, Joseph. How to survive in industry: cost justifying library service. *Special Libraries*. 77(2): 61-70; 1986 Spring.

   Discusses the need for determining the extent to which the library saves clients' time. Describes two studies of this type of measurement in an aerospace library.

5. Zachert, Martha Jane; Williams, Robert V. Marketing measures for information services. *Special Libraries*. 77(2): 61-70; 1986 Spring.

   This paper on marketing techniques includes discussions on ways to audit the effects of marketing efforts. Through examples, urges the use of calculating the return on investment.

6. Echelman, Shirley. Libraries are businesses too. *Special Libraries*. 65(10/11): 409-414; 1974 Oct./Nov.

Explains how the library manager can benefit by learning about the tools and outlook of the business world.

7. White, Herbert S. Organizational placement of the industrial special library: its relationship to success and survival. *Special Libraries*. 64:(3): 141-144; 1973 Mar.

Discusses the relative merits of having an administrative supervisor versus one engaged in research. Also considers the personal makeup of different top executives versus their influence in the organization.

Chapter 6

Planning and Budgeting

In identifying managerial responsibilities, planning and budgeting would rank high on the list. Planning consists of taking steps that would bring about needed changes, or, as the book by Stueart puts it, planning is "the process of getting an organization from where it is to where it wants to be in a given period of time by setting it on a predetermined course of action."[1] Budgeting involves drawing up plans for expenditures of limited resources, for a given time period, usually one or two years.

Since these two responsibilities relate very closely to each other, it seems fitting to discuss them in a single chapter. One cannot make definite plans without a budget to support the plans, and one cannot make up a suitable budget without knowing for what purpose the funds would be needed. This chapter will show how the two functions fit into the operations of special libraries and information centers. In small units the manager must do all of the planning and budgeting, whereas in larger ones some of the work could be assigned to appropriate staff members. Only in large academic or public libraries would one find a staff member who does just planning and budgeting.

The Planning Process

As might be expected, much has been written about the planning process. Over the years different techniques or styles of planning have attracted attention.

Participatory Management.   In recent decades a management technique known as participatory management has enjoyed popularity. In essence it consists of seeking out opinions of employees, the object being to obtain input that would enable the manager to make better decisions. This includes, but is not limited to, planning decisions. There is nothing very startling about this technique; in a sense it may have grown out of the old-fashioned "suggestion box" that has been used for many decades (sometimes still functioning very well in some organizations), with or without monetary incentives. The difference is that participatory management makes a well-organized effort to draw employees into the planning effort, not just hope that someone will drop a useful suggestion in a box. Group participation in the typical application is well organized, including use of committees and special study groups. The underlying assumption here is that employees perform better if they have a sense of participation.

As is the case with most techniques, success depends a great deal upon how it is implemented. For example, take a manager, Ms. Smith, who has a lukewarm attitude about this technique. She could sabotage the system. She might appoint inappropriate people to head study groups, give study groups too little time away from the job to accomplish much, or, perhaps worst of all, ignore the suggested plans the employees propose. A manager is not bound to follow the proposed plans, but to ignore them completely would stifle all incentive for future study groups. The manager must be open-minded enough (and smart enough) to recognize the merits of excellent employee proposals, yet at the same time avoid the implementation of faulty plans that would lead to problems.

Most business management texts include a discussion about the basic concepts involved in participatory decision-making. For library applications, Webb has written a paper about the need for preparing the staff for taking part in management studies, a prudent step if one wants things to go smoothly.[2]

Management by Objectives. Still another technique is known as Management by Objectives (MBO), a phrase first used by Peter Drucker in 1954. It consists of an approach for delineating an organization's ultimate goals or objectives, a determination made jointly by a manager and the people in the manager's unit. The technique involves strong group participation and cooperation. A general account of the benefits and pitfalls of MBO appears in the book by Humble.[3] Library applications are discussed in two articles by Stanton and Jones, which describe the use of MBO in two sci-tech organizations, one corporate and the other academic.[4,5]

Of course, as with participatory management, using a popular technique of this sort offers no guarantee of managerial success. Using whatever techniques, the best managers undoubtedly achieve more than do mediocre managers who use the latest procedures. On the other hand, a mediocre manager would undoubtedly achieve more by using modern techniques than by trying to work without any specific plan of action.

Quality Circles. An extension of participatory management, quality circles, began in Japanese factories approximately 40 years ago but was not tried in the U.S. until 1974. A quality circle consists of a small group of employees who meet regularly and voluntarily to talk over their work problems and to discuss possible solutions. They seem to function best in situations where a profit relates to measurable output. An article by Mourey describes the system in detail and points out its benefits and its drawbacks.[6] Library managers who have used the system state that, properly used, it works well.

Some Basic Concepts. In addition to the special techniques described above, several basic concepts apply regardless of the technique used.

First, written goals make planning easier and more accurate—too much room exists for error otherwise. A written plan simplifies by breaking a large project into units, each of which has a benchmark, a means of measuring progress. Say the goal were to increase the output of a cataloging department by 50 percent by the end of the year. To reach the goal someone must estimate in advance the total number of books cataloged by the end of each month. Closely related to this point is the need to set deadlines for each part of the project so that one can monitor progress toward goals set for each major step of the way.

The above procedures work best when all the departments and units are using the same system. Problems would arise, for instance, if the library manager were the only one in an organization who was using MBO. Implementing a technique in only one unit presents problems.

Time Management

Managers commonly complain about not having enough time to accomplish everything that needs doing. Some do better than others, but most managers could profit by paying more attention to how they manage their time. The smaller the staff, the more important it is for managers to use time wisely. An article by Berner is written for the heads of small libraries.[7] He lists several misconceptions they may have about managing their time; these include the belief that one must work under pressure to be efficient or that the number of hours one works is more important than the quality of the work.

A book by Winston provides some useful pointers for ways to improve the use of time on the job:[8]

1. *Set priorities.* "First things first" may be an old adage, but it definitely applies to the use of time.
2. *Unclutter desks.* A neat desk is no guarantee of efficiency, but it saves a lot of time in not having to rummage around looking for a particular report (or even a pen).
3. *Don't procrastinate on decisions.* Once one has examined all the issues and considered the results of alternate plans, there comes a time when procrastinating becomes easier than making a decision. This wastes time by dragging the process out unnecessarily.

Typical Examples of Library Planning

Planning activities have traditionally been classified on the basis of the length of time involved. Long-range plans, usually called strategic plans, often are defined as covering five to ten years. Short-range plans cover briefer periods, such as those for next year or two years from now. One common example of the latter would be annual budgets. Both types have their place in library operations. Two typical examples might be as follows:

• *Library facilities.* Many librarians, particularly those in special libraries, find themselves involved in the planning of a new, or a remodeled, facility. Though exasperating at times, the reward comes when one sees the completed facility. The work involved includes preparation of an analysis of what the library needs in the way of space, special equipment, and arrangement of equipment and furnishings. Time schedules for completion of the various steps would also be needed. Working with an architect and others on the planning team can prove to be a very challenging responsibility. (More on this topic will be found in Chapter 23.)

- *Online search service.* It is not uncommon for librarians to have to prepare a proposal for instituting some particular service, such as planning for the inauguration of online searching. This would involve a study of what kind of service is needed, staffing requirements, necessary equipment, and so on.

A staff member would need to spend a lot of time and energy preparing a high-quality proposal for either of these examples. The librarian's skills in writing and communicating receive a good test when such projects come along. A useful review of the techniques involved in preparing a proposal for instituting online search service in a corporate setting appears in the paper by Martin.[9]

Besides planning for specific one-time projects the manager must be able to deal with routine operations that take place year in and year out, such as the annual budget. As you will see later in the chapter, budgeting is a crucial process that presents a real challenge for managers. For example, preparing a budget in which two new clerical workers are requested may not be as stimulating as planning a new library; nevertheless such routine documents are indispensable and offer satisfaction when produced successfully.

Not every project requires preparation of a formal proposal. The manager's supervisor can usually answer questions about the degree of formality required in a given instance.

Budgeting

It is virtually an inescapable responsibility for library managers to prepare budgets, usually done annually. The timing depends upon when the fiscal year begins in a particular organization—not all are on a calendar year basis. Whatever the time frame, it is a vital process because the budget determines more or less what the library can accomplish in a given year. The preparer must use foresight. Say a budget does not allow for increases in serial subscription costs. Then a time will come when either certain journals will have to be discontinued or money "borrowed" from other funds, neither of which would be desirable. A careful planner would have foreseen this problem and put the needed extra funds in the budget.

A paper by White discusses the relationship between corporate finance and library operations.[10] He points out the need to understand funds allocation among different departments in a typical corporate setting and gives examples of several situations. A useful article on understanding budgets that includes examples of budgeting techniques is by Sellers.[11]

In recent years more and more managers have discovered the value of preparing budgets by using spreadsheets designed for personal computers. One of the most popular versions is Lotus 1-2-3; Machalow wrote a helpful book for the library manager who wants to use Lotus.[12] A spreadsheet of this sort offers the advantage of making changes in both amounts or kinds of items to include in the budget. The software also allows one to make tentative changes and then see what effect they would have on the budget. Often called the "what if" feature, one can see what the results would be if a given change were made. If the manager does not wish to make the change, the budget returns to the original figures. As you can see, Lotus and the competing software encourage creativity in manipulating data on spreadsheets.

Types of Budgets

Several types of budgets are in common use. Koenig has written an article that describes five types of budgets and discusses ways of preparing and justifying them.[13]

In the business world, budgets involve estimates of revenues and expenditures for a given unit or organization for a given time period, usually the fiscal year. Budgets may cover time periods longer than one year, but this is uncommon. Most special libraries/information centers have virtually no revenue; in this case the budget is confined to expenditures.

Another way of looking at budgets involves seeing them as vehicles for presenting top management with proposed programs of action. Subsequent approval of the budgets would indicate approval of the programs. The latter concept probably has the most validity in organizations in which management prefers to have new programs presented as part of the annual budget process rather than dealing with them in separate, one-time documents. However, it should be noted that a manager is usually free to submit plans for new projects at any time in the fiscal year.

Various types of budgets have been identified in the literature, but four variations prevail:

1. *Line Item Budget.* This common format includes a line-by-line listing of items for which funds are allocated. There is no specific indication as to how funds are to be used. The simplicity of this type of budget is its greatest advantage as well as its greatest disadvantage.

   Here we see a typical line budget:

Salaries.	$80,000
Fringe benefits	35,000
Books and subscriptions	6,000
Binding	3,500
Office supplies	5,100
Rental of equipment	6,000
Telephones	4,300
Travel	2,000
Total	$171,900

2. *Lump Sum Budget.* Even more simple than the line item budget, this type consists of one sum of money with no breakdown into categories of expenditures. Fortu-

nately, it is not a commonly used method. It places a great deal of responsibility on the manager to use the sum wisely, and it does not stand up to scrutiny by top management.

3. *Formula budget.* A few organization use formulas to determine how funds will be allocated. A well known example of this is the Clapp-Jordan formula for budgeting collections at university libraries.[14] Although not widely used, it offers a good example of an attempt to take the guesswork out of budgeting for academic libraries. The formula is based on the number of graduate students, faculty size, number of doctoral degrees granted, number of departments served, and other elements. For each element a lump sum is allotted. Obviously, the results are no more accurate than the factors built into the formula. Other formulas have been proposed that deal with the number of staff members needed for a certain size clientele served by a special library. One reason that such budgets are not widely used is the difficulty of arriving at formulas that work.

4. *Program Budget.* This is the most complicated type of budget to prepare, but it is also the most useful. It has the advantage of supplying much information about the uses of funds in relation to *specific* programs or projects. Program budgets are best used to inform top management of services or projects in relation to their costs. It is possible to get a very good concept of a particular activity from this sort of budget. An example might look like this:

	Reference Service	Current Awareness	General Purposes	Organizing Materials	Total
Salaries	$80,000	$5,000	$35,000	$25,000	$145,000
Books	4,000	5,000	20,000		29,000
Serials		2,000	26,000		28,000
Supplies			2,000	3,000	5,000
Telephone	3,000		2,000		5,000
Online costs	4,000	3,000	1,000	4,000	12,000
Overhead	15,000	3,000	15,000	10,000	43,000
Totals	$106,000	$18,000	$101,000	$42,000	$267,000

Other Types of Budgets

One well-known version of program budgeting is the Program Planning and Budgeting System (PPBS), which originated in the federal government in the 1960s. It involves, essentially, the same process used in preparing a program budget, except that PPBS usually requires evaluating different options for achieving a particular goal before deciding upon the allocation of funds. Since libraries are obviously smaller than organizations such as the Department of Defense (in which the PPBS originated), very few have options as to who will do what. An article by Tudor describes this type of budgetary system as applied to libraries, along with a discussion of the preparation of an actual budget.[15]

Still another budgeting system is Zero-Based Budgeting (ZBB). Though similar in style to a program budget, a ZBB budget begins each budgetary period with no preconceived plans for items to include. It thus takes a fresh look at each proposed item. The system received great acclaim in governmental circles at one time, but it has had little success in smaller organizations. One reason for this is that there are not many alternatives in small organizations as to what activities will need funding. Everyone knows that collections must be enlarged (adding new issues of serials, for example) or that reference service should be offered; this is unlike large organizations, which have countless alternatives to evaluate. Another criticism is that for small organizations a careful application of ZBB takes more time than it is worth. An article by Sarndal describes her experience with the system.[16]

Preparation of Budgets

Before preparing an annual budget, a manager needs to consider what changes to make in services and the collection. It is not a process that can be rushed if it is to be done well.

Another preliminary step involves gathering statistics to help determine the basis for costs included in the finished budget and to prove the viability of the figures; one never knows when top management might question them. For example, the librarian should not overlook data on costs of literature, information published annually in journals, particularly *Publishers Weekly* and *Library Journal*. Percentage increases in costs over recent years become invaluable in estimating costs of publications for the future.

Little exists in the way of accepted standards in special libraries/information centers for certain important portions of the budget, such as the appropriate number of staff members to serve a given number of clients. The ratio of people served per professional varies tremendously from one special library to another, even if the user population is identical in size. Thus the budget maker should not count on finding some authoritative source that would serve as a justification for staff size. Some figures, such as professional salaries, listed in the annual SLA study, are easier to justify than others.

In preparing a budget, the delicate subject of padding inevitably arises. In some sectors it is expected that the budgets proposed will contain a certain percentage of padding, which, when allowed for, leaves the true figures for funds actually required. In other circles management definitely discourages padding. The manager must tactfully find out the practice at his or her organization. In passing, we might add that padding contradicts the often-expressed goal of accuracy in planning.

In establishing projected costs the manager must consider many factors, some more obvious than others. Inflation will probably not get overlooked. Other cost increases may be due to changes in operations, such as the use of more elaborate data processing equipment to speed up operations. This change in equipment would undoubtedly include higher costs for equipment lease or rental. Impending expansion of a company into new fields will certainly lead to increased costs for bringing the collection into line with the expanded subjects.

Cost Centers Versus Cost Recovery

In some special libraries/information centers the costs of operating are prorated among the various units of the sponsoring organization; estimates of the expenses incurred in serving each department are calculated annually and divided among departments. Such a library/information center would be called a *cost center*.

A variation on the cost center is the *recovery center*. It is found in organizations whose libraries serve outside customers for a fee; the charges are usually computed on an hourly basis. In a typical recovery center up to seventy percent of the annual costs of the library/information center is charged to outside companies, with the balance charged to the sponsoring organization.

Tweed has written an article that explains the difference between cost centers and recovery centers, as well as variations on the two types.[17] He also reviews some of the basic ways of producing enthusiastic customers for library services.

Talavage has written an article about cost recovery practices in industrial information centers.[18] An article by White points out the need for the manager to gain a better understanding of the role of the library in relation to cost benefit analysis.[19]

Operating Within Budget

The budgeting process would be a farce if the various units with an organization were able to overspend their budgets with no repercussions from top management. However, this seldom happens; in most organizations top management cares a great deal about operating within the budget.

Managers could take several steps to help ensure that the library/information center operates within its budget:

- Make sure the budget is as accurate as possible. If the budget that is finally approved presents hardships, talk to the supervisor at once so that cutbacks in planned expenditures can be made before the unit runs out of funds. The supervisor might even be able to have some funds restored, if it becomes apparent that the unit cannot do all it would like with a smaller budget.
- Inform the staff early in the fiscal year of any special problems that the approved budget presents. You will not be able to live within a budget if those on the staff with authority to commit funds are not kept fully informed of financial limitations. To avoid raising false hopes, do not promise relief for a reduced budget until the changes are approved.

- Monitor expenditures regularly throughout the budget year to avoid suddenly discovering that the budget is being spent too quickly. Make a monthly review and then perhaps make weekly checks during the last quarter of the fiscal year.
- Find out in advance if the organization will allow for overexpenditures in one budgeted area if counterbalanced by underexpenditures in another. Many organizations readily permit this, but not all do.
- If there are still problems living within the budget, decide which cutbacks would be feasible with the least effect on the unit's operation. Tudor's article lists dozens of possible ways in which budgets can be cut, some being more applicable to a midyear application than others.[20]
- Make sure that costs are examined to see if they can be charged to accounts outside library funds. For example, one librarian had paid for the cost of rented terminals used in the library. To her regret, she found out one day that she could have been charging them over the years to a capital budget not associated with the library.

It should be apparent that the manager must devote sufficient time and effort to keep fully aware of how well the library is adhering to the budget and, furthermore, must keep his or her supervisor advised of any problems that might arise. Like most aspects of management, the sooner one addresses a problem, the less likely it will develop into a more serious difficulty.

In the event a library must adopt a smaller budget, an article by Bell provides several ideas for enabling a library manager to provide adequate service and still survive budget cuts.[21] He describes five areas in which budgetary constraints could be less binding, ranging from seeking ways to share services with other units to increasing productivity.

References

1. Stueart, Robert D.; Moran, Barbara B. *Library management*. 3d ed. Littleton, CO: Libraries Unlimited; 1987. 376 p.

Provides an explanation of the responsibilities of the manager in regard to planning. The book also covers different types of planning and the role of goals or objectives.

2. Webb, G. M. Preparing staff for participative management. *Wilson Library Bulletin*. 62(9): 50-52; 1988 May.

Discusses ways to interest a staff in participatory management, using workshops, task forces, and other devices to enlist their activity. Stresses the value of determining staff needs in order to set goals for the process.

3. Humble, John W. *How to manage by objectives*. New York: Amacom; 1973. 150 p.

Reviews the principles of management by objectives and also points out the common mistakes made in applying the system. Contains many "real life" examples of its use.

4.   Stanton, Robert O. Applying the management-by-objective technique in an industrial library. *Journal of the American Society for Information Science.* 26(6): 313-317; 1975 Nov./Dec.

Describes the use of MBO at the library/information center at Bell Laboratories; a typical list of objectives for a supervisor is shown and comments on same are included.

5.   Jones, William. An evaluation of the use of MBO procedures in a library. *Special Libraries.* 66(7): 306-312; 1975 July.

Discusses the application of MBO techniques at the engineering library at Northwestern University; includes descriptions of jobs, schedules, training techniques, and evaluations.

6.   Mourey, Deborah A.; Mansfield, Jerry W. Quality circles for management decisions: what's in it for libraries? *Special Libraries.* 75(2): 87-94; 1984 April.

Gives the history of the technique, describes its operation, then relates how several libraries have used it. The authors also include an outline of conditions lending themselves to this method.

7.   Berner, Andrew. The importance of time management in the small library. *Special Libraries.* 78(4): 271-276; 1987 Fall.

Points out the need for careful attention to how one uses time on the job; describes fallacies about the use of time, such as the belief that time management stifles creativity.

8.   Winston, Stephanie. *The organized executive: a program for productivity: new ways to manage time, paper and people.* New York: Norton; 1983. 345 p.

A readable book written for the manager who needs to become more productive and efficient. Has many examples that illustrate its points.

9.   Martin, Jean K. Preparation of proposals for online bibliographic services in academic, government and industrial libraries. *Science & Technology Libraries.* 1(1): 7-17; 1980 Fall.

Discusses the various steps involved in preparing proposals once the key factors are identified. The article also points out the contents of the ideal proposal.

10. White, Herbert S. Special libraries and the corporate political process. *Special Libraries.* 75(2): 81-86; 1984 April.

Describes the effects of political decisions on the financial positions of corporate libraries. The competition for funds between the library and other departments is analyzed and solutions suggested.

11. Sellers, David Y. Basic planning and budgeting concepts for special libraries. *Special Libraries.* 64(2): 70-75; 1973 Feb.

Points out the importance of mastering budgeting techniques and gives illustrations of their use.

12. Machalow, Robert. *Using Lotus 1-2-3: a how-to-do-it manual for library applications.* New York: Neal-Schuman Publishers; 1989. 166 p. (How-to-do-it manuals for libraries number 1)

and Information Centers   **51**

Provides guidance for the librarian who knows nothing about Lotus, then proceeds to give numerous examples of its possible uses in libraries, such as the department budget, the book budget, and timesheets.

13. Koenig, Michael E. D. Budgets and budgeting. *Special Libraries*. 68(7/8): 228-240; 1977 July/Aug.

Describes and illustrates several types of budgets; also discusses the methods of preparing budgets in terms of library applications.

14. Clapp, Verner W.; Jordan, Robert T. Quantitative criteria for adequacy of academic library collections. *College & Research Libraries*. 26(5): 371-380; 1965 Sept.

A well-known formula that attempts to put rational calculations to work in budgeting rather than using more casual methods. Although designed for academic libraries, special librarians should at least be familiar with it.

15. Tudor, Dean. The special library budget. *Special Libraries*. 63(11): 517-527; 1972 Nov.

Explains the features of the Program Planning and Budgeting System (PPBS) as applied to libraries. Includes a discussion on how to prepare the budget document.

16. Sarndal, Anne G. Zero-base budgeting. *Special Libraries*. 70(12): 527-532; 1979 Dec.

Besides describing the features of zero-base budgeting, the author also discusses the problems and the advantages it offers.

17. Tweed, Stephen C. The library as a profit center. *Special Libraries*. 75(4): 270-274; 1984 Oct.

Gives examples from different types of libraries in areas such as charge-backs of service costs, availability of profits from customers outside the organization, and variations of sources of library funds.

18. Talavage, Joseph. Financial aspects of industrial information centers: a survey. *Journal of the American Society for Information Science*. 30(3): 154-160; 1979 May.

Reviews results of a survey of 175 industrial information centers. Stresses the importance of cost recovery.

19. White, Herbert S. Cost-effectiveness and cost-benefit determinations in special libraries. *Special Libraries*. 70(4): 163-169; 1979 Apr.

Stresses the need for library managers to understand the financial interests of the organizations they serve. Discusses the need to pay special attention to cost-benefit analysis.

20. Tudor; *op. cit.*

21. Bell, Steven J. Cutback management for special libraries: strategies for library survival. *Special Libraries*. 75(3): 205-213; 1984 July.

A careful review of ways to cope with budget cutbacks, such as resource development (seeking ways to increase income sources and/or charge back more to users); productivity (use planning and staff training to ensure efficiency on the job); economy measures (use modern equipment/techniques and reductions of staff salary increases); interorganizational cooperation (find ways to share purchasing, space, and services); and reorganization (consider mergers, centralization, and purchase of services, if more economical than doing them in-house).

Chapter 7

Organizing and Staffing

A well-organized and well-staffed special library/information center will undoubtedly be more successful than one having a poorly designed organizational framework and an inadequate staff. A manager, no matter how effective, can do only so much—the rest depends on the staff. This chapter will review ways to organize a unit and build a good staff. The text by Stueart and Moran covers these topics well.[1] Some attention also will be given to the special nature and problems of staffing the one-person library.

Organizational Pattern

If a unit had twenty employees, one possible method of organization would be to have all employees report directly to the manager. This would be an inefficient pattern since it would keep the manager tied down by each person's problems and would not take advantage of the skills and supervisory talents of staff members. No effective manager would organize a unit in this fashion.

How, then, might you, as manager, set up an effective organizational structure? Here are some suggestions:

- Establish clear-cut lines of authority. Normally, a person should have only one supervisor.
- Distinguish between line and staff positions. People in line positions have authority to supervise others; those in staff positions serve in an advisory capacity.
- Have an adequate number of supervisors.
- In larger units do not have an excessive number of people reporting directly to the manager.
- Have an organization chart which is made freely available to employees in the unit; make sure it is kept up to date.

These suggestions may aid the manager in planning an organization. Bear in mind that much of the success of a unit depends upon the type and quality of the people involved. An organization that seems perfect on paper may not function as well as one less skillfully organized if the people involved in the "perfect" organization are not well suited to their positions.

The following examples of organization charts may prove to be useful to the reader; one is for a relatively small staff (the ABC Library) and the other for a larger unit (the XYZ Information Service).

Note in the ABC Library that the secretary occupies a staff position and does not supervise anyone, whereas the reference librarian and the cataloger have line positions since each supervises one person. Note also that the chart bears a date; this makes it clear when a particular organizational plan was adopted. Job titles should be as descriptive as possible; that is, the titles "Circulation Clerk" and "Cataloging Clerk" are preferable to "Clerk," which does not indicate the area where the person works. Also consider indicating on the chart which of the two professionals reporting to the library manager would serve as the acting manager, should the need arise. Some organizations may not wish to indicate this on a formal chart; the assignment may depend on the qualifications of the incumbents.

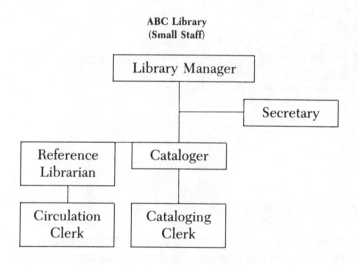

ABC Library
(Small Staff)

Library Manager

Secretary

Reference Librarian

Cataloger

Circulation Clerk

Cataloging Clerk

July 1979

Following is the chart for the XYZ Information Services, representing a much larger organization.

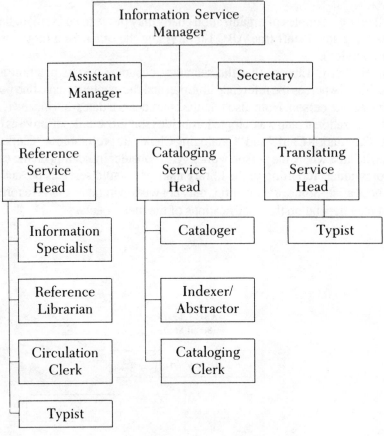

April 1980

Note that the assistant manager reports directly to the manager, as do the three heads and the secretary. Each of the unit heads supervises from one to four employees.

While the boundary lines between sections are distinct, during certain periods employees could be temporarily shifted from one unit to the other. Unusual work loads, temporary staff shortages because of illness, vacations, or unfilled positions are typical instances in which the manager must be flexible about assignments.

Effective staff organization contributes to efficiency. At the same time consider the position of the library/information center in the sponsoring organization when setting up the unit's organizational structure. The manager usually has little say about where the unit is to be placed in the general scheme of things, although on rare occasions top management may ask for recommendations. (For further information on this topic, see Chapter 5.)

Staff Composition Size

Staffing a library/information center would be simplified if there were accepted standards or formulas to determine the type and number of positions for a given number of users of the services. However, no such standards exist, since there are so many factors involved. To make these decisions, the manager can only confer with other managers serving similar organizations in view of the fact that staff sizes vary tremendously from one type of organization to another. One prominent research organization, serving hundreds of engineers, has only one librarian on the staff, whereas in the New York City financial world it is not unusual for a well-known company to have a ratio of twenty financial analysts per library staff member. Most examples are less lopsided, but even so, a person who could devise a workable formula for staff sizes would win the undying gratitude of countless managers.

There is similar disagreement as to staff makeup. One can identify several types of skills needed—reference skills, cataloging, indexing, translating, editing, systems development, and perhaps one or two others. Beyond these, other specialties are unusual, regardless of a unit's size. Subject specialization is another matter, as the subject concentrations of special libraries and information centers cover the alphabet, from art to zoology.

One staffing situation to avoid is that of having too few clerical workers; otherwise the professional staff is apt to spend too much of its time keyboarding, filing, or sorting. Having such highly priced "clerks" not only wastes the sponsor's money but it also devastates professional morale. An experienced manager can usually predict when such a situation has been created or is apt to arise, at which point top management must be convinced of the wisdom of hiring more clerks. The manager must be sure that all appropriate labor-saving devices are being used; in some cases it is easier to obtain funds for new equipment than for hiring more employees.

Job Descriptions

Job descriptions are necessary to inform employees what is expected of them and to indicate the relationship of their jobs to the rest of the unit. Requirements for positions are also usually part of the descriptions, as are titles. A variety of job titles are currently in use, some examples of which are:

Professional		Paraprofessional	Clerical
Assistant Manager	Cataloger	Library Assistant	Secretary
Assistant Librarian	Indexer	Cataloging Assistant	Cataloging Clerk
Reference Librarian	Abstractor	Reference Assistant	Reference Clerk
Information Specialist	Translator	Library Technician	Typist
Systems Analyst	Editor		Clerk-typist
			Shelver

Professional positions normally require at least one college degree for those who are translators, indexers, editors, and systems analysts. Library positions usually require at least a master's degree. Having a degree in a subject pertinent to the sponsor's field of interest is usually a great advantage for a prospective applicant. Positions as information specialists in certain subject areas may even require a doctorate.

Paraprofessionals are expected to have some college training, although not necessarily a degree. Clerical skills are usually clearly specified because the duties for paraprofessional positions invariable involve typing and filing along with more demanding tasks.

Clerical employees are required to have high school diplomas or the equivalent, as well as certain clerical skills.

For all kinds of positions, job descriptions should indicate the previous experience in appropriate work that is expected. It is assumed that all employees will be able to work harmoniously with others (an assumption that does not always prove true). Such a qualification may be included in a job description.

Job descriptions may indicate the pay range for a position, although not the pay of the incumbent. Pay scales are set by the personnel department of the sponsoring organization. Such departments may request the assistance of the manager for establishing pay scales for new positions in the unit and also may confer on this matter with their counterparts in other organizations. Different levels of positions will have varying levels of pay. For example, there may be four grades for clerical salaries, five or six pay grades for professional non-managerial positions, and a dozen pay grades for managerial positions. They often overlap, so that a newcomer to a second level pay grade may be earning less than an experienced person in the first grade.

Two typical examples of job descriptions may illustrate these points.

Note the variation in the two examples as to the listing of duties. There is no generally accepted format for job descriptions; each organization sets its own style. Also note the inclusion of a duty to perform related tasks as assigned—this is advisable to avoid difficulties if there is a need for the employee to perform tasks which are within his or her range of abilities yet do not happen to be specified in the job description. No one can foresee what new tasks may come along that would be appropriate to assign to a particular job. (see Figure 1)

Procedure Manuals

A necessary companion for a job description is a procedure manual. This is a detailed listing of duties to be carried out by each employee, along with enough descriptive information to enable a person to perform the duties with little supervision. Such manuals are invaluable aids in training new employees, particularly if the last incumbent is no longer available to aid in the process. The manuals must be kept current to avoid time-consuming updates.

Procedure manuals should be organized into broad categories of duties, then subdivided into smaller tasks. The inclusion of sample forms is an aid to clarity. Naturally, manuals for

MAJESTIC CHEMICAL COMPANY

Position:	Reference Librarian I	**Reports to:**	Head, Reference Section
Department:	Information Center	**Date:**	January 1990

Basic Functions: Assists library clientele by locating requested information and preparing bibliographies, using printed and online search tools. Recommends pertinent sources of information to appropriate clientele. Assists in the selection of information materials for the collection in assigned subject fields. Supervises one clerical position.

Duties and Responsibilities:
1. **Supervision:** Supervises one clerk-typist, who files materials, keeps circulation records, and types bibliographies.
2. **Literature Searches:** Locates requested information, using both printed sources and online sources. Upon request will prepare bibliographies on specified topics, creating or supplying abstracts if desired.
3. **Collection Development:** Assists in the selection of materials for the collection by selecting items in assigned subject areas. Peruses book reviews, publishers' brochures, and other selection aids.
4. **Current Awareness Service:** Maintains awareness of current information and notifies clientele in prescribed subject areas of items of interest.
5. **Special Projects:** Assists head of reference section in the preparation on long-term literature searches, bibliographies, and similar projects as assigned.

Special Qualifications: Master's degree in library science plus bachelor's degree in a physical science. Ability to work well with clientele. May have knowledge of one or more foreign languages (German or Russian preferred.) Three years of supervisory experience required.

ROSARIO & COHEN (Law Firm)

Position:	Clerk-typist B	**Reports to:**	Head, Cataloging Section
Department:	Library	**Date:**	June 1990

Basic function: Types records and inputs data into computer. Assists at circulation desk as needed. Performs related tasks.

Duties and Responsibilities:
1. Types records, working from data supplied.
2. Inputs catalog data into computerized catalog.
3. Prepares monthly statistical reports, using data supplied.
4. Files returned reports in vertical files.
5. Assists at circulation desk as needed.
6. Answers simple reference questions; refers more complicated ones to Reference Librarians.
7. Performs related duties as assigned.

Special Qualifications: High school diploma or equivalent. Must type 60 WPM. Must pass filing test given to check accuracy of filing. Must have one year of clerical experience. Must have ability to work with clients.

Figure 1.

professional jobs would have less in the way of detailed "how-to-do-it" instructions than one for a clerical post. A looseleaf format facilitates updating.

An article by Wender[2] describes the nature and use of procedure manuals and also stresses an important point, namely the need for supervisors to make incumbents in positions comfortable about recommending ways for improving procedures at any stage of their employment. She feels that a despotic library manager could so dominate the process of establishing and recording procedures that employees would never be consulted and would develop a feeling of antagonism towards the manager-decreed rules.

One-Person Libraries

A large percentage of special libraries are so small there is only one person on the staff; some small units can afford the "luxury" of an additional person to round out the staff. In many cases the person in charge is a professionally trained librarian, while the second person is a clerk or clerk-typist.

In spite of the small staff size, the person in charge has almost all the problems of a manager of any size unit except that of organizing the staff. There is still a budget to prepare, plans for user services to make and carry out, top management personnel to deal with, and other such responsibilities. In addition, the head of the library must perform all the functions done by professionals—collection building, reference service, cataloging, and representing the library to the organization.

A well-written summary of the nature of operating a one-person library was prepared by St. Clair.[3] He points out the freedom in such units to decide one's own schedule and to set one's own priorities, a feature which might appeal to many librarians. He also describes the drawbacks of such positions. Promotional opportunities within the organization are nearly zero, unless one takes a position outside the library unit. Another problem is that there is usually no one in the organization with whom to confer when seeking the comments of a person knowing anything about library matters, as would be the case when other professionals were around. A new librarian on his or her first job would have no experienced colleague on the staff from whom to learn, which could inhibit growth unless the librarian went out of his or her way to keep in close touch with colleagues in other libraries. The dangers of getting bogged down in unimportant clerical tasks in a small library, neglecting professional responsibilities, are noted in an article by Holladay.[4]

References

1.   Stueart, Robert D.; Moran, Barbara B. *Library management*. 3d ed. Littleton, CO: Libraries Unlimited; 1987; Chap. 4.

Describes different kinds of organizational plans for libraries and presents sample organization charts. Discusses staffing as related to performance evaluation, job descriptions, and pay scales.

2.   Wender, Ruth W. The procedure manual. *Special Libraries*. 68(11): 407-410; 1977 Nov.

Explains the techniques of creating procedure manuals and also sets forth the purpose of such documents. Relates experience with these records at a health-sciences library.

3.   St. Clair, Guy. The one-person library: an essay on essentials revisited. *Special Libraries*. 78(4): 263-270; 1987 Fall.

Discusses the responsibilities and privileges of one-person libraries. Reviews the means for obtaining education in this special field.

4.   Holladay, Janice. Small libraries: keeping the professional position professional. *Special Libraries*. 72(1): 63-66; 1981 Jan.

Points out the priorities to be given to professional tasks that are at a high level. Includes ways to enhance the status of the special library.

Chapter 8

Supervising

Supervising—directing the work of others—is an important aspect of management. Although simple to define, supervising is not simple to perform. Some managers excel at supervising; others do not. There are no formulas that guarantee to make every manager a good supervisor, but following certain principles and practices can certainly help.

This chapter will review the practices involved in supervision and briefly discuss the importance of a positive attitude for those in such positions. The size and type of library or information center have a lot to do with how certain aspects of supervising are carried out, but, whatever the conditions, the quality of supervision is crucial. In all but the smallest units (such as the one-person library) people must receive direction; many new graduates of library schools may find themselves at their first job supervising other employees. For that reason, one must know what this process involves. Those interested in a basic discussion of supervising would find the book by Stueart helpful.[1] He covers all aspects of the topic, including leadership.

Attitudes of Supervisors

Not all people, librarians included, like to supervise others. They may prefer to do their own work, not being responsible for the performance of their colleagues. Others, on the other hand, enjoy the challenge of directing the work of others, not for the sense of power or influence the position may seem to offer; rather they enjoy the satisfaction of creating a smooth working team that accomplishes a great deal. Such supervisors, who get their rewards from seeing the group as a whole do well, are usually quick to give credit to the employees. Good supervisors realize that without reliable, hard-working employees little would be accomplished; they consider excellent performance of the organization a result of a team effort.

In general, good supervisors tend to be very aware of the feelings and morale of their employees. People who would take advantage of kindly supervisors do not fool such managers; nevertheless they pay attention to the needs of sincere employees. Such supervisors usually find their employees giving their best effort on the job, knowing that their supervisors are fair and care about them. The harsh, unfeeling boss may accomplish certain goals by virtue of instilling a sense of fear or stress in employees, but, in the long run, the considerate supervisor will undoubtedly achieve more through intelligent concern for employees than the overbearing martinet accomplishes in an atmosphere of tension.

Good supervisors are not considerate of other people simply to get more work done but because being considerate is the way they deal with everyone; it's part of their life style.

Hiring the Staff

Assuming approval of the organizational plan for the unit and preparation of job descriptions, the supervisor and the personnel department decide where and when to advertise the jobs. Newspapers, professional journals, nearby library schools, maintained by local library chapters—these are some of the means by which the openings can be made known. The wording of the ads must be decided on jointly by the supervisor (or manager) and the personnel department. They also must decide whether or not to use a blind ad—one in which the name of the organization is replaced by a mailing address or box number. However, applicants generally dislike this approach. In using a blind ad the employer does not have to answer disappointed applicants, but this offers little consolation to applicants who would at least like to know to whom they are applying.

Only those most qualified should receive a personal interview, with the manager or supervisor present. It is devastating to the morale of applicants to speak only to personnel staff during interviews. If a serious applicant lives some distance away, the organization should pay travel expenses to the interview, if funds permit.

Interviewing applicants is a fine art that not every supervisor has mastered. One must not let personal bias of race, sex, country of origin, and the like influence the process. Even personal questions, such as marital status, religion, age, race, and living style are taboo. Laws prohibit practices of this. The applicant should be encouraged to describe relevant interests and experience in an informal way. By selecting key words for questions, such as those involving the why, what, and how of past experience, the supervisor can keep the interview moving along in a fruitful manner. At the end of the interview the interviewer should tell the applicant what will happen next. For example, some jobs, especially clerical ones, require performance tests. If given, they should be objective, standardized, and given to each applicant for such jobs.

Successful applicants are seldom a perfect match for the job; usually a compromise is made on some requirements or qualifications. A less-than-perfect educational background, for example, may be compensated for by very strong work experience. References from former employers are usually checked somewhere along the line; speaking to those who know the applicant is a very satisfactory first check, when feasible. Of course, not all applicants get hired, but it is only courteous to advise unsuccessful applicants of the outcome, especially those who were notified that they were being considered.

Shaughnessy has written an article that considers the effect of new technology on the changing of jobs, and shows how most positions are becoming more complicated.[2]

In recent years there has been an increase in the number of libraries which hire temporary workers as well as use staff members furnished on a contract basis by private companies designed for that purpose, the latter case being more common in government libraries than in the private sector. In either case the library manager should be involved in the acceptance of new staff members. Unsatisfactory performance, if that were to occur, should provide no different situation to the manager than if the person involved were hired on a permanent basis as an individual, unrelated to any outside company. The employer should be free to treat all individuals the same way.

Evaluation of Staff Members

Every well-organized employer has a system for periodic evaluation of employees. Employees generally are on probation for various time periods—the more responsible the position, the longer the probation period. A typist's probation might last only one month, while a professional's may be six months. Newly hired employees should know about the period when hired and told how it will affect their employment.

Most organizations have standardized forms for evaluating employees which the supervisor fills out. After an evaluation is done, whether at the end of probationary periods, on the annual anniversary date of a person's date of hire, or at the end of a fiscal year, the employee should be shown the evaluation and asked for comments before the document is sent to the manager of the unit and the personnel department. The employee should have the right to discuss an unfavorable review with others in management besides the supervisor who prepared it. All evaluations should strive for fairness and frankness. They should not stress only negative points; the employee's strengths should also be included. Decisions on salaries and promotions should not be made without full use of evaluations, where available.

Training of Employees

The speed and ease with which new employees learn the duties of their positions depend largely upon the quality of the training they receive from supervisors. A carefully planned program leads to thorough training that is accomplished with the least amount of time. Training ranges from a general orientation concerning basic facts about the sponsoring organization to very small details regarding the employees' specific duties.

Besides brochures and leaflets available from the personnel department, the employee should be furnished with adequate information about the special library/information center, such as the organization chart, any statement about the goals of the unit, and a procedures manual. These materials, while helpful, provide minimum help to the new employee; the chief need involves clear explanations and guidance until tasks are learned. A supervisor could ask an experienced employee to help in the training process, but the responsibility still belongs to the supervisor. The supervisor should periodically have short talks with the employee, allowing more and more time between conferences as the person learns the work. The slower the person is to learn, the more attention should be given by the supervisor or an experienced employee. If tests are appropriate to check the results of training, every step should be taken to make the person feel at ease. If the employee is not doing well, problem areas should be explained and clarified as soon as possible. Obviously, errors should be pointed out only in private and presented in as considerate a manner as possible. The employer should reserve stern admonitions for the employee who is not making an effort to do the job well.

Firing Staff Members

Most supervisors dislike dealing with employees who are not suited for their positions; it is much more pleasant to have employees succeed at their jobs. In addition to the difficult task of dismissing an employee, the supervisor must juggle the schedules of other employees to maintain the workload in the unit until the vacant position is filled, and even more difficult, has to justify to superiors the cost of hiring a new employee. Interviewing, hiring, and training a new person all represent time taken away from accomplishing normal duties. Depending upon the amount of training needed in a specific job, sometimes quite a while goes by before new employees begin to earn their salaries. Despite all these drawbacks, sometimes a person must be asked to leave.

Someone might be fired for personal reasons, such as inattention or laziness. Others do not learn their job in what the employer has established as a reasonable time period. In the latter case, the employee may have had an exemplary probation period as far as personal characteristics were concerned but perhaps was in a job unsuited for his or her skills and aptitudes. In other cases, a long-time employee may have deteriorated in work performance to such an extent that efforts by the supervisor to improve the person's level of work failed. Such a person is often the hardest to let go, but the patience and efforts of an employer to help such a person are not unlimited. Once employees leave, it takes a master of diplomacy to respond truthfully to any reference requests from other employers regarding that person. In recent years many organizations no longer provide information about a former employee; perhaps they might say only that he or she was employed for a particular time period. Uneasiness about possible law suits is generally the cause for such a policy.

Labor Unions

In some sponsoring organizations some or all of the non-supervisory employees in a special library/information center may be members of labor unions, whether by choice or by law. In such cases, in order to have smooth relationships with employees, the supervisor must keep certain conditions in mind. In some instances union membership makes little or no difference to daily operations; in others it makes a great deal of difference.

Unions have gained recognition because employees were dissatisfied with working conditions, such as salaries, hours of work, and fringe benefits. Some unions brought about improved working conditions and tried to help employees having difficulties holding or advancing in their jobs. Other labor unions were not so helpful; some of them, it must be said, brought an atmosphere of tension to organizations and left little to show for their efforts. The wise supervisor should accept unions as a common part of the modern scene, while still standing up for the rights of management to manage its business with reasonable rules and procedures. It would be foolish to overlook the fact that in the past there have been errors on the part of both management and union. Some organizations have not treated their employees fairly, and some unions have been involved more in disruption than in improving conditions. Ideally, both sides should conduct their business in an atmosphere of respect and reasonableness.

Unionization usually brings about a very rigid set of job descriptions for each position. A supervisor who regularly asks an employee to do a task belonging to a higher job rating would probably be faced in time with a union steward asking for a promotion for the person. Any favoritism shown toward one or more employees would also be likely to draw the attention of the union (an understandable result)—the practice is not to be condoned. Extra pay for overtime is carefully maintained, as are days off for sickness, vacations, and jury duty. Unions keep steady pressure on management for better pay.

In general, clerical and paraprofessional employees are more apt to be members of unions than professional members, although both groups may be union members in some organizations. It is more difficult to measure output and performance of professionals than of clerks. On the other hand, professionals may depend more upon their own ability on the job for furthering their advancement than do clerks, who may feel less attachment to their routine tasks.

Supervisory Responsibilities

Probably the main duty of supervisors involves providing leadership to their employees. What is leadership? It can be defined in many ways, but one good definition is the ability to move a group towards its goals. This assumes that the group has goals and is adequately staffed and trained.

Leadership involves many functions. First of all, one must use the staff in the best way possible, which requires knowing the abilities and talents of employees and making proper use of these skills and interests. Not all employees have what they consider an ideal job, but a good supervisor tries to find the best assignment possible for each person.

Another supervisory function involves motivating employees to achieve their goals. A dull and lethargic supervisor can hardly expect the people in the unit to build up much enthusiasm for their work. Conversely, we have all known leaders who are so enthusiastic for the project at hand that others following them also become enthusiastic. Enthusiasm does not have to be of the boisterous "cheerleader" type; it can be quiet yet at the same time evident and sincere.

Supervisors also have the important responsibility of assigning work to employees. Even when each employee has a well-defined job description and a detailed procedure manual, a need exists to vary routine duties when the situation calls for it. "Crash" programs are needed at times, even in the best libraries/information centers, and a good supervisor must be able to switch people's duties to meet the need of the moment. Likewise, when the staff is temporarily shorthanded because of vacancy, illness, or vacation, the supervisor must be able to assign duties in such a way that the most important functions are still accomplished. When strict union rules exist about the level of work each person can accomplish, the situations challenge supervisors even more; on occasion, supervisors may have to take on certain tasks themselves for a short period.

Burnout Problems

In recent years the term "burnout" has appeared regularly in the literature. In essence it refers to emotional exhaustion resulting from stress on the job. Here we are concerned with work-related aspects of burnout. An article by Blevins describes some of the symptoms as irritability, paranoia, and cynicism, often accompanied by angry outbursts, exhaustion, and sometimes drug and alcohol abuse. [3] Her article also considers some preventive measures one could take. One method involves seeking more outside interests, such as hobbies or professional development in librarianship, or taking continuing education courses, or even developing new, attainable goals for oneself. Blevins also recommends that during recruitment for job openings the interviewer point out the stressful aspects of a position so that a potential new employee could prepare for them emotionally.

Another article on burnout, written by Smith and Nelson, points out that some special librarians suffer burnout because of the pressure of constantly seeking to help library clients. [4] The authors discuss the symptoms of burnout and how to cope with this kind of pressure.

The introduction of new technology has begun to create a special kind of burnout called "technostress." An article by Bichteler describes it as the stress due to a person's inability to deal with computers and other forms of technology. [5] She examines its prevalence in special libraries and offers some solutions. Insufficient training in new equipment is seen as one cause.

An interesting survey on burnout among corporate librarians was described in an article by Smith and Nielsen. [6] They found much evidence of burnout, often occurring when librarians felt a lack of appreciation for their efforts.

Most writers delegate the responsibility of avoiding burnout to the individual, feeling that it is avoidable. The literature offers many suggestions for coping with stress successfully before the effects become critical.

References

1.   Stueart, Robert D.; Moran, Barbara B. *Library management*. 3d ed. Littleton, CO: Libraries Unlimited; 1987; Chap. 5.

    Besides discussing the various styles of supervising, the authors also cover such topics as motivation of employees, leadership techniques, and staff training methods.

2.   Shaughnessy, Thomas W. Redesigning library jobs. *Journal of the American Society for Information Science*. 29(4): 187-190; 1978 July.

Still a timely article in that it discusses how technical advances change the nature of jobs, making them more productive but perhaps more difficult at the same time. Points out the need of management to keep abreast of the times.

3.   Blevins, Beth. Burnout in special libraries. *Library Management Quarterly*. 11(4):17-22; 1988 Fall.

Describes the effects of burnout in special libraries and some probable causes. Ways of preventing it are also discussed. Includes a useful bibliography.

4.   Smith, Nathan M.; Nelson, Vaneese C. Helping may be harmful; the implications of burnout for the special librarian. *Special Libraries*. 74(1): 14-19; 1983 January.

Discusses the symptoms of burnout and how to cope with it. A table summarizes solutions offered by more than a score of authorities.

5.   Bichteler, Julie. Human aspects of high tech in special libraries. *Special Libraries*. 77(3): 121-128; 1986 Summer.

Explains the nature of technostress and cites results of a survey of several dozen members of online user groups and other employees involved with computers. Offers some solutions.

6.   Smith, Nathan M.; Nielsen, Laura F. Burnout: a survey of corporate librarians. *Special Libraries*. 75(3): 221-227; 1984 July.

Provides findings on a survey of 150 corporate libraries. They found that lack of personal accomplishment was the greatest cause of burnout, commonly occurring when there was inadequate positive feedback from clients or when there was a lack of control over library operations. Presents quite a bit of data on the subject.

Chapter 9

Marketing

There are many definitions of marketing; wise library managers will get familiar with the subject once they realize the importance of the process. Skill in marketing can make a great difference in the degree of success special libraries and information centers achieve.

Many librarians think of marketing as limited to the advertising process; some of them even consider advertising as an activity having little or no place in a special library. Yet when the clients of such libraries do their work largely unaware of what the libraries have to offer in the way of services offered or collections available, these same librarians may begin to see the need for advertising, also known as promotion of services. So even those who have a very limited concept of marketing often come around to acknowledging that the process does relate to library operations.

Main Aspects of Marketing

A thorough discussion of the nature of marketing and its implications for special libraries is found in the paper by Zachert and Williams.[1] They identify these five main aspects of marketing:

1. *Marketing segmentation.* Identifying markets (actual and potential) as well as non-markets within the organization. Some groups have a strong need for library services while others have little need for them. It is necessary to determine the proportion of both those having a definite need for service as well those with few or no needs. Conducting surveys, described in the next chapter, is probably the best way to determine these figures.
2. *Market positioning.* Determining the priority of serving the needs of primary users, developing both long- and short-range goals. Sources of funds to handle costs must be determined.
3. *Consumer analysis.* Measuring the extent of the needs of different groups and their preferences for various services. Quantitative data must be gathered.
4. *Marketing program.* Choosing the proper mix of services and costs along with promotion of the services. Deciding what will be offered and making sure users are aware of important services.

5. *Marketing audit.* Evaluating plans and their implementation. Measurements should be made of the efficacy of the marketing program, while allowing for future revisions.

This paper includes a brief discussion of cost-benefit analysis as one major aspect of marketing audits—the process helps one determine if the benefits of a particular library activity are more or less than the costs, in dollar figures.

It can be seen from the aforementioned elements that marketing deals with more than just promotional activity. It involves much attention to learning what clients need and understanding the best ways to meet those needs. Certainly it would be foolish to place a lot of emphasis on advertising services if one weren't sure that the average client wanted those services in the first place. One way to become aware of user needs is for the library manager to sit in on meetings of supervisors, where it would not be difficult to inquire about the degree to which the library is meeting the needs of its clients. Sometimes a manager must conduct a quiet campaign to reach the point of being accepted as worthy of a seat at management meetings.

Promotional Activities

Although marketing is a multifaceted activity, promotion, or advertising, is an important aspect of it. The author knows of many libraries whose clients are unaware of what services are available because these libraries did little or no promotion. An article by Keeler includes suggestions of some ways to advertise services, including several time-honored techniques.[2]

Some methods for advertising include:

1. Library newsletters—informing users of new services and new equipment, along with listings of selected new acquisitions.
2. Posters and signs—announcing new programs as well as demonstrations of new equipment or new databases. A bonus of this method is its low cost.
3. Dissemination of information to pertinent users—sending notices of new books or listings of appropriate articles/reports to interested clients. A proactive stance is better than a reactive one when meeting users' needs.
4. Instructional sessions with new employees—introducing the library and its features to newly hired people is a good way to make sure they are aware of what the library has to offer.
5. Bookmarks or book bags (for inclement weather)—providing still another way to inform clients. Announcements of library services could be printed on these products, which would be an inexpensive promotional device.
6. When the library has given unusually good service to a client, discreetly ask the one served to write a short note of thanks "for the record" in order to build up a file of concrete examples of services rendered. Many clients will agree to this simple request.

Creative Activities

Promotional activities can be as varied as the imagination and creativity of the staff permit. Some librarians seize on some seemingly obscure event or situation and turn it into a promotional success. As an example, when the 1,000th (or 500th) online search was performed for a client, such managers would feature the event in the local house organ or in the library's bulletin. If one of the staff won an award, they would note this as a news item. Some libraries are located in towns or cities where a local newspaper would print news items about library events. Many of the employees, or their families, might see such items and feel pleased at seeing their company in the news. Such techniques rarely save the day for a library during severe budget cuts, but they don't do any harm and may influence an executive toward providing support.

New techniques are constantly being created that can be utilized in promotional activities. For example, instead of a conventional lecture to new employees in an orientation, a videotape, even if only a few minutes long, could probably hold the audience's attention longer and be more meaningful. A few words before and after running the tape could give extra emphasis to major points and invite to use library services. The same method could be used with a tape/slide show about the library and its services.

An article by Shapiro discusses ways of promoting library services, listing specific techniques that could be useful.[3] He stresses the importance of giving careful thought to this activity. An approach recommended by Echelman is that of using the library's reference service as a "salesman" for the library, particularly when a top executive has been aided by its service.[4] She points out the need for approaching library operations in a businesslike way, including giving ample regard to marketing techniques.

References

1.   Zachert, Martha Jane; Williams, Robert V. Marketing measures for information services. *Special Libraries*. 77(2): 61-70; 1986 Spring.

Discusses the five key marketing concepts and their application to special libraries. Besides promotional activities, identifying needs of user groups, determining the proper mix of services, and evaluating marketing activities are explained in relation to libraries. The role of collecting pertinent data is also stressed.

2.   Keeler, Elizabeth. Mainstreaming the new library. *Special Libraries*. 73(4): 260-265; 1982 October.

Discusses the role of marketing, including advertising, in corporate libraries. The need for professionalism is stressed along with some ideas about specific types of advertising.

3.   Shapiro, Stanley J. Marketing and the informational professional: odd couple or meaningful relationship? *Special Libraries*. 71(11): 469-474; 1980 Nov.

Reviews promotional techniques and points out applications in special libraries.

4.   Echelman, Shirley. Libraries are businesses too! *Special Libraries*. 65(10/11): 409-414; 1974 Oct./Nov.

Stresses the need for the manager to be able to speak the language of business and to operate the library in a business like way. Marketing is seen as an important part of library activities.

Chapter 10

Evaluating Operations

The alert manager of a library or information center constantly observes and evaluates the progress and the problems of the unit. Smugness over past successes, as well as a reluctance to face up to current problems, can lead to difficult times for a manager. As long as no one in authority is concerned about the status of operations, it is very likely that small problems will grow into large problems. The longer one waits to tackle those problems, the worse they become.

This chapter presents three ways to evaluate operations. The first method involves a formal committee of users who are encouraged to present comments and ideas for bettering the library. The second consists of formal evaluation of user comments, gleaned through the use of questionnaires and interviews. The third avenue relies on hiring a consultant, one who is conversant with library operations, to make evaluations.

Library Committees

An article by Katayama provides the outlook of an experienced special librarian on the value of library committees.[1] She strongly recommends creating such a committee and cites advantages, such as learning the opinions of users on library operations. This information could provide an early warning to the manager of problem areas before they become serious. With the committee acting as a sounding board for testing new ideas, the manager can keep in touch with user opinions.

Katayama feels that the library director must be a member, and, if possible, the manager's supervisor should also attend. Ideally, committee members should be active library users themselves, not only low-ranking employees whose time could be spared for attendance at meetings. This points out the need for support by top management so that the committee is taken seriously. She recommends that major departments be represented on the committee, if having every department represented would make the committee too large.

It should be emphasized that the role of the committee should be to offer advice to the library manager, not to actually supervise or manage the library. Responsibility for operating the library still must remain with the manager.

Formal Surveys

While library committees have proved to be valuable for communicating with representative library users, a library manager should consider making a formal survey if more detailed information about user opinions is desired. The usual way to accomplish this is through questionnaires or interviews; a common approach is to use both.

Management's Role. It is important that the manager consult with his or her supervisor before initiating any formal survey or evaluation. Sometimes a brief statement of management's support of a forthcoming evaluation placed in a house organ or internal newsletter will ensure cooperation of clients of the library/information center. If the process involves extra costs or requires more than a few minutes of each participant's time, management's approval is all the more desirable. Evaluations sometimes require the use of an outside consultant; in such cases it is imperative to have the prior approval of management.

Types of Evaluation. Printed questionnaires and interviews are two basic methods used for obtaining information in evaluating a unit's performance. The choice of a method would depend upon circumstances.

Printed questionnaires vary greatly in complexity and length, but it is advisable to make them short enough so that participants will not feel imposed upon by being asked to fill them out. They should be clearly written and simple to answer. The forms may be distributed in random fashion or to all the clientele. If carefully planned, replies on completed forms can be tabulated quickly by using machine methods.

Interviews usually involve sessions of about fifteen minutes apiece with representatives of various groups of the clientele. A predetermined set of questions must be used, and the interviewers should be selected with care. Unlike questionnaires, it is difficult to design interview questions which do not require rather slow techniques of analysis in view of the lengthy replies commonly made during interviews.

In most instances it is wise to use a combination of both techniques in making an evaluation since each has a different value as an information source. Questionnaires invariably allow one to reach a larger audience in a shorter time than do interviews, but interviews allow for in-depth comments not possible with questionnaires. Interviews invariably involve a smaller number of participants than questionnaires because of the longer time required for interviews and analysis of responses.

Timing. Some time periods are better than others for conducting an evaluation. For example, a few days prior to the deadline for submission of budgets, or just before or after a holiday period, or any time before or after a major change in the structure of the organization are bad times to conduct evaluations. An evaluation ought to be conducted when clients are not pressured by other concerns or disoriented by changes. They then will be ready to give their complete attention to the evaluation.

There is no ideal frequency for conducting evaluations. Generally, every two or three years might suffice, unless the sponsoring organization was so badly served by its special library/information center in the past that more frequent evaluations are necessary to find out what improvements in service clients demand. Remember, the more often a survey is made the more opposition one may find among participants, who could well question (and with some justification) the need for frequent evaluations.

Confidentiality.   It is essential that participants be offered the option of anonymity in their responses. Anonymity may increase the truthfulness of responses since it eliminates the possibility of disapproval by management of critical comments. This is not usually the case, but it could happen if management is sensitive about certain points. On the other hand, some participants may prefer that their names be clearly known by those analyzing the data. In some cases, identifying a particular point of view with an important person in the organization (who is not worried about privacy) might strengthen the hand of the library manager when summarizing the results of the evaluation.

Content.   This is obviously a very important aspect of any evaluation, for the focus of the questions will determine the usefulness of the information. The manager must give careful thought to the subject matter involved, as well as to the style and wording of the questions. There are several pitfalls to avoid, such as phrasing questions too broadly or making them so detailed and complicated that participants find them confusing. In the case of questionnaires, where informal, open-ended verbal comments are rarely possible, some idea of the range or depth of a respondent's feelings may be ascertained by a simple rating system, such as using a scale of 1 to 10. One example might be:

How would you rate the selection of periodicals currently received: (Circle the number which best expresses your views.)

Poor				Average				Excellent	
1	2	3	4	5	6	7	8	9	10

The same sort of question might be suitable for an interview, when respondents then could be asked to explain their response. The explanations offered in interviews might very well be open-ended statements that will take time to summarize. However, the information gleaned from such responses may prove to be invaluable to managers.

By carefully designing the content of questionnaires, the answers can be readily converted to machine-readable form, if there are enough responses to justify this method. In many small surveys, however, it would not be cost effective to tabulate information using data processing equipment. If the size of the number of clients is rather large, a random sample would probably be more suitable than taking the extra time and effort to survey all clients.

Conducting Evaluations.   All those conducting the surveys must be briefed in advance so that they understand the purpose and importance of the process. It is best to avoid assigning to a survey any staff members who might cause difficulties when meeting with respondents. Cheerfulness, politeness, and tact make the process proceed smoothly. Forms must be carefully designed in advance, must be neatly prepared, and must have adequate instructions.

Each manager must decide the number of days questionnaires are to be distributed if, for example, they are given out to all those entering the library over a given time period. Otherwise, if they are to be mailed to participants, it is necessary to decide how to choose the sample (if one is used) and how large the sample should be. Adequate time should be allowed for responses, if answers are not to be given immediately, and some system for keeping track of unreturned forms may be necessary.

Likewise, interviews must be carefully planned to control the selection of interviewees, the time allocated for interviews, and the schedule of the interviews. In addition, the location of the interviews should be carefully considered so that privacy is assured for participants as they come and go and as they speak. If only known "friends" of the unit are chosen to be interviewed, answers could be slanted in a favorable direction. While this may give the library a higher rating, it will do little or nothing to uncover areas where improvements are necessary.

Analysis of results. The next step is to tabulate the answers, using either manual or machine methods as dictated by the number and type of responses. Responses from interviews are almost impossible to tabulate by machine methods if open-ended comments are included. Such responses require the services of someone who is familiar with the topic and can summarize seemingly diverse replies.

Once the data are summarized, the all-important task of analyzing them in a formal report must be done. The library manager should interpret the results so that they can be readily understood by his or her supervisor, who would probably appreciate a concise summary. If the results show that certain improvements need to be made, the manager should include in the summary report an estimate of the impact on the staff and on the budget of making the needed changes. This aids the manager's supervisor in deciding on what action to take.

Numerous studies have been made of the problems involved in evaluating libraries/information centers. Several papers point out the need for careful planing of evaluations so that the efficiency and the effectiveness of the organization are measured. Ladendorf, for example, makes clear the difference between the two terms—a unit could be very efficient without concentrating on the proper activities, and thus be ineffective.[2] She emphasizes the need for adequate statistics to make good measurements. Wooster surveys the literature that deals with the effectiveness of information analysis centers, including methods of measuring their value[3] He finds that surveys are a popular means of evaluation but notes the difficulties of making accurate measurements through this process. An article which gives the results of an actual survey is Fatcheric's account of an evaluation made in an industrial laboratory in which thirty-two people from twenty-one different departments were studied as to their use and evaluation of the library.[4] It would be hard to find an account which describes the activities involved in making a survey as well as this paper does.

Another set of problems is treated in a paper by Schwartz, who points out the difficulties of comparing different libraries.[5] He mentions three aspects of a library whose characteristics might be compared—relationships with management, staffs, and users. His paper raises some interesting points for evaluators to consider.

Use of Consultants

There are times when outside consultants are needed in evaluating special libraries/information centers. They may be called in when management is dissatisfied with the way the units are being operated, when a change of managers is being contemplated, or when the staff of the unit is too busy to make the evaluation itself.

Whatever the reason for calling in an outside consultant, the manager has no choice but to give full cooperation to the evaluation process. If the manager's position is in jeopardy, lack of cooperation with a consultant will only further damage his or her future status.

A useful set of guidelines for outside consultants was written by Albert, who lists possible questions to be considered by consultants.[6] They cover such areas as administration and library operations. Many points in the article would be useful to those planning to make their own evaluations.

References

1. Katayama, Jane H. The library committee: how important is it? *Special Libraries*. 74(1): 44-48; 1983 Jan.

   Describes the value of a library committee to the library at MIT's Lincoln Laboratory. Comments and ideas from committee members proved valuable, especially when complex projects, such as automation, were undertaken. Operation of the committee is discussed.

2. Ladendorf, Janice. Information service evaluation: the gap between the ideal and the possible. *Special Libraries*. 64(7): 273-279; 1973 July.

   Analyzes the problems involved in evaluation of services. The theoretical and the practical aspects are discussed. Points out the need for collecting meaningful statistics.

3. Wooster, Harold. An information analysis center effectiveness chrestomathy. *Journal of the American Society for Information Science*. 21(2): 149-159; 1970 Mar./Apr.

   The author surveys the literature on the effectiveness of centers and analyzes the determination of goals and methods of measuring their effectiveness.

4. Fatcheric, Jerome P. Survey of users of a medium-sized technical library. *Special Libraries*. 66(5/6): 245-251; 1975 May/June.

   Describes the items studied in a survey of selected employees of the Bristol Laboratory as to their use and evaluation of the services offered by the library; also discusses the results discovered. Items evaluated include SDI service, collections, computer facilities, and physical facilities.

5. Schwartz, James H. Factors affecting the comparison of special libraries. *Special Libraries*. 71(1):1-4; 1980 Jan.

   Points out the problems in comparing different libraries. Suggests alternatives to compare within the organization.

6. Albert, Dorothy. The special library consultant: some pragmatic guidelines. *Special Libraries*. 63(11): 507-510; 1972 Nov.

Lists the services, administrative matters, and specific details which should be examined by an outside consultant. Points to be followed in preparation of a final report are cited.

Chapter 11

The Role of Technology

Essays or texts on the effects of science and technology on society usually include mention of the greater speed with which new inventions reach the marketplace and take their place in our homes, our offices, and even our libraries. What once might have taken five years to move from a laboratory experiment to commercial sales now might make that transition in two years. As a consequence, new ways of doing things come along at a fast pace. At one time in the past twenty years virtually the only change in traditional library equipment was the introduction of the photocopier. A few years before that, the microfilm reader-printer was considered an innovative device. Then came card-driven computers; they were large, bulky, and definitely not for the librarian to operate. This situation held sway for quite a few years, with only a few large libraries having their own computers.

It was the advent of the microcomputer, the PC or personal computer, that really touched off an avalanche of changes in library operations. Although some librarians during the early days of computers were afraid computers would replace them, time has proved that new technical advances tend to eliminate many tedious jobs while at the same time making it feasible to perform many new, creative operations. Thus there is a general upgrading of jobs due to the advent of computers, and it become possible to perform certain services that would have been impossible without computers.

No librarians, particularly managers, can long survive in special libraries without some knowledge of new technology, particularly if they are seeking new positions or hoping for promotions. The purpose of this chapter is to summarize the various aspects of technology that have affected libraries as well as review some of the special managerial techniques that have become invaluable in this age.

Managerial Techniques

Statistics.   The term *statistics* has two meanings, both of which can be applied to the management of special libraries/information centers. One meaning is simply that of data collected on library operations, such as the number of interlibrary loans made in a given month by a particular library. The other meaning refers to the science of statistical analysis, a branch of applied mathematics that has long served the pure sciences, the social sciences, and other major fields. Statistical analysis is usually taught at the collegiate level, and more and more library schools encourage or require their students to take courses in this subject because of the practical help it provides in analyzing managerial problems.

In a cursory treatment of the subject it is impossible to describe its characteristics in depth, but a few instances will suffice to show its potential applications. One important segment of statistical analysis is probability, which allows a manager to predict with some confidence the likelihood of a particular occurrence. For example, if data on library loans showed an increase of thirty-five percent in one week, the use of statistics in analyzing circulation data might determine the likelihood of a recurrence of such a phenomenon.

Another application is sampling theory. In almost every effort to make surveys or to gather representative data, the question arises as to how many samples need to be taken and how large a percentage they should be of the total number of items to be studied. For example, if there were a total of 800 engineers in five departments served by an industrial library, how many engineers from each department should be included in a survey involving interviews or questionnaires? If some of those to whom questionnaires were sent did not respond, what percentage of the total would be needed so as to have a statistically valid set of data? Statistical analysis provides this sort of information.

The results of the statistics depend entirely on the skill of the manager in gathering data and making careful analysis of them. Careless efforts will result in misleading conclusions, so that manager must proceed using the proper methods of analysis. Those wanting an introduction to the subject can consult various texts, such as the one by Hafner.[1] He presents basic data, illustrated with applications pertinent to libraries. His book does not require expertise in mathematics to understand.

In regard to the gathering of statistics, the manager of a special library/information center will profit from making sure that a select number of activities of the unit are measured and/ or counted regularly. While the keeping of statistics can be overdone in some instances, one needs to have as much evidence as possible concerning the type and amount of use made of the unit. There will undoubtedly never be one single method by which one could ascertain with mathematical certainty the number of outstanding ways in which the special library/ information center helped its users. The instances involving a direct relationship between a service performed by the unit and a subsequent saving to the sponsoring organization are so rare that one cannot count on obtaining such examples. While this sort of significant service does happen, few clients take the trouble to acknowledge the role of the library in the success of a particular plan or operation. Therefore, the manager must rely on more prosaic types of statistics to prove the worth of the unit.

Useful examples of the kinds of statistics worth collecting and the ways in which relationships among items can be developed appear in an article by Randall.[2] Among the elements he measures are collection sizes, annual rates of acquisition, the number of items loaned, and budgets for both salaries and collections. He then compiles ratios, such as the number of loans per borrower and the relative amount of the budget spent on serials as compared to monographs. The results of his article are no longer usable, but his methodology offers valuable reading. An article by Strain explains the reason behind her selection of statistics worth collecting.[3] She also presents illustrations of each type.

Besides tabulating data, a manager should be familiar with the technique of preparing graphic analyses of data. In many instances, a well-prepared graph is more useful in presenting data than a table. In most cases graphs must be accompanied by explanations as to their significance; even so they almost always make a given situation more clear to a reader than does a table of data. Figures 1 through 3 illustrate, respectively, examples of a line graph, the familiar pie chart, and bar graph.

For special presentations where a great deal is at stake, the manager should not hesitate to draw on professional talent in the sponsoring organization, such as an art department or a staff editor, to make the most professional charts or graphs possible. Some are best prepared on paper, while others are more effective as slides or transparencies for overhead projectors. Keep in mind that color adds to a presentation's attractiveness and clarity. Whenever making slides or transparencies, the manager should make sure they will be clearly readable by the entire audience. There is nothing more frustrating to an audience than to be shown a slide or transparency in which the scale is so small in proportion to the size of room that attendees are unable to read the data easily.

In recent years the process of making graphs and charts has been tremendously facilitated by the existence of personal computers as well as the wide accessibility of newer software programs, which simplify the handling of graphics. Not every library may have the requisite software, but more and more programs are appearing all the time, with prices coming down in many cases.

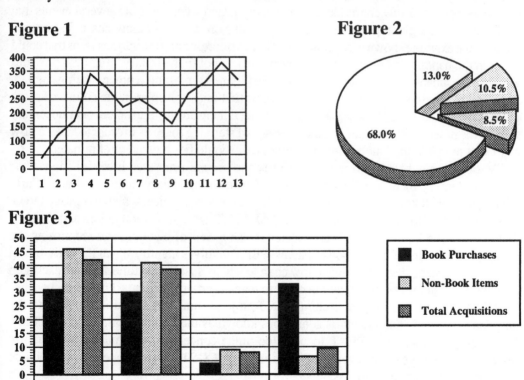

Figure 1

Figure 2

Figure 3

Book Purchases

Non-Book Items

Total Acquisitions

R & D   Marketing   Sales   Other

Systems Analysis

At the beginning of World War II a new method of problem solving related to military matters was developed in England; it was known as operations research. It was practiced primarily by scientists and mathematicians, and their contribution to the war effort is generally conceded to have been significant. After the war, the techniques of operations research were adopted by business firms. One of the features of this new tool was reliance on models of real situations or activities; experiments were done with the models in the search for ways to improve the activity being studied. Emphasis was on using the scientific method to solve problems in organizations.

Since then, another management tool known as systems analysis has developed which is closely related to operations research. Moore has defined systems analysis as involving "collection, organization, and evaluating facts about a system and each subsystem and the environment in which they operate."[4] She points out that the objective of the analysis is to learn enough about a system to permit the design of a better system, if feasible. Moore discusses the use of surveys of existing conditions (largely through interviews), the reviewing of documents on the matter being studied, the preparation of flow charts and organization charts, and the reliance on reports of similar projects.

Flow charts are often rather mysterious sounding to an inexperienced analyst but are actually simple in nature, although not always simple to prepare. In essence, a flow chart is a string of symbols arranged to show the sequence of events in the course of a particular activity or process. Flow charts can become complicated when there are several events that could happen at a given point. An article by Bolles on the use of flow charts in libraries contains the example shown in the following figures, representing the various steps that could occur in the handling of a request for a journal article not in the library.[5] Figure 4 provides a code to the meaning of the symbols used while Figure 5 represents a process being studied. Flow charts provide a clear picture of the events that must transpire in the course of some process or service while showing, at the same time, if there are any inefficient or unnecessary steps in the process. Sometimes just the necessity of studying routines in order to make a flow chart will reveal immediately some processes that should be changed or eliminated.

Various terms have been used to identify the special processes involved in systems analysis. Among them are linear programming, quening theory, and the Monte Carlo technique. A well known method for controlling events in a project which has proven to be useful in some library applications is called PERT (Program Evaluation and Review Technique). The United States Navy created it as a means of planning and monitoring the development of one of its weapons systems. PERT involves identifying all the activities in a particular project, then preparing a flow chart to which is added the time at which each step of the process should be completed in order to meet a certain deadline. Of course, because PERT tends to be used for very complicated projects, much time and effort go into the decisions involved. The system is sometimes known as the Critical Path Method (CPM). Because of criticisms that PERT focused too much concern on schedules while slightly minimizing matters of cost, a version known as PERT/COST was developed so as to include expenses in the planning process.

Another aspect of management that has been receiving much attention in recent years is cost-effectiveness analysis and cost-benefit analysis. Cost-effectiveness is a ratio of the performance (effectiveness) of a service on a system to the cost associated with it. Thus there are two ways to increase the cost effectiveness of a system:

- Increasing its performance level while keeping costs constant.
- Decreasing its cost while keeping the level of performance constant.

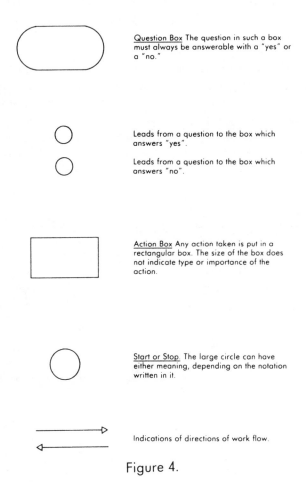

Question Box The question in such a box must always be answerable with a "yes" or a "no."

Leads from a question to the box which answers "yes".

Leads from a question to the box which answers "no".

Action Box Any action taken is put in a rectangular box. The size of the box does not indicate type or importance of the action.

Start or Stop. The large circle can have either meaning, depending on the notation written in it.

Indications of directions of work flow.

Figure 4.

Cost-benefit analysis is more difficult to measure. It concerns the benefits a system provides (and the cost associated with the benefit). The problem arises with measuring the benefit. It is not an easily determined quantity like the performance of a specific system, which can often be measured in terms of documents indexed per hour, cards printed per minute, and the like.

Perhaps the use of an imaginary (and absurd) example will demonstrate the difference between the two kinds of analyses. Suppose an ingenious (but misguided) special librarian invented an electronic device that would automatically record the color of each new book in the library, so that at any moment one could push a button and learn how many of which color had been added. Perhaps in the first year this service cost twenty dollars per month, but improvements during the second year led to costs of only ten dollars per month. As a result, the system became twice as cost effective as it used to be. But in regard to cost benefits, it is obvious that the sponsors and users of the library would have no interest at all in knowing about the colors of books. Thus, the system would have a cost benefit of zero, no matter how cost effective it had become.

In real life, it is rare that a service or system can be evaluated so easily in terms of its benefits. This remains a difficult measurement to make, but an important one nevertheless. While it is necessary to make our service as cost effective as possible, it is just as vital to be sure that certain activities are worth doing.

Stueart's text summarizes the main features of the various techniques currently used in library management.[6] An article by Main discusses both CPM and PERT, including illustrations of library applications.[7] Software, the name for computer programs, is also mentioned.

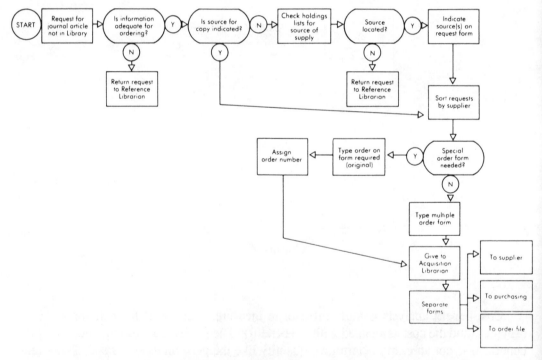

Figure 5.

Role of New Technologies

Our societies and institutions, including libraries, have gone through remarkable changes in recent years due to the influx of new technologies. Libraries are certainly no exception. For example, it is becoming increasingly rare to find an information professional who has not had some contact with computers, due to their greatly increased use in libraries and information centers of all sizes. Most library schools offer either optional or required courses dealing with computers. Students planning to become special librarians are being advised to take several such courses, and those planning on working even more closely with computers often take all the offerings possible. In one library school known to the author at least 80 percent of the MLS students take the optional course in online bibliographic databases, so important has online searching become these days.

The new technologies are not confined to computers; we find products based on lasers, optical storage, new ways of magnetic storage, and a number of other technologies available for library applications. The flood of new products makes it difficult at times just to keep up with understanding the rudiments of new devices, much less to master their use. Obviously in one chapter it is not possible to present a comprehensive review of new technologies, but this chapter seeks to summarize some of the techniques for choosing new products wisely and to point out some of the problems inherent in their applications.

Those wishing an overall look at the problems of automation and other aspects of new technology would profit from reading the book by Boss, who covers general topics and applications.[8] An article by Molholt points out the effects of new technologies on libraries.[9] She sees new technologies as compensating for inadequate staffs in such areas as online acquisitions or online bibliographic utilities by offering quick identification of requested literature. Another aspect of automation deals with the growing role of librarians in teaching clients how to use new systems. Widening of access to graphic materials could lead to innovative library applications. For example, new software permits searching for chemical compounds by using a representation of their physical structure, rather than words and traditional symbols. Computerized systems also free staffs from certain tedious chores while enlarging opportunities for sharing information in spite of time and distance restraints. Her paper also discusses some long-range trends in libraries, including the integration of techniques as exemplified by hypertext, which allows the combining of textual and graphic data at a terminal. Still another trend involves allowing users more individual choices in how they use libraries, such as the ways in which they conduct their searches. The other trend involves the reduction in the need for library collections as we now know them—alternative sources of texts may diminish our reliance on conventional printed sources. Moholt sees librarians in the future serving chiefly as partners with information scientists in the development of new systems and as interpreters of systems to clients.

New technologies are not an unmixed blessing, an example of their effect being the increased stress among those who have responsibilities for working with computerized equipment. An article by Bichteler on "technostress" describes a survey of library employees whose purpose was to learn what side effects automation had on their lives; some possible solutions to difficulties are given.[10]

Planning for Automation.   One can now find a sizable amount of literature about planning for automation. These projects are generally complex and involve relatively large amounts of money in terms of library budgets. A paper by Smith and Borgendale discusses the major pitfalls to avoid in planning a local online search system.[11] It is clear that a great deal of thought must be given to such projects, with topics ranging from choices for online display of instructions to the calculation of the costs of converting data to a new system.

Several papers on the problems and benefits derived from installing ready-made (turnkey) computer systems are to be found in a special issue of a journal devoted to sci-tech libraries.[12] Five papers describe the details of the projects, while one paper is more general in nature, discussing factors to be kept in mind in planning for adaptation of a system. This article, written by Friewer, identifies the following steps to be taken in obtaining proposals for a turnkey automated system:[13]

1. Once an automation team has been appointed, identify the information needs of the organization; prepare a written statement of the problem and from this material define the scope, specific objectives, and constraints of the proposed system; be sure to define the existing situation.
2. Gather information about potential turnkey vendors; examine advertisements in journals, stop at equipment exhibits at conferences, or visit vendors' customers. Try to determine if vendors will supply what the system needs (for example, can their equipment perform all the functions needed?).
3. Develop a listing of all the functional criteria required of the system, such as data transactions to perform (circulation, serials checking), speed of operation, creation of statistics, and so on. Identify each criterion as to its importance (required, highly desirable, or moderately desirable), system backup that the vendor would provide, software maintenance, and the like.
4. Prepare a request for proposal (RFP) that will include objectives, technical requirements, types of equipment, demonstrations required, criteria to be used in evaluating proposals, and time schedules.

As can be seen, preparing a businesslike RFP takes time and effort, but the results should be worthwhile. A poorly written RFP can lead to the selection of systems that do not accomplish what is needed or to the choice of second-rate bidders for the project.

The book by Boss covers most of the above steps in preparing the RFP, then adds the following steps:[14]

1. Contracting with a vendor includes providing a detailed list of all performance standards agreed upon as well as terms of payment. A plan for acceptance tests must also be included, as should terms for maintenance programs for the hardware and software.
2. Training of staff members would probably be shared by both vendor representatives and local staff, following training by the vendor.

3. Converting data to fit the new system should be started as soon as possible. It is embarrassing to announce a new system having very little data in it.
4. Selling the system to library users is an essential step; several techniques are advised. See Chapter 9 for descriptions of several methods to use.

How can managers involve the general staff of a library in the early stages of the process? It is generally agreed that they must be given some role, if for no other reason than to do them the courtesy of keeping them informed of what will happen. Of course, this eliminates a lot of needless worry on their part. On the positive side a manager should expect to get useful input from a staff when they are involved in the planning of the project. A paper by Shaw describes a study made at a state library of the opinions of the library staff on the subject of automation, taken before planning for a proposed project got underway.[15] A year later another survey was made after the staff had been involved in automation planning. Results showed an improvement in their attitude about the need for automation; participation seemed to make the difference. It only stands to reason that staff members will be more supportive of a project in which they had an opportunity to share their ideas.

Computerized Databases.   One of the fastest growing information tools has been the computerized database. From their introduction to the public in the 1960s, databases have grown in number from a handful to well over 4,000 in 1990. They are the basis of a multibillion dollar business and have become indispensable in libraries of all sorts, particularly in special libraries. Practically any subject one can think of is represented by one or more databases; some popular subject areas, such as business, have been inundated with scores of files from which to choose. Some corporate libraries annually spend hundreds of thousands of dollars for online searching; the speed and thoroughness of the searches leave them no choice.

After the advantages of computerized databases became evident, it was not long before organizations sought ways to create their own databases. For example, a corporation might have unique internal records and data, hence not on any public database. Furthermore, an organization not wishing to disclose the data would find that commercial databases were no solution. The obvious answer would be to create a local database, for corporate use. This practice is now quite common, and more information is being published on the subject. For example, a paper by Moulton describes in considerable detail the recommended steps to take in creating a database.[16] She covers the process from inception to completion; it clearly requires careful planning.

Closely tied to the creation of new databases is the growth of a new position in libraries, namely database manager. An article by Chapman describes the role of such a position in the creation and management of local databases at the Exxon Corporation.[17]

CD-ROMs.   In the past few years an alternative to online databases, namely the CD-ROM, has appeared on the market; the number of files in this medium grows larger every week. They consist of a diskette that bears information imbedded in it by a laser device, a computer, and a player to reproduce the data on the computer monitor. The start-up costs are only for the playback equipment and the charge for a subscription to the service for the CD-ROM. There are even directories devoted entirely to listings of CD-ROMs, so rapidly has the number of them increased. *CD-ROMs in Print* (Meckler) is an index for these products; in early 1990 there were more than 300 titles available.

CD-ROMs have the advantage of allowing unlimited searching at no cost, as contrasted to the usual charges for each minute of online databases. On the other hand, most CD-ROMs are at least three months old by the time they are distributed, since most are updated no more frequently than quarterly. Unless one has a special drive that allows more than one disk to be used at the same time, a queuing problem for multiple users will occur. Those wishing to learn more about the different types of optical disks, along with a description of how they work, are referred to the book by Elshami.[18] It covers a wide range of topics in readable style.

Electronic Mail and Electronic Bulletin Boards.   The proliferation of personal computers and special telecommunication channels designed for data transmission rather than voice traffic have combined to facilitate the creation of electronic communication techniques that would formerly have been very difficult to establish. One is a system called *electronic mail,* which simply relies on establishing a code number for each participant in the system. All that each person needs is a computer, a number in the system, and a connection to a telephone network. The network might be as small as within a given company or a given university, while it might be as large as a national network. The sender sends the message by a computer through a telephone network to the recipient's location and code number. Various systems allow for special features, such as a signal to the recipient that there is a message waiting. This sort of communication is very rapid; some people use it almost exclusive of regular voice transmission, one reason being that there is no need to send the message more than once, thus avoiding the frustrations of "telephone tag" in which two people call each other numerous times before both are at their telephones at the same time.

Electronic bulletin boards consist of an arrangement whereby those having the right password can dial it to find out information on a number of subjects. One may use the bulletin board for a variety of purposes, including professional reasons. Along the latter line, an article by Tinsley describes an electronic bulletin board used in an academic library for displaying contents pages of several journals at Carnegie Mellon University.[19] Faculty members can get a listing on their computers of selected contents pages, then order a photocopy by electronic mail, if desired, with the copy coming to his or her campus address. Only a minimal charge is made. Future goals include purchase of an optical character scanner to digitize the contents pages so they can be posted automatically rather than relying on volunteer workers.

A summary of the nature and history of electronic mail can be found in a paper by Whitaker.[20] Electronic bulletin boards are also discussed.

Facsimile Equipment.   Facsimile equipment (commonly known now as fax equipment) has been in use in businesses for at least forty years, but not until the 1980s did the performance of the equipment reach the point at which commercial use was practical and economical. Fax relies on electronic scanning of a record or document, followed by transmission of the data on telephone lines to a receiving unit. Fax has greatly speeded up the delivery time for documents, assuming the senders and recipients both have access to the equipment. An article by Brown summarizes the use of fax in libraries.[21] He points out all the benefits it provides and also lists its problem areas, such as level of legibility, paper jamming, and costs.

A recent phenomenon, known as "junk fax," is the large quantities of unwanted advertisements and other miscellaneous material being sent to fax machines, taking up the recipients' precious time. As long as fax numbers are readily available through various directories, there is little one can do to eliminate such nuisances. No sure-fire solution to the problem has been found to date.

Artificial intelligence and expert systems. The development of digital computers led to the appearance of two fields that hold great promise for the future. A paper by Alan Turing in 1950 is said to have been the first one written on artificial intelligence, a term describing the use of computers or other devices which can be made to function in a fashion similar to humans. Since that time progress has been made in creating devices that show evidence of the process, although no one claims to have equalled human intelligence on a grand scale. One area of study concerning how humans process data, is aimed at providing a means of developing decision-making, problem-solving models for computer applications. A brief summary by Manning of artificial intelligence (or AI, as it is often referred to) lists several fields of research: pattern matching, in which AI systems look for patterns that match data in the computer; solution searching, involving different ways the system performs a search; and knowledge representation, concerned with developing computer programs for solving particular problems.[22] Her article touches on several applications, such as expert systems, which have been defined as aids to decision making and problem solving. They are knowledge systems which attempt to provide solutions to problems by going through processes similar to those used by human experts. One of the first expert systems was a program developed in 1947 that allowed a computer to play chess. It is estimated that by 1988 up to 3,000 expert systems were in daily use.

An article by Sowell discusses the development and testing of an expert system for use in collection development in an academic library.[23] He devised a system that would facilitate the selection of classical Latin literature, using a six-step method. Four possible decisions were available for each monograph, ranging from "Must be bought" to "Should not be bought." Testing of the system against known decisions allowed for adjustments so that the machine's output more or less matched the previous decisions made by humans.

Hypertext. A much-cited article written by Vannevar Bush in 1945 has received increased attention in recent years because of its relationship with a quickly developing field. Bush mused about the advantages of having all the information one would need contained in a computer, with unrelated bits of knowledge capable of being called up as required by pushing a button. His concept is said to have become the basis for a new type of database called "hypertext." The term was coined in the 1960s by Ted Nelson, who was active in English literature studies. There was no great interest in the subject until the advent of powerful personal computers in the late 1980s made it feasible to think of new ways of linking bits of data through computerized databases. One early version involved Apple computers that ran special software called "Hypercard," which allowed one to link discrete bits of information from different documents. Since then efforts have been made to allow users to link all sorts of data, whether textual or graphic, to mimic human thought processes, which are not bounded by text lengths or data format. Hypertext has been defined in various ways; one person explained it as a nonlinear, nonsequential text that is used to link data in one document.

A readable summary of the background, meaning, and outlook for hypertext appears in the paper by Borgman and Henstell.[24] It should be noted that their article is one of seven recommended papers in an issue devoted to the subject. An article by Nyce and Kahn analyzes the extent to which hypertext systems achieve the objectives implicit in Bush's pioneering paper.[25]

Local Area Networks.   In the past decade one of the fastest growing activities in librarianship has been the development of the local area network (LAN). The need for better communication among groups of computer users within an organization has led to their development. In simplified language, they consist of a linkage between two or more computers using any of a variety of methods of connecting them. Such a system allows for sharing of hard disk storage among the various stations, which may also share a printer (usually a high-quality one). Typically they serve a rather small area compared to national networks. Inside a given organization, a small-sized LAN might serve to link computers less than 200 feet apart. A medium-sized LAN typically serves a unit in which the computers are on two different floors, while large-scale LANs might serve a university campus or different buildings of a corporation. Even the larger sizes of LANs are essentially limited to one organization, which makes them quite restricted in scope compared to the types of networks previously described. Nevertheless, LANs represent a vital type of network, albeit limited in scope as far as the number and geographical location of participants is concerned. LANs offer more efficient use of data within an organization, enhanced reliability, and better utilization of equipment.

A well-written book on the subject by Kemper describes the nature of LANs, their design and equipment, and their implementation.[26] One useful feature is a series of checklists to consider in planning a LAN. The book also contains a number of practical guidelines, such as the necessity of maintaining proper documentation on any system installed; such records are useful for training users and for maintaining a high level of efficiency.

A thoughtful article on the stages of development through which LANs have passed is by Hoehl, written in terms of the operation of a LAN at a health sciences library in a hospital.[27] The title of her paper refers to phase III; she explains the meaning of this by describing the stages through which her LAN has moved. The first stage was simply that of automating as many activities as possible. The next stage involved changing what the library did as well as how it accomplished the work, all due to the automation of library operations. The third phase refers to the long-range picture of the effect of LANs, namely the way in which technology changes all of society. For example, the development of linkages between disparate vocabularies currently in use in various information systems, or the increased role of expert systems in online retrieval, could have significant effects on the operation of our libraries and on their relationship to clients.

References

1. Hafner, Arthur W. *Descriptive statistical techniques for librarians*. Chicago: American Library Association; 1989. 261 p.

Clearly written, providing basic data on such topics as methods of data summary and communicating data before delving into the traditional subjects of sampling, probability, and various statistical tests. Each chapter has a number of problems all related to library applications. Should be suitable for all librarians.

2. Randall, Gordon E. Randall's rationalized ratios. *Special Libraries*. 66(1): 6-11; 1975 Jan.

Discusses the type of statistics regularly gathered by various IBM libraries, covering such areas as collection sizes, number of loans, number of borrowers, and book budgets. Shows how useful ratios can be prepared, such as the number of loans per borrower or expenditures for serials compared to monographs.

3. Strain, Paula M. Evaluation by the numbers. *Special Libraries*. 73(3): 165-172; 1982 July.

Illustrates and describes the type of statistics collected by a sci-tech special library (MITRE Corporation), such as annual cost of library operations per employee in the organization, number of library uses per employee, number of requests handled by the library staff per hour, and the like.

4. Moore, Edythe. Systems analysis: an overview. *Special Libraries*. 58(2): 87-90; 1967 Feb.

Discusses the use of systems analysis as an effective management tool. Benefits are enumerated. Directed towards those with no previous experience.

5. Bolles, Shirley W. The use of flow charts in the analysis of library operations. *Special Libraries*. 58(2): 95-98; 1967 Feb.

Describes the nature of flow charts and shows how they can be used in typical library situations.

6. Stueart, Robert D.; Moran, Barbara B. *Library management*. 3d ed. Littleton, CO: Libraries Unlimited; 1987; Chap. 6.

Describes the various control techniques, including cost-benefit analysis, operations research, and PERT.

7. Main, Linda. CPM and PERT in library management. *Special Libraries*. 80(1): 39-44; 1989 Winter.

Reviews the basic aspects of the two techniques and shows possible uses in library operations. Includes descriptions of software available for using them.

8. Boss, Richard W. *The library manager's guide to automation*. 2nd ed. White Plains, NY: Knowledge Industry Publications; 1984. 167 p.

Covers a wide range of topics, including hardware, software, databases, options for automation, planning/implementation, and future trends. Easily understood; includes a useful 16-page glossary.

9. Molholt, Pat. Libraries and the new technologies: courting the Cheshire Cat. *Library Journal*. 113(19): 37-41; 1988 Nov. 15.

Describes three types of effects new technologies have on libraries, then points out particular areas of importance, such as availability of artificial intelligence, development of networks, and the relationship of librarians to systems design.

10. Bichteler, Julie. Human aspects of high tech in libraries. *Special Libraries*. 77(3): 121-128; 1986 Summer.

Reviews results of a survey of librarians who work with computers to ascertain adverse effects that might result. Presents some solutions to reduce stress.

11. Smith, Barbara G.; Borgendale, Marilyn. The second time around: the next generation local online system. *Library Journal*. 113(12): 47-51; 1988 July.

Reviews the main considerations in planning a new online system, covering such aspects as determination of the technical requirements, methods of conversion of data, provision for backup systems, security issues, and user interface decisions.

12. Mount, Ellis, ed. *Adaptation of turnkey computer systems in sci-tech libraries*. 116 p. New York: Haworth Press; 1988. (Also issued as *Science & Technology Libraries*. 9(1): 1988 Spring.)

Contains six papers devoted to the experiences of sci-tech libraries in installing turnkey systems for such purposes as online catalogs, circulation, and acquisitions.

13. Friewer, Karen A.; Vinande, Robert G.; Bruns, Michael J. Protocol for the selection of a library automation system. *Science & Technology Libraries*. 9(1): 3-10; 1988 Spring.

Describes the important steps to be taken when proposals for automated systems are sought from turnkey vendors, based on work done at Dow Chemical Company's Technical Information Services.

14. Boss, *op cit.* p. 110-115.

15. Shaw, Debora. Staff opinions in library automation planning: a case study. *Special Libraries*. 77(3): 140-151; 1986 Summer.

Shows results of surveys of staff members taken before and after participation in automation planning. Results generally showed participation was responsible for greater support of automation. Includes copies of survey forms.

16. Moulton, Lynda W. Constructing databases—professional issues. *Special Libraries*. 78(4): 281-287; 1987 Fall.

Discusses the various aspects of creating a database, beginning with assessing goals and needs, estimating costs, defining benefits, preparing requests for proposals, implementing the system, instituting startup procedures and maintaining the databases.

17. Chapman, Janet L. The information scientist as database manager in a corporate environment. *Special Libraries*. 77(2): 71-79; 1986 Spring.

Reviews the steps needed to create internal databases in a sci-tech corporate environment. Both design and operation of the databases are covered, along with a description of software used.

18. Elshami, Ahmed M. *CD-ROM technology for information managers*. Chicago: American Library Association; 1990. 280 p.

Explains how optical disks of all sorts work, then discusses the hardware needed to use CD-ROMs, their role in networks, and typical commercial products for libraries that are available. A thorough treatment of the subject.

19. Tinsley, G. Lynn. An electronic bulletin board. *Special Libraries*. 80(3): 188-192; 1989 Summer.

Explains the use of an electronic bulletin board to list the tables of contents of current issues of periodicals of interest to the computer science department of a university. Each faculty member can query the bulletin board and retrieve the listing of titles of interest. Allows for electronic ordering of a photocopy of any article listed.

20. Whitaker, Becki. Electronic mail in the library; a perspective. *Library Trends*. 37(3): 357-365; 1989 Winter.

Summarizes the history, applications, costs, and benefits of electronic mail.

21. Brown, Steven Allen. Telefacsimile in libraries: new deal in the 1980s. *Library Trends*. 37(3): 343-356; 1989 Winter.

Reviews the advantages offered by fax equipment, as well as costs and recent developments. Problems are also discussed, but the benefits to libraries are seen as significant.

22. Manning, Helen. Artificial intelligence: an overview. *Specialist*. 12(9): 1, 3, 9, 11; 1989 Sept.

A brief but readable summary of artificial intelligence and its applications, such as expert systems, speech analysis, and symbolic processing.

23. Sowell, Steven L. Expanding horizons in collection development with expert systems: development and testing of a demonstration prototype. *Special Libraries*. 80(1): 45-50; 1989 Winter.

Discusses the creation of an expert system for use as an aid in selecting monographs for a classical Latin literature collection at Indiana University. A six-step procedure was devised; the project was felt to be successful following testing and adjustment of the system.

24. Borgman, Christine; Henstell, Bruce. Hypertext—what's in a name. *Bulletin of the American Society for Information Science*. 15(5): 22; 1989 June/July.

A summary of the origin, meaning, and applications of hypertext, presented in very readable style.

25. Nyce, James M.; Kahn, Paul. Innovation, pragmatism, and technological continuity: Vannevar Bush's Memex. *Journal of the American Society for Information Science*. 40(3): 214-220; 1989 May.

Reviews the significance of Bush's writings and the degree of progress of hypertext systems toward meeting the goals of the Memex.

26. Kemper, Marlyn. *Networks: choosing a LAN path to interconnection*. Metuchen, NJ: Scarecrow Press; 1987. 279 p.

A thorough coverage of the design, equipment, and applications of LANs. Includes a glossary and a 20-page bibliography.

27. Hoehl, Susan B. Local area network implementation: moving toward phase III. *Special Libraries*. 80(1): 16-23; 1989 Winter.

Discusses the development of LANs, then describes the operation of one at the Health Sciences Library of Allegheny General Hospital. Includes drawings showing the types of terminals and the connections used between terminals.

Part 3

User Services

To many clients of special libraries, the most important feature of such organizations is the type and quality of the services provided. This does not mean that the size and appropriateness of the collections are unimportant, nor that the appearance and comfort of a modern facility offer no interest. But, in general, what matters most is what the library does for the average user.

This section discusses four aspects of user services. Chapter 12 deals with information retrieval, while Chapter 13 concentrates on methods of alerting users to current data of interest. In Chapter 14 the emphasis shifts to the techniques of circulating materials to library users; Chapter 15 contains descriptions of the various services having to do with writing and preparing data for use.

Chapter 12

Retrieval Services

One of the earliest types of service provided by special libraries involved retrieving information for library requestors. Until the past decade, printed publications, such as abstracting and indexing services, card catalogs, and printed reference tools, were the sole resources. With the advent of online bibliographic databases in the 1970s, reference service took on a new look that makes present-day retrieval methods far different from traditional ones. Although the means of retrieving data have changed, some aspects of retrieval service have stayed the same. For example, retrieval service tends to consist of a mixture of so-called quick answer questions (requiring only quick use of a reference book) and long, complicated literature searches, perhaps lasting for months at a time. In between the two extremes are services such as identifying incomplete references, conducting searches of moderate length, or obtaining interlibrary loans. Some of the principles governing retrieval services appear below.

Principles for Searching Data.   The following points illustrate the many factors involved in data retrieval:

- *Reference interview.* No matter how one searches, the information professional needs to have a clear understanding of what is being sought. Having a fuzzy or inaccurate concept could result in a worthless search. However, understanding the subject or object sought is only part of the story. Other factors enter in, such as knowing what is desired by the client in regard to the language of the information, its publication date, or its format (patents vs. books, for example). A reference interview is an important first step to take. Knowing the purpose for which the information is to be used will strongly influence the nature of the search.
- *Sources to use.* Choosing the best sources can make the search more efficient and less costly as well as make the difference between finding the data sought and not finding it.
- *Format for data located.* It is important to know whether the requestor wants merely citations for the literature retrieved or needs full-text versions of the items cited. The appearance of the final data provided also needs consideration; does the requestor desire a bibliography in polished format or would a simple list of citations found suffice?
- *Time schedules.* Knowing when information is needed is another vital bit of data to have; a search taking three hours may be far too late for some requestors. The searcher

must ascertain when data are needed, making allowances for some requestors who seem to think everything they ask for is needed "yesterday" or at least almost immediately.

Online Search Techniques. As this brief section indicates, being skilled at information retrieval involves several aspects not apparent to the neophyte. In many instances important decisions hinge on the outcome of searches, so it is imperative they be performed skillfully. An article by Shaver and others points out some of the ethical aspects of online searching that bear consideration.[1] For example, the authors state that searchers have several obligations to their clients, such as keeping abreast of new developments in online databases, maintaining search skills, avoiding bias in choosing databases to search, making sure the scope of the search is fully understood, and notifying the requestor of possible limitations of the databases or possible errors arising during the search. Ethical considerations of this sort are gaining increasing importance in special libraries.

A paper by Willard and Morrison gives a picture of the many duties of information specialists in special libraries, noting that heavy involvement in online searching was a vital part of their duties.[2] One of the authors spent up to 50 percent of her time at this task. The article describes some of the equipment used as well as recommended methodology for doing the search.

Choice of Search Methods. As mentioned above, the special librarian's search is no longer limited to traditional printed materials. The advent of online databases has revolutionized retrieval methods. In addition, the past few years have seen the availability of still another product, CD-ROM files, which allow unlimited searching of a disk with no further charges. No doubt other options will be created as further advances are made along these lines.

A paper by Tenopir deals with the decisions that reference librarians must make as to which method of retrieval to use.[3] For example, an online search would be recommended if the collection on hand lacked printed reference materials on the subject, or if the requestor required immediate access to full-text versions of retrieved documents not in the collection. If the request does not involve the past two or three months of data, a CD-ROM search might be in order because searching can be done more inexpensively than with online searches.

Some searches may be so simple that merely perusing printed reference materials would suffice; for example, it is not necessary to go online to determine the spelling of the names of certain cities or to find the names of the two senators from Montana. Many reference books contain such information; using them may in many instances be quicker than an online search.

Maciuszko made an interesting study of the relative merits of searching a topic using both printed materials and online searches.[4] She discussed the options of seeking material particularly pertinent to needs of the requestor (known as the "precision" of a search), versus conducting a search that would concentrate on retrieving a greater quantity of material, which may or may not be pertinent to the requestor (a measurement known as "recall"). Most experienced searchers are fully aware of the need to plan a search such that one goal or other (high relevancy versus a large quantity of retrieved documents of possibly less relevancy) is a factor in planning the search. Such decisions govern both online and manual searches.

A common problem for online searchers is that of deciding which database system to use. That is, should they do the search on DIALOG, or BRS, or WILSONLINE, or STN, or another system? A paper by Tenopir considers this matter.[5] She describes the impact of several factors on making a choice of a system. These include the number of files in the system, the subject matter they emphasize, the availability of full text, the amount and ease of help available by telephone calls to a support desk, response time during peak hours, and costs of the system. As is apparent, there are quite a few factors that should be considered in making these choices.

End-user Training. More and more libraries are finding it desirable to train their clients in online search techniques. This often gives the library staff more time to concentrate on difficult searches because those who have received the instruction are more likely than before the training to run their own searches. An account of end-user training at a corporate sci-tech library is found in the paper by Kirk.[6] She found that many attendees at the lectures wanted simply to learn about the availability of data in online systems. Only the most dedicated and/ or computer-oriented attendees opted to participate in the hands-on sessions that followed. Those who did begin to do their own searching were in need of continuing education so as to keep abreast of new developments.

A similar paper by Dedert and Johnson pointed out that many of those who had received library training were much more apt to do a search in their office than to take the time to describe their needs to a library staff member for a library search.[7] This paper gives a detailed account of the planning, implementation, and analysis of an end-user training project in a laboratory.

In order to maintain high standards of search service it is good to obtain evaluations of the quality of searches from those who requested the service. It need not be more complicated than a simple form attached to the printouts provided the requestors; the form can ask for comments, suggestions for improving the service, or both. Any search, whether online or manual, should be done as well as possible, and seeking feedback offers a good way to find out what requestors think of the service.

Interlibrary loans. Obtaining loans from other libraries has long been a regular duty in special libraries' reference sections. With the rising costs of serials causing restrictions in the size of local collections, tied to the greater awareness of materials cited in online searches, the need for interlibrary loans is actually increasing. One librarian noted a 50 percent increase in the number of interlibrary loans requests after online search service began in her library.

A key point to remember about interlibrary loans is that one must usually be willing to make loans if one expects to borrow from other libraries. Exceptions exist, of course, but this general rule seems to hold. While most libraries will not lend certain classes of materials, such as reference books, or very expensive materials, or periodical issues, one can find a cooperative spirit among special librarians that encourages reciprocal borrowing and lending.

In many cases it is simpler and cheaper to make a single photocopy of a journal article than to lend the volume. Some academic libraries prefer to make photocopies for special libraries on a fee basis because there is little that academic libraries would want to borrow from special libraries. There are some for-profit organizations whose business consists entirely of selling photocopies. It is taken for granted that all participating parties are following copyright regulations.

In seeking interlibrary loans it is imperative that the borrowing library verify in some way the accuracy of the citation, thus avoiding causing either a delay in obtaining it or causing the loaning library needless time in correcting the citation. The large online systems such as OCLC and RLIN are good sources for correct citations and list likely sources from which to borrow. The borrowing library must take extra care to return loaned items on time and in good condition.

Competitor Intelligence. During the past few years a new type of retrieval service has developed—obtaining information about competitors in a certain field. Executives of a firm often need to know more about other companies in competitive fields, such as the number of employees they have, new product lines under consideration, sales figures, new plants being opened, and similar data. Such data are invaluable in strategic planning by top executives. A paper by Greene summarizes the field well, pointing out that the service is perfectly legal and not at all unethical.[8] She lists the many types of data sought as well as likely sources for locating items. In addition she discusses the type of computer systems recommended for this type of service.

As you can imagine, the for-profit sector has the greatest need for this service. Even so, there are instances where not-for-profit organizations would benefit by having a well-organized set of files on the activities and characteristics of other groups in the same field.

Database Management. Besides being heavy users of online databases, an increasing number of special librarians have developed local databases for their organizations. Having used databases for retrieval would make such people aware of what makes a good database and thus alert to pitfalls in planning a new one. An article by Chapman describes the design and operation of a local database.[9]

A paper by Warner discusses the details of developing a database using a particular database management system named Revelation.[10] The article is well illustrated, showing many types of displays created by the system. Benefits and weaknesses of the system are explained.

References

1. Shaver, Donna B.; Hewison, Nancy S.; Wykoff, Leslie W. Ethics for online intermediaries. *Special Libraries*. 76(4): 238-245; 1985 Fall.

   Describes the ethical problems involved in online searching, such as maintaining reasonable skills, using good judgment in choosing sources to search, and respecting the confidentiality of the search.

2. Willard, Ann M.; Morrison, Patricia. The dynamic role of the information specialists: two perspectives. *Special Libraries*. 79(4): 271-276; 1988 Fall.

   Summarizes the duties and responsibilities for positions in a one-person special library versus those in a larger information center.

3. Tenopir, Carol. Decision making by reference librarians. *Library Journal*. 113(16): 66-67; 1988 Oct. 1.

   Describes the factors that influence choices between using printed materials, online databases, or CD-ROMs in a search. Speed of retrieval, costs, and type of data sought are some of the factors to weigh before choosing the system to use.

4. Maciuszko, Kathleen L. The case for coexistence: hardcopy and online searching. *Library Journal*. 114(6): 55-57; 1989 April 1.

   Gives results of a study of the relative effectiveness of searching online versus using only printed reference sources. Both methods were found to offer certain advantages, depending upon the criteria used.

5. Tenopir, Carol. Evaluating online systems. *Library Journal*.113(10): 86-87; 1988 June 1.

   Presents some of the factors that should govern the choice of a database system to use in a given search, such as the number of files available in the system, the time period covered, the features that speed searches, and costs of search time.

6. Kirk, Cheryl L. End-user training at the Amoco Research Center. *Special Libraries*. 77(1): 20-27; 1986 Winter.

   Discusses the two-part approach used for training end-users in online searching. This consists of classroom instruction for a group of users, followed by individual tutoring in hands-on searching. Results are given.

7. Dedert, Patricia L.; Johnson, David K. Promoting and supporting end-user online searching in an industrial research environment: a survey of experiences at Exxon Research and Engineering Company. *Science & Technology Libraries*. 10(1); 25-45; 1989 Fall.

   Presents an account of the type of end-user training given in a multidisciplinary research laboratory. Results of the training as well as costs and benefits to the company are discussed.

8. Greene, H. Frances. Competitive intelligence and the information center. *Special Libraries*. 79(4): 285-295; 1988 Fall.

   Describes the factors that create a need for competitive intelligence, the types of data included in such a process, and ways to organize and retrieve the data.

9. Chapman, Janet L. The information scientist as database manager in a corporate environment. *Special Libraries*. 77(2): 71-79; 1986 Spring.

   Traces the steps taken by the author at a research organization in developing a database, ranging from becoming aware of the need to creating the fields, to determining the operational requirements, selecting the software, and maintaining the database.

10. Warner, Amy; Wenzel, Patrick H. Management of bibliographic data using Revelation. *Special Libraries*. 80(3): 198-205; 1989 Summer.

    Explains the use of software in creating a computerized file of literature; it was to be a relational file, supporting information retrieval and Boolean searching. Many illustrations show the features of the system.

Chapter 13

Current Awareness Services

Most clients of special libraries are interested in keeping abreast of new developments in their specific fields. Consequently they expect their library to provide ways of doing this. Over the years several methods have been developed for accomplishing this updating, with improved techniques constantly evolving. It is important for the reader to be aware of the various ways currently used to provide this sort of service.

Library Bulletins

One of the most common ways to alert clients to recent additions to the library collection is through issuance of a library bulletin. They are sometimes called accession lists, although they are most useful (and more interesting) if they include along with the listings such features as announcements of the inauguration of new services, or the addition of a new piece of software, or the completion of some library project. All these features attract more attention than a mere listing of new books, new serial subscriptions, new reports, and similar materials, although such information is well worth publicizing. The library manager should not miss the opportunity to call the clients' attention to special features, as mentioned above.

Some libraries hold newly listed publications in the library for perusal for a week or so after distribution of the bulletin to allow clients to browse through new books while they are all held in one convenient location in the library. It is discouraging to would-be readers to be told that all the new books are already circulating before clients can get in to see them.

Another common feature of bulletins is a listing of future national, regional, and local conferences of interest to readers. Occasionally a bulletin could also be used to remind readers of some under-utilized service or publication; most clients need a periodic reminder of this sort.

Still another service to alert users to new developments consists of having one or more library employees examine the morning newspapers and clip articles apt to interest managers. Items from wire services are also frequently included in the compilations. It is not uncommon for these to be distributed to the offices of top executives by 9 a.m. In an article about similar services Thury describes the number and type of compilations prepared by library staffs.[1] In some instances more than one set is prepared during a day, with one summary of the news and wire service highlights going to some 3,000 middle and top managers.

It is desirable to simplify the process whereby clients order items from the bulletin. Ideally it could be done by internal electronic mail, assuming the equipment for this is in place. Lacking access to this sort of electronic equipment, the least the library could do for its users would be to include a form in the bulletin on which item numbers for desired publications can be jotted down, followed by mailing the form to the library.

A paper describing the benefits of using electronic mail to distribute the daily collection of news items has been written by Levinton.[2] The daily news items selected in a bank library are placed in a "shared folder" which each employee may access on his or her office terminal, on an optional basis, available as early as two hours after the start of the bank's workday. It has proved to be a very popular service.

Selective Dissemination of Information

Long before the United States Department of Defense began to use the initials SDI to stand for Strategic Defense Initiative, libraries had been using these letters as an initialism for Selective Dissemination of Information. A form of current awareness, SDI usually means supplying library clients with current information that matches previously prepared lists of topics of interest to each client. For example, a person might want to receive automatically any recent data on the uses made of a particular chemical in the food industry, or on the strength of miners' unions in Bolivia. A description of the range of topics of interest for each person is usually called the person's profile of interests. Before the advent of computers, the only way this service could be performed was through manual searching of pertinent journals and/or newspapers, usually performed by a member of the library reference staff. There were limits to the number of topics a given librarian could keep in mind while perusing the current literature, and it was difficult to locate data on certain complicated questions by manual searches.

Not long after the creation of public access to the major databases the vendors of the files began to offer online versions of SDI service; the clients requesting this service would inform the library staff of his/her fields of interest, which fields would then be matched by the computer with topics that appeared in the appropriate types of literature that were indexed by that database. Usually the SDI process is automatically carried out each time the database(s) involved are updated, whether that is weekly, monthly, or less frequently. This process ensures that the requestor receives notice of the latest information soon after it is entered into the database. Records that match the requestors' profile are either printed and mailed or perhaps sent electronically, to be printed on the library's computer. Some services will mail records directly to the end-user's address.

Because people's interests change, it is important for the library staff to devise a way to check with each requestor periodically to make sure the profile of interests is still valid. Some users don't bother to inform the library of changing interests, even though there is a charge by the database vendor for each batch of "hits" obtained with this service.

The service saves a great deal of searching time for the library staff or the user; it is done without regard to the amount of rush projects taking place in the library; and, since the searches are done off-line, they do not incur connect charges. An article by Ojala provides a thorough review of the advantages and disadvantages of SDI service.[3] She points out that it is best for locating more or less routine data, but, if the information must be obtained immediately, the client would not want to wait for the next updating period before getting data. She expresses the need for real-time electronic delivery, which is at present available on at least one system, NewsNet; it operates continuously 24 hours a day, seven days a week.

Contents Pages of Journals

For years special libraries have routed issues of current periodicals among their clients. A separate routing list is required for each issue, and in many cases journals are so popular that several extra subscriptions must be ordered. Besides the costs of extra subscriptions, there are other drawbacks to this procedure, such as frequent delays in routing. Some delays are caused by employees on vacation or on business trips, while others are caused by procrastinators who just don't pass along the periodical issues promptly. Another problem is the need for constant updating of routing slips as people come and go in the organization.

As an alternative to this traditional practice, many special libraries instead distribute photocopies of the tables of contents of journals to clients. This can be a very efficient way of quickly informing clients of what is available in new journal issues. Before beginning to distribute contents pages, a library should make a survey of readers to learn which titles are enough in demand to make it worthwhile to include them. There are always some journals in which there is a relatively low number of clients interested, in which case routing the actual issues would be a more practical solution.

Libraries who use the contents page process would be well advised to obtain permission from the journals' publishers, to ensure that copyright regulations are being followed. Still another way to provide this service is to order copies of commercially produced sets of contents pages, such as *Current Contents*, which is available in several areas of science and engineering. Other fields are covered by different publishers. One problem with buying such publications, besides costs, is the lack of choice of journals to include in the program. By doing the entire process locally, this would no longer be a factor.

An example of the involvement of E-mail and electronic bulletin boards in the use of contents pages is found in the paper by Tinsley.[4] She describes the use of an experimental electronic bulletin board (named "Library") at the computer science department at Carnegie Mellon University. It allows for production of a list of the tables of contents of some 30 periodicals, and posts the list on the department's network. Carrying the use of electronics one step further, interested readers can order a photocopy of any article by use of electronic mail, with the article sent to his or her office.

References

1. Thury, Eva M. From library to information center: case studies in the evolution of corporate information resources. *Special Libraries*. 79(1): 21-27; 1988 Winter.

    Reviews the services offered by corporate information centers, including the preparation of sets of clippings for executives at various times during the day.

2. Levinton, Juliette. Electronic news delivery. *Special Libraries*. 81(3): 180-182; 1990 Summer.

    Explains the operation of providing clients with a customized abstract of current news items using electronic mail. The system uses a VAX minicomputer with All-in-1 office automation software, available on clients' DEC VT220 terminals in their offices. The "shared folder" system allows each client to peruse the clippings at his or her option. Employees in Puerto Rico are also able to access the service.

3. Ojala, Marydee. SDIs: the Star Wars of business searching. *Database*. 11(6): 82-89; 1988 Dec.

    Discusses the reasons for using SDI service, along with a review of the characteristics of the services offered by the major database vendors, including costs, speed of providing records to clients, and frequency of updating (some can be done on a daily basis).

4. Tinsley, G. Lynn. An electronic bulletin board: Library. *Special Libraries*. 80(3): 188-192; 1989 Summer.

    Describes use of an electronic bulletin board for displaying the tables of contents of more than 30 periodicals received in an academic library. Interested faculty members can order photocopies of articles by using electronic mail. Future improvements are mentioned.

Chapter 14

Circulation Services

Managers of special libraries do not make a fetish of circulation statistics, recognizing that how the collection was used is more important than how many times it was used. Nevertheless, the amount of use of the collection is one measure of how the library's clients relate to its operations and is thus a topic of considerable interest to librarians. Different types of circulation are covered in this chapter as well as the related topic of copying materials.

Circulation Policies

Users of special libraries generally expect to be able to borrow freely from their libraries; they tend to dislike restrictions on circulation that they consider unnecessary. Thus the librarian who attempts to introduce rules that may have been suitable in other types of libraries would undoubtedly find a lot of resistance among clients. This section reviews some of the policies that are commonly followed in special libraries.

Most users of special libraries are reasonable about sharing library materials with their colleagues at work. If the rules are apparently based on common sense, the average user seems content to follow the rules. For example, many special libraries allow several months to pass before sending overdue notices; however, if another person should request an item that is out on loan, the average special library would request it be returned after having been on loan for at least two weeks. Rules of this sort are generally acceptable to the average special library client, but most clients tend to rebel at being asked to return a book simply because they have had it on loan for a few weeks if no one else has requested to see it. What might seem reasonable in an academic or public library might very well seem too restrictive in a special library.

One technique to use to keep material from being out for many months, if not for years, is to ask for a routine return of all materials which have been on loan for a rather long period, say for three months, with another loan period allowed if the client still wants the material. In practice this has usually worked well.

The use of fines for overdue material would be unheard of in most special libraries, and it would be foolish to establish them. The loss of library materials, however, is commonly recognized as a basis for an accounting for the materials involved. It is not uncommon for the borrower's department to be charged with the costs of replacing and processing any item that is not returned by the borrower after a suitable interim has elapsed since the item was first recalled. This policy covers not only the case of lost materials but also acts as a spur for procrastinators to return items they just haven't managed to return when so requested. Officially it can be assumed the items were lost, even if the likelihood of procrastination is strong.

Permanent Loans

The term "permanent loan" may seem contradictory, but it has been used successfully to indicate materials which are permanently on loan to a given department, often to a certain person in a department. It provides a way for people to have permanent use of a given book or journal subscription without regard to circulation rules. Many employees find they need certain basic books, reports, journals, and other materials on a long-term basis. Rather than take the time of the library staff and of the reader to regularly fill out renewal records for materials of this sort, a permanent loan would allow for the use of materials for as long as they are required; this eliminates a lot of paperwork.

The writer once instituted such a system at a corporate library where there had been no proviso for long-term use, and where the library staff and the clients were both dissatisfied with trying to operate under normal rules. The library committee readily agreed to the plan when first proposed, and the committee helped establish a plan for calculating the amount of money to be allotted annually to each department for books or subscriptions. Under the plan adopted, most departments received an annual sum based on the number of professional employees in the department; in the case of small, specialized departments, such as the patent department of the firm, a fixed figure was chosen that would take their needs into consideration. Other departments, where there was little or no research, were given small allotments or even no funding. Over the years it was necessary to review the size of the allotments to allow for changing conditions, such as inflation or reorganization of the departments. The departments were free to use their allotments for obtaining whatever their quota would allow, whether it was used for books or for subscriptions.

Other organizations using such a plan have differing viewpoints about cataloging these materials and including them in the organization's catalog, whether in card form or computerized. One school of thought is that in an emergency it would be unfortunate to do without a piece of literature simply because there was no knowledge outside the department that the item was on hand. On the other hand, listing an item in a catalog might lead to trivial requests for an item presumably not vitally needed outside the department owning it. One compromise position might be to list items in the catalog with a minimum of entries, enough to identify them in an emergency but not enough to locate them (the location could be omitted from the catalog entry). A client requesting to see such material could be told the location of the item should his or her need for it seem to a library staff member to be worthy of referral to the owning department.

Circulation Records

Many special libraries do not have automated circulation records because the total number of items borrowed per day is so small that manual records suffice. Other libraries operate with software systems which includes a module that was designed to handle circulation records. In such a case, it would be foolish to operate on a manual basis.

One advantage of an automated system is the ease and speed with which the library staff could determine what is charged out to a given client. In the event employees are leaving the organization, it is prudent to check the records to see if the persons had any outstanding library materials; this can be done very quickly with an automated system, unlike the slow, laborious task of checking circulation records manually.

An example of a computer-based system for simplifying the process of requesting items from the library is explained in the article written by Hodges.[1] She explains how clients can use electronic mail for requesting library materials (as well as requests for online searches). Copies of request messages sent on the UNIX-based system are included.

Restricted Information.   Circulation records are vitally important in a library containing military documents bearing security restrictions—usually called simply secret documents, although they might be classified at a lower level than secret. Security regulations require that each person who has access to a classified document have a personal clearance as well as what is called a "need to know" for the document. This rule ensures that the documents are seen by those who have a legitimate need to do so, denying access to those who are merely curious. Only libraries serving organizations which are working on federal contracts involving restricted military data are apt to be affected by regulations of this sort.

Another large class of documents might be restricted due to commercial considerations. Certain types of information pertaining to businesses, law firms, or other commercial enterprises may need to be restricted as to who could see or possess it. Unauthorized access to what is sometimes termed "company confidential" data might be very harmful to commercial organizations.   There are few government regulations governing this sort of material; each company sets its own rules. In practice the libraries of these organizations would need to follow the instructions as to whom such information could be lent as well as how and where it would be stored. It is not uncommon for a firm to have a vault for storing the data; only certain employees would have access to the vault or its contents.

Librarians are usually unaware of the requirements involved in the handling of restricted information since such topics are seldom discussed in most library school programs. A book by Mount and Newman describes the steps that must be taken to safeguard restricted information of both a military and a commercial nature.[2] Pertinent laws are cited along with recommendations for establishing good library practices. In addition, ways of legally obtaining federal information covered by the Freedom of Information Act are discussed. Librarians working with the public should be aware of the possibilities offered by the latter law for access to certain federal information, as well as being familiar with similar statutes in effect at the state level in most states.

An article by Shores describes a system of document control established in a corporate library for handling classified military data.[3] She covers the nature of the software used for this purpose as well as important points in library operation involved with safeguarding such information. A paper by Graham is devoted to the handling of proprietary information in corporate libraries.[4] She presents the pros and the cons of handling this sort of data; the article includes a discussion of the various steps that are necessary, such as document identification, indexing methods, retention policies, document storage, and search systems.

Photocopying

For years it has been taken for granted that libraries provide photocopying service for its clients and for its staff. In most organizations the choice of equipment is made by a staff manager, such as head of the purchasing department or some such manager. If the library manager were to have a voice, it is likely that certain features would be sought that might not be thought of in other departments. One valuable asset of a library photocopier would be a design that allows a book to fit easily over one edge of the glass where copying occurs; such a feature enables the operator to copy far into the inner margins of bound pages without straining the binding. Flat glass screens invariably cause damage to bound materials because their spines must be pushed down rather hard in order to copy the inner margins properly. Another important feature is quiet operation; just as important is reliable service and good maintenance service if needed.

Most special libraries post a warning notice at photocopy machines regarding the need to comply with the copyright law. Making a single copy for non-commercial use is generally acceptable; clients should check with an attorney if other uses are contemplated.

Photocopies of articles requested on interlibrary loan are often sent in lieu of the original; it is not expensive and eliminates tieing up a bound volume for several days at a time. The use of facsimile further speeds up the process of handling interlibrary loan requests.

References

1.   Hodges, Pauline R. Reference in the age of automation: changes in reference service at Chemical Abstracts Service Library. *Special Libraries.* 80(4): 251-257; 1989 Fall.

Reviews the uses of computers in the library, including the application of electronic mail by clients for ordering items from the library.

2.   Mount, Ellis; Newman, Wilda B. *Top secret/trade secret: accessing and safeguarding restricted information.* New York: Neal-Schuman Publishers; 1985. 214 p.

Describes the regulations and practices involving the safeguarding of data covered by military or commercial restrictions. One section is devoted to protection of data contained in computer files. Also discusses ways of legally obtaining data through freedom-of-information statutes.

3.   Shores, Patricia M. Classified documents in the corporate library. *Special Libraries*. 79(1): 15-20; 1988 Winter.

Explains the operation of a computerized system for keeping track of classified documents, including their status as to who borrowed them and present location. Reports can be generated arranged by titles, document numbers, an individual's borrowing record, keywords, etc.

4.   Graham, Margaret H. Management of proprietary information: the trials and the treasures. *Special Libraries*. 73(4): 281-285; 1982 Oct.

Analyzes the positive and negative aspects of handling proprietary information in a corporate setting. Emphasizes the importance of the outlook of management and information professionals in creating a suitable environment for proper care of this sort of material.

Chapter 15

Editorial Services

In many special libraries/information centers a great deal of staff activity involves such editorial services as writing, abstracting, and translating. Educational requirements may be as high as a subject doctorate, particularly in the case of highly technical fields, such as chemistry or biology. Besides the need for competence in certain subject disciplines, many of the editorial duties require the skills normally associated with professional librarians, such as the ability to write clearly or to prepare abstracts of reasonably complex material. In order to maintain high standards, the manager must be familiar with what constitutes high-level editorial work, even if, in some cases, subject specialists on the staff may perform most of the editorial duties.

Writing

Every manager is required to write routine reports for top management; these may be annual reports, special project reports, or requests for budget increases. It is assumed that managers are able to write clearly, if not brilliantly. Brevity of style and accuracy are essential in business writing; a flair for excellent writing is a bonus.

Managers of special libraries/information centers may be assigned projects outside the realm of the routine. For example, it is not unheard of for a top executive to ask the manager to prepare a draft of a speech, saving valuable executive time. Requests of this sort would not generally be made until or unless the manager had previously proved to have ability in similar assignments.

Other types of writing projects are closely tied to reference service, such as the preparation of analyses, state-of-the-art reports, and reviews of the literature. For example, a state-of-the-art report might be concerned with the current outlook for the production of microprocessors. It would probably discuss various techniques for their preparation, their costs, and the names of important suppliers; this would require not only writing skill but also good judgment and considerable knowledge of the field. The preparation of a review of the literature also would call for more than superficial knowledge of the field. In a typical case, a reviewer might examine the literature of the past five years, and select the best items to cite and summarize. Services of this sort used to be performed chiefly in information centers, with the work done by persons with experience or graduate training in the field. In recent years, some good special libraries also have been able to offer such services, a situation that is typical of the blurring of differences between special libraries and information centers. The article by Meyer covers many of the major aspects of providing literature reviews.[1]

Information specialists with good experience or graduate degrees in marketable subjects, such as the sciences, engineering, and certain social sciences, can usually command high salaries. Although the advent of computerized databases is adding a new dimension to information retrieval, there will always be a need for a thoughtful analysis of a subject prepared by a well-trained specialist.

Abstracting

Many types of materials in special libraries/information centers are of so much importance to their clientele that abstracts (sometimes called annotations or summaries) must be prepared. Periodical articles (in journals not covered by published abstracting services), local technical reports, and patents are three types of materials commonly abstracted in these organizations.

The preparation of a concise but thorough abstract calls for certain skills different from those needed for writing reports. The abstractor must be able to reduce many pages of prose, graphs, tables, and charts to a clear statement of the purpose and nature of the items being analyzed. An article by Weil describes the nature of abstracts and how they are prepared.[2] As mentioned in Chapter 2, there are two distinct types of abstracts although many abstracts fall somewhere between the two. Indicative abstracts summarize the main points of information without going into details about specific points. Informative abstracts indicate the main highlights of the item but also give sufficient details to make clear what the contents include.

The following examples use an imaginary periodical article on highway safety to illustrate both types of abstracts:

- *Indicative Abstract:*   Presents a summary of steps being taken to increase safety on highways in Connecticut. Statistics showing effectiveness of the measures taken are cited.
- *Informative Abstract:*   The Connecticut Department of Highways annual report for 1980 shows that the following steps have been taken in an effort to reduce highway accidents in that state: better lighting at main intersections; improved design of guardrails in dangerous locations; modernized design of highway signs; stricter enforcement of laws regarding speeding; and stopping the use of intoxicating beverages by drivers. In 1980 deaths from highway accidents were reduced 14 percent from 1979 figures, based on the same number of man-miles driven. Future plans include a continuation of the present program.

Informative abstracts clearly give more information but require more time to prepare and take up more space. Since more details are included, a higher degree of competence in the subject is required so that facts are not misstated.

While any kind of abstract adds to the cost of a listing or bibliography of items, most readers find them more helpful than a mere listing of bibliographic elements.

Besides abstracts which summarize the contents of an item, there is a higher level of abstracting which involves a critical analysis of the contents. This requires a high level of competence in the subject matter. More information is available in the national standard for writing abstracts.[3]

Translating

In many special libraries/information centers the clients must be kept aware of developments found in foreign language publications. There are several ways of accomplishing this, such as the publication of cover-to-cover translations of major journals, or the publication of translations of occasional articles or books of major importance. In many cases the time lag caused by waiting for others to make translations for general distribution is far too long, requiring the special library/information center to employ one or more translators. This requires subject competency, translating skills, and competence in writing, if abstracts or digests are involved.

Those who have translating skills in complex subjects are generally highly paid, but providing timely, accurate translations is usually well worth their cost to the organization. Most staff linguists spend their entire time translating. In addition to writing abstracts or complete translations, they are often called upon to read an abstract or to summarize orally the contents of a periodical article or patent to a fellow employee who requires an idea of the contents rather than a formal written summary.

As an alternative to having a staff translator, some organizations rely on outside commercial translating firms or reliable free-lance translators. While this eliminates the need for the usual fringe benefits usually paid to full-time employees, the cost of translations done on a free-lance basis may be so high that an organization with frequent need for such services might find it cheaper and more convenient to have a staff translator. A study of the current rates charged for translations by professional translating firms showed that they currently charge $80 per 1,000 words in the case of the major European languages; there is an extra charge of $8 per 1,000 words for non-Roman alphabets.

Those interested in a summary of the sources of translations, the role of translating firms, and translations handling at an indexing service should consult a book edited by Mount that covers the topic.[4]

Equipment

Practically all special libraries are equipped with one or more personal computers; prices are so reasonable now there is no excuse for not having at least one. When the computer is equipped with one of the many software packages for word processing, the staff can prepare all the reports and other written documents they are apt to need. Letter-quality printers make the finished product fully acceptable for all uses. In some instances the output can also be a diskette, particularly in the case of long documents if the recipient intends to incorporate them in a different publication. Another use is to download data from online searches so that records can be edited, rearranged, and otherwise made more attractive before being presented to clients.

Since these same personal computers can also be used for such purposes as mounting an online catalog, for serial records, or circulation records, there should be little opposition by management to providing the funds for equipment that offers so many advantages.

Another essential piece of equipment is a high-quality photocopier. The ability to prepare attractive copies is taken for granted. Those selecting a copier should require that it not only provide good quality copies but also be able to collate pages so that copying documents with several pages can be done quickly when multiple copies are needed.

Desk top publishing, which includes formatting text to incorporate graphics, tables, etc., is possible with the right software and almost any type of personal computer. Library accession bulletins or library reports would profit from being made more attractive. There are many programs from which to choose, some being much simpler to use than others. Most of them allow for formatting documents so they can be printed using a laser printer, which produces a very clean, crisp-looking document.

References

1.   Meyer, Roger L.; Schwartz, James H., The literature survey; policy for performance, evaluation and use. *Special Libraries*. 61(3): 122-126; 1970 Mar.

Provides a list of many questions which could be used as a means of evaluating search services, particularly complex literature reviews. Discusses the qualifications of various types of employees for performing literature searches.

2.   Weil, Ben. Standards for writing abstracts. *Journal of the American Society for Information Science.* 21(5): 351-357; 1970 Sept./Oct.

Explains the principles of writing abstracts and provides several samples.

3.   *American national standards for writing abstracts, ANSI Z39.14-1979.* New York: American National Standards Institute; 1979. 15 p.

Describes the different types of abstracts and gives examples of each type.

4.   Mount, Ellis, ed. *Translations in sci-tech libraries.* New York: Haworth Press; 1982. 94 p. (Also published as *Science & Technology Libraries,* vol. 3 no. 2, 1982 Winter.)

Presents several papers on translations, including sources for obtaining translations, operations of a commercial translating firm, handling of translations at *Engineering Index*, and the activities of the former National Translation Center.

Part 4

Technical Services

Many users of special libraries have little comprehension of what are usually called technical services, yet these people would be very aware if technical services were not carried out in a satisfactory manner. Without a smoothly functioning technical services department, the library would not be likely to provide a well-designed current catalog of library holdings, nor an efficient method of obtaining information from outside sources, nor a collection in which the items were kept in good repair and useable condition.

This part of the book contains a description of technical services, commencing with cataloging and indexing activities in Chapter 16, including examples of the different types of catalogs and indexes. Chapter 17 is devoted to the topic of ordering or otherwise acquiring additions to the collection, covering both print and nonprint materials. Chapter 18 is concerned with the care and preservation of materials; it discusses serials, microforms and other formats of data.

Chapter 16

Cataloging and Indexing

If a collection consisted of a disorganized array of materials, one in which there was no logical method of locating information, the term "library" would hardly apply. Organization of data is taken for granted in libraries and information centers.

Each library manager normally decides what methods to use for organizing materials and the degree of organization to employ; thus there are differences of emphasis from one organization to another. University and public libraries generally differ from the average special library as to their techniques and goals. Even within the ranks of special libraries there are differences. Some special libraries pride themselves on their carefully organized materials, while others devote just enough attention to get by. In some special libraries certain types of materials, such as patents or technical reports, may receive a great deal of attention so that they will be kept in a well-organized fashion, while other libraries may treat them very casually, if they collect such items at all. The decisions made depend upon the expected use of the materials in a particular library. This chapter will discuss the most likely methods of organizing materials with the understanding that a choice of techniques and systems is going to be a matter for each organization to make.

One of the choices to be made is that of the degree to which internal expertise would be used to create computerized or manual systems for organizing materials versus using commercial systems ready for installation. The size of budgets also plays a major role in these decisions.

Cataloging

In this book the term *cataloging* includes the processes of descriptive cataloging, subject cataloging, and classifying, for the purpose of creating an information retrieval tool. In school, public, and academic libraries, the traditional card catalog, or one of its more modern variations, is the only tool for locating materials by author, subject, or title. In special libraries and information centers there are usually special indexes available in addition to the traditional catalog.

Most libraries rely on abstracting and indexing services, published by commercial or government organizations, for bibliographic control of periodical articles or certain technical report series. The sheer bulk of these materials forces libraries to depend on such tools for access to this data. Catalogs are generally devoted to monographs, serials (overall treatment, not contents of issues), and occasionally such miscellaneous items as maps and slides. However, special libraries frequently have very large collections that are not covered by commercial indexes, forcing them to prepare special indexes. While the method they use may result in a catalog, the treatment given each item is often so detailed that it is more accurate to describe the retrieval tools as indexes. They may be in card form, book form, or online.

Descriptive cataloging refers to identifying and recording the key bibliographic elements of a work (author, title, series data, imprint, etc.), while subject cataloging refers to the selection of subject headings. Classifying, for those libraries whose books are shelved by classification numbers, refers to the selection of the appropriate class number from a classification system, usually either the Dewey Decimal System or the Library of Congress System.

While many special libraries/information centers are able to use conventional subject heading lists (such as the multivolume set prepared by the Library of Congress), such conventional headings are sometimes too broad. Thus, many libraries must devise their own subject headings for greater specificity. Palatsky's article describing subject headings prepared in a major museum library is an example of this.[1] These efforts require considerable experience with the nomenclature of a particular subject field. Frequently librarians can use existing indexing terms, but new terms may still be needed. In a related article, Ho describes other cataloging methods used at that same library for the handling of exhibition catalogs.[2]

Many special libraries/information centers create their own classification systems because the conventional systems are not detailed enough or are dated. The new systems are usually confined to major areas where the bulk of the collection is treated. An article by Craft discusses the classification scheme devised for a collection of plant drawings maintained by a library at Carnegie Mellon University.[3] Categories allowed for in the system include classes for each species, for parts of plants, for horticulture, and for folklore. There are few general libraries which would need such a detailed scheme, but it was appropriate for this particular library.

Types of Catalogs.   Hundreds of years ago, library catalogs were written by hand and cumulated when the lists became too unwieldy to use. The advent of card catalogs near the turn of the century, along with the sale of catalog cards by the Library of Congress, made the card catalog the most common type of library catalog. This system allowed for easy expansion of the file, required no special equipment, and was simple to use. Most card catalogs were arranged with author, subject, and title cards all interfiled in one large alphabet. When catalogs became very large they were often simplified by separating subjects from author-title entries.

Early in the twentieth century, several libraries in the United States turned to a variation on the traditional card catalog, called the classified catalog. Used in many European libraries, its main feature was the arrangement of subject cards by the notation (usually numerical) of a classification scheme. The parts of such a catalog were an alphabetical file for authors (and titles, where the main entry is a title), a classified subject file (arranged by classification numbers), and an alphabetical file that served as an index to the classified subject file. For example, one would look in the alphabetical subject index to learn that the number for aircraft engines was 629.87, then locate the cards filed under that number in the classified subject file. Advocates of the classification scheme appreciate the logic of putting like things next to each other, as opposed to arranging items alphabetically by subject headings. For example, in a conventional alphabetical subject file the terms related to aviation would be scattered all over the alphabet, such as a (aileron), l (landing gears), j (jet engines), f (fuel), etc. In the classified catalog all would be in the same class number, 629, and filed next to logical topics. One special library using such a system is the Engineering Societies Library in New York City. Their catalog, while based on the Universal Decimal Classification (UDC), actually uses modified Dewey numbers because the UDC system has not been kept up-to-date in recent years. This is a typical problem for libraries that do not use the LC or the Dewey systems—the problem of finding ways to keep the classification schemes updated as needed.

There are now sources besides the Library of Congress for obtaining printed catalog cards. Commercial firms have proved to be viable competitors for LC, offering quick service and tailoring such details as the number of cards made, and call numbers suited to user needs. The most recent source of catalog cards are large, online databases which produce computer-printed cards, the most prominent probably being OCLC, which produces millions of cards each year for subscribers.

Another way of describing catalogs is by physical format. The most familiar is the card catalog, but other versions also have been developed. One type uses microforms, often prepared by converting an existing card catalog, with supplements issued at regular intervals thereafter. This system reduces the cost of upkeep since there are no cards to file and it makes the catalog readily available in several locations if desired.

Book catalogs are another type of catalog in use in recent years. Modern book catalogs are generally computer-prepared. The simplest type of book catalog consists of inputting data into the computer, which prints entries according to the specifications set by the designers. One format is to have full entries arranged in alphabetical order by main entry, with additional subject and/or title indexes. They can be cumulated as frequently as desired, with extra copies photocopied as needed. In more elaborate systems, the computer operates a photocomposition machine, providing a variety of type faces. One great benefit of book catalogs is that they can be read without the special viewers required for microform catalogs. They provide the added advantages of being easily updated and being suitable for multiple copies (although the full-size format used would be more expensive to reproduce than microforms).

During the past few years a dramatic growth has occurred in the number of commercial firms who sell automated systems to libraries. Their software is usually procured to be used in such areas as online catalogs, circulation records, acquisition records, and serial records. Online catalogs are particularly of interest now since most libraries desire to have this sort of catalog. These ready-made automated systems are often called "turnkey" operations because theoretically the vendors install the systems and the librarians merely "turn the key" to get the systems operating. Of course, it is not this simple a matter; there are always snags to unsnarl, or special needs in each library that require readjustment of the "standard" system. A well-written account of the selection and installation of a turnkey system at the Los Alamos National Laboratory Library is found in the article by Stoll.[4] The care taken in the crucial step of preparing a request for quotation from various vendors is fully explained. In general the system worked very well, but the author points out that one failure in the planning stage was the lack of awareness of the length of time it would take to phase out manual systems; one reason for this was a lack of manpower to convert old records into the new system. The same periodical issue containing this paper also features experiences with turnkey systems at several other libraries.

In the past twenty years several large computerized databases containing millions of records of cataloged items have come into being. They are often called bibliographic utilities. One of their chief values is that of serving as a source of cataloging data which libraries having access to the utilities may copy, if they wish.

Two prominent utilities are the OCLC network, based in Columbus, Ohio, and the RLIN system (Research Libraries Information Network), owned by the Research Libraries Group. OCLC has many public and academic library members, although an ever-increasing number of its members are special libraries. It was created in Ohio in 1967 by the Ohio College Library Center, having as its primary purpose at the time to provide a means for libraries in that state to share resources. Membership grew rapidly, and by 1978 it had become so widely used that a new organization was formed, this one national in scope. The initials were retained, but it was renamed Online Computer Library Center. Today there are over 16 million records in the system, along with some 260 million holding symbols of its members. A periodical article by Little emphasizes the international activities of OCLC, beginning with the United Kingdom in 1981 when OCLC Europe was founded.[5] Since then activities have been extended to the Asian/Pacific area and Canada. The article points out the benefits of this expansion to U.S. and non-U.S. libraries as well as some of the problems involved, such as differing standards for entries, different languages, and different library traditions. In general the overall outlook is that the potential benefits are significant.

RLIN was created in 1978 when the Research Libraries Group, at that time a rather small group of large research libraries, saw the need for a common database for its members. It grew rapidly; by 1988 it had acquired nearly 23 million bibliographic records representing more than 9 million unique entries. Like OCLC, it also adds records from such sources as the Library of Congress, the National Library of Medicine, and the Government Printing Office as well as from its members, now totaling more than 80. Bales and Tucker have written a paper that reviews the current status and future outlook for RLIN.[6] Many changes have been made since its inception, such as the availability of Oriental and Cyrillic records in their original characters, a special index to architectural periodical articles, and an art sales catalog database. In 1991 RLIN was closed by RLG for financial reasons.

Since the development of OCLC and RLIN there have been countless debates about the quality of the cataloging done for entries in these two databases. Many librarians felt that OCLC's early years, in which emphasis was on building its database rather than on quality of entries, still characterized current conditions. A paper by Intner throws a different light on the subject.[7] She reports that a 1987 study of 215 matched pairs of catalog records contributed by members of OCLC and RLIN revealed the number of errors was practically identical (537 versus 530); thus the impression that OCLC was less accurate and had inferior cataloging to RLIN was untrue. Many of the errors involved punctuation, although the largest number involved errors in application of AACR2 rules. Only a small number of the errors that occurred would have affected retrieval in an actual search.

There are many utilities having national status in addition to OCLC and RLIN. For example, the Library of Congress produces the MARC (Machine Readable Catalog) records, distributed weekly in magnetic tape format to subscribers. The records are widely known and used; both OCLC and RLIN include such records in their files.

The copying of data from bibliographic utilities allows for transferring data from an online database to a library's local files, a process called downloading. So popular has this mode of cataloging become that a special name has evolved: cataloging with copy (although printed sources of cataloging data could just as well be included as another source of cataloging information). This activity is important because of the time and costs it saves as compared to doing original cataloging. A book by Taylor is devoted to the practice of cataloging with copy, including such topics as searching for online records, entering new records online, and training of staff members.[8]

An important feature of any cataloging system is an authority file, essentially a list of approved subject headings, or authors, or descriptors; such a list helps ensure that the cataloger uses the best term for a particular concept. It also helps avoid using synonyms for approved terms. Occasionally libraries develop cataloging systems without having an adequate authority list. As a result, the catalog user can never be sure approved terms are the ones on which to search if non-standardized terms were sometimes used in that system. If synonyms were used, the searcher would not know which one to choose for a search.

An example of this situation is found in an article by Bellamy and Bickham.[9] They describe a situation in a corporate library in which the cataloger realized after a year of cataloging that the subject headings were in need of revision; the main problem was inconsistency. They were based on both the Library of Congress system and the National Library of Medicine System. The paper discusses the process of developing a reliable authority file, done in the style of a thesaurus. A thesaurus is superior to a straight listing of terms; thesauri show relationships, such as broader terms, related terms, or narrower terms. They have become indispensable for searching online databases.

Indexing

It is not easy to distinguish indexes from catalogs, but indexes generally provide a much greater depth of analysis than catalogs. Whereas books are usually cataloged with no more than three or four subject headings per book, an index might have many more points of access for subjects (sometimes dozens of subject terms are assigned to each document) as well as including bibliographic elements not normally used for retrieval from catalogs, such as publication dates, publishers, and languages in which written.

Special indexes are generally reserved for items for which commercial or government-published indexes are not available. For example, while there are numerous government-generated indexes for certain major report series, there are many reports not covered by these indexes; a special library/information center must do its own indexing in such cases. Locally prepared reports are prime examples of this sort of material, as are reports from agencies not associated with government technical report production. Slides, drawings, maps, and other formats, such as laboratory notebooks, usually require local indexing. On the other hand, patents, both foreign and domestic, are now carefully covered by several commercial indexing firms.

Thesauri.   A basic necessity for a good indexing system is a thesaurus of terms used for the process. The detailed relationships between words, shown by a thesaurus, are not found in an ordinary dictionary. For example, a thesaurus on the subject of aviation might include the following entries and initials:

> aircraft
> > UF airplanes
> aircraft wings
> > UF wings
> > BT aircraft structures
> > RT aerodynamics
> > NT ailerons

The reader may not be aware of the meaning of the symbols used in most thesauri, as follows:

> UF—used for (indicating a term that is not used)
> BT—broader term
> RT—related term
> NT—narrower term

Terms in thesauri are invariably much more detailed than subject headings used for books. The nature of the items being indexed, such as technical reports, patents, etc., requires that narrow terms be used; otherwise the index could not distinguish between publications concerned with the same general subject category. In the library of an electronics firm, there might be so many reports on radar, for example, that they would all have the same subject heading if LC subjects headings were used. An array of specific terms is needed to differentiate one item from another. This is true whether the subjects involved pertain to technical, business, social science, or humanistic fields. The problems of creating a thesaurus for a diffuse subject area are explained in an article by Freeman, whose library dealt with the broad topics of leadership, management, and organizational behavior.[10] He describes how terms were selected, recorded, and updated.

Types of Indexes.   Just as there are several types and formats of catalogs in current use, there are several choices of formats available for indexes, card indexes, book-form indexes, microform indexes, and online indexes. Each has the same merits and weaknesses described in the section on catalogs. Because special libraries and information centers generally include materials for which ready-made catalogs and indexes do not exist, they are more apt to prepare special indexes than are academic or public libraries.

The planning of a computerized index for technical reports at an Exxon information center is described in an article by Landsberg and Weil.[11] The system makes use of phrases for indexing, rather than single terms, and a computer rearranges retrieval words, prints pages, and makes retrospective analysis of the patterns of index use.

Some locally produced indexes rely on commercially produced indexes for providing selected entries to be incorporated in the local product. An article by Wang and Alimena explains how reports from the National Technical Information Service are combined with those from their own company (Bell Laboratories) to prepare announcement lists and allow for a computer-based retrieval system.[12]

Computer-based indexes can be designed by using conventional indexing terms or by using keywords found in titles. The keyword system has been widely used because it provides subject access with little or no professional indexing time involved. Essentially, all that is needed is to input titles into the computer; the program does the rest. This system can be no better than the terms used in the titles, and there are many deficiencies due to this problem. For example, synonymous terms would each have to be looked up in the index, as would spelling variations (such as the British *colour* versus the American *color,* or the terms *lifts* versus *elevators).* Use of titles as the sole basis for an index has been rather inelegantly described as a "quick and dirty" method for producing an index. It is quick, but it is neither thorough nor precise. Nevertheless, there are times when an index of this type is adequate for providing a reasonable means of retrieval. The savings in preparing such indexes may offset their less effective performance.

References

1.   Palatsky, Celine. Art library subject headings system: Metropolitan Museum of Art. *Special Libraries.* 67(8):371-376; 1976 Aug.

Discusses the selection of terms for the system and provides examples.

2.   Ho, Lucy Chao. Cataloging and classification of exhibition catalogs in the Library of the Metropolitan Museum of Art. *Special Libraries.* 66(8): 372-377; 1975 Aug.

Explains the descriptive and subject cataloging decisions involved in handling exhibition catalogs, including examples of main, added, and analytic entries. Some mention also is made of the classification system developed by the library.

3.   Craft, Mary Anne Snavely. Subject classifying botanical art. *Special Libraries.* 68(1): 18-23; 1977 Jan.

A description of a classification scheme devised for use in the Hunt Institute of Botanical Documentation at the Carnegie-Mellon University for drawings and prints of botanical plants. Detailed categories were established to provide for the many species involved as well as parts of plants.

4.   Stoll, Karen S. Installation of the Geac System at Los Alamos National Laboratory Library. *Science & Technology Libraries.* 9(1): 11-19; 1988 Fall.

Relates the steps taken to choose, install, and operate a turnkey computerized system that handles circulation records, acquisition records, serial records, and the online catalog.

5. Little, Thompson M. OCLC's international initiatives and the online union catalog. *Cataloging and Classification Quarterly.* 8(3/4): 67-78; 1988.

Summarizes the international activities of OCLC in several parts of the world. Describes the benefits of and the problems resulting from the addition of foreign data.

6. Bales, Kathleen; Tucker, Alan. The RLIN database: current status, work in progress, future developments. *Cataloging and Classification Quarterly.* 8(3/4): 79-89; 1988.

Describes the contents, the means of access, the authority file, the non-Roman characters, and the future plans for the system.

7. Intner, Sheila S. Much ado about nothing: OCLC and RLIN cataloging quality. *Library Journal.* 114(2): 38-40; 1989 Feb. 1.

Presents results of a test of the relative accuracy of entries cataloged for both the OCLC and RLIN databases. Findings show that the number of errors was almost identical for the two databases, indicating that their quality was essentially equal.

8. Taylor, Arlene G. *Cataloging with copy.* 2d ed. Littleton, CO: Libraries Unlimited; 1988. 335 p.

A text which concentrates on the techniques of copying catalog records from appropriate sources, such as the national bibliographic utilities. Savings in costs are considered in conjunction with a possible lessening of quality of cataloging.

9. Bellamy, Lois M.; Bickham, Linda. Thesaurus development for subject cataloging. *Special Libraries.* 80(1): 9-15; 1988 Winter.

Explains the methods used to construct a thesaurus for use in cataloging a corporate biomedical book collection. It was based on the principles of the National Library of Medicine's medical subject headings.

10. Freeman, Frank H. Building a thesaurus for a diffuse subject area. *Special Libraries.* 67(4): 220-222; 1976 Apr.

Construction of a specialized thesaurus for the Center for Creative Leadership is described, for use in indexing documents in the field of management and other areas of the social sciences. Recommendations for thesaurus construction and updating methods are included.

11. Landsberg, Karen; Weil, Ben H. Managing Exxon's technical reports. *Science & Technology Libraries.* 1(4): 55-64; 1981 Summer.

Describes the use of special indexing techniques for Exxon reports, with examples of pages from their report announcement bulletin. The role of computers is stressed.

12. Wang, Amy; Alimena, Diane M. Managing the Bell Laboratories Technical Report Service. *Science & Technology Libraries.* 1(4): 27-39; 1981 Summer.

Incorporation of government-indexed reports in a system that includes locally produced reports is discussed, with details given of a numbering system for different types of reports. A description is also given of a computer-based system for generation of an announcement bulletin and for retrospective retrieval of reports.

Chapter 17

Acquisitions

Print and nonprint materials for the collections of special libraries/information centers are obtained by purchase or by gift on routine and emergency bases. It is important that organizations have efficient, effective ways of adding needed materials to their collections.

Purchases of Materials

In the average special library/information center most materials are added to the collection through purchases, whether individual or blanket orders (an order for all titles in a given series, for example). Once it has been established that certain titles are to be added, the acquisition section of the unit decides how they are to be obtained. In many cases, individual items are acquired one by one, admittedly an inefficient process but one that allows for differences in the type of material acquired, the speed with which it is obtained, and sources from which it can be obtained. When an item is needed urgently, cost considerations may play a very small role in decisions about how to proceed, whereas for routine items it would be foolish to use methods that are more expensive than necessary.

For routine purchases of monographs, libraries usually have one or more favorite wholesalers or jobbers, who deal in the books of most publishers. Discounts may be small or nonexistent, but these firms may more than make up for that by the quality of their service. Many will accept telephone calls, which is a great convenience for the library. Jobbers are often adept at obtaining materials, working quickly, and billing accurately. However, since not every library is fortunate enough to have a good jobber, the search for a better source is frequently a perennial matter of concern.

When monographs are needed urgently, the method of acquisition depends on such factors as where the library is located in relation to stores and/or the original publisher. It is sometimes feasible to send a messenger to a bookstore or publishing firm for an urgently needed item. In other cases, a telephone call and use of speed-mail will bring the wanted item soon enough. In still other instances, the source may be so inaccessible, and time so limited, that the best the library can do is to borrow a copy or make photocopies of pertinent pages.

For smaller items, such as technical reports, government publications, patents, and pamphlets, there are expediting services which (for a rather large fee) will help make wanted items quickly available. Facsimile (fax service) is often the best method where there are not huge quantities of titles involved. It is the fastest method yet devised.

In recent years another source of material has come into its own—ordering items in the course of online searches. Several sources sell photocopies of articles or other items for users of databases. The searcher merely indicates at the terminal, when connected to an online database, what is needed and the code for the designated source. The next day the source agency responds to requests received at its terminal overnight. Special rush service is often available, at an additional fee.

Subscriptions to serials are generally concentrated so the library will deal with as few periodical subscription services as possible. This reduces the number of purchase orders and payment checks required and simplifies handling of missing issues. A good subscription agency will consolidate the charges for a library's titles into one large annual bill so that hundreds, or even thousands, of titles can be checked against one large invoice and paid for with one check. This is a tremendous time and money saver for the library.

However, it is sometimes not possible or wise to place certain subscriptions with one dealer. An example is a publisher in which the library's sponsor has a company membership, giving it special rates and discounts for the publications of the publisher, often a society or institute. In other cases, the publications are so irregular that commercial dealers will not take the trouble of handling orders, in which case the library may have no choice but to deal directly with the publishers. A few publishers will not deal with jobbers, requiring that orders go to them. Some agencies will not handle titles from certain geographical areas, so that another agency that does handle such materials must be sought.

Special techniques must be used when searching for out-of-print materials. Different dealers are involved, longer waiting periods may ensue, and prices may be higher than expected when a dealer locates an item being sought.

Gifts and Exchanges

A few libraries are in the enviable position of receiving large quantities of monographic works and serials as gifts and/or exchanges. Quite often they receive materials without cost because they are in a position to prepare and publish reviews of the books in publications under their control or with whom they have close relationships. One example is the Engineering Societies Library, which can submit reviews to any of the dozens of technical periodicals published by the several engineering societies which support the library. Because of this, it receives gift copies of monographs from many of the publishers in whose books they are interested.

Most special libraries/information centers do not receive more than a few new gift books per year, and they usually come from friends of the unit, rather than from publishers. However, almost all libraries are occasionally offered older books from friends. Unless all items are really needed for the collection, it is important to reserve the right to dispose of unwanted items. There are few commercial outlets interested in buying old books, unless they have unusual features. A few periodical dealers will purchase discarded serials, particularly complete runs of titles in certain subject areas. Some libraries offer discarded books to their clients on a "first-come, first served" basis, but other libraries may be bound by rules that prohibit giveaways. In recent months there have been signs of revival of an agency (formerly known as the U.S. Book Exchange) that used to distribute used books and periodicals to Third World libraries. It was an ideal outlet for unwanted materials that might have aided libraries in underdeveloped areas.

Another way in which libraries can receive free material is through exchanges, in which the two sources involved have publications to trade. Unless a library is sponsored by a group which regularly publishes useful materials, the opportunity to participate in exchanges is limited.

Acquisition Records

For many years special libraries/information centers had no choice but to maintain all the voluminous records required for the acquisition process by manual means. With the advent of less expensive computers, certain data could be put in machine-readable form, thus making clerical tasks more efficient. Not all libraries have made these improvements, and the larger the library the more difficult it is to completely institute computerized operations because of the greater complexity of the system and the larger number of records involved.

The following are some of the ways in which libraries have used computers in acquisitions activities:

- Preparation of an order for a book automatically reduces the fund for book purchases by the amount of the order, and processing of cancelled orders automatically increases this fund.
- Lists of dealers, their addresses, and phone numbers can be easily prepared whenever desired.
- Acceptance of a filled order automatically prepares a check from the organization for the amount of the order.
- A list can be maintained of each order's status (on order, received, in cataloging, processing completed, etc.) for use by both the staff and clients. Such status data can also be displayed on terminals in an online system, making it even more current.
- Records for serial subscriptions can be input into a system that automatically prints lists of subscriptions coming due in a given time period, or lists of the titles ordered from a given agent.
- Receipt of journal issues can be recorded in the system, which is programmed to prepare claim slips automatically following a delay in receipt of an issue.
- Prior to ordering a book, a search of a bibliographic utility such as OCLC would in many cases afford a check of the accuracy of order information and at the same time provide cataloging information for use when the book has been received.

A paper by Nagle describes the many uses to which an automated system could be put in a special library, many of which involve technical services.[1] She notes that the system aided the following services: acquisitions, serials control, cataloging, authority record management, database management, circulation, and a public access catalog. The staff searches OCLC for pre-order data, downloading it to the catalog if located; the entries thus obtained can be manipulated and enhanced between the time of the placing of an order and its receipt, cataloging, and processing for circulation.

References

1.   Nagle, Ellen. Implementing the NOTIS integrated library system at the Dana Medical Library of the University of Vermont. *Science & Technology Libraries*. 9(1): 43-59; 1988 Spring.

Describes the selection, installation, and uses of an integrated library automation system at a university health sciences library. Both user services and technical services were involved.

Chapter 18

Care and Preservation of Materials

All special librarians need to be aware of the problems involved in the preservation and care of materials in their collections. Without giving proper attention to such matters, it is quite possible that deterioration, wear and tear, or accidents could damage or even destroy valuable items in the collection. Some materials are much more fragile and susceptible to damage than others, and some materials are more valuable than others, making protection more important than otherwise.

More and more attention is being given to preservation of informational materials; many librarians, architects, planners, and publishers are giving consideration to the role of preservation insofar as it affects their work. Even the public is aware of one of the most far-reaching preservation problems, that of the deterioration of paper because of its acidity. Publishers and paper manufacturers, partly due to the urging of library and conservation groups, are beginning to use permanent paper, but the problem of preserving older publications has been only partially solved through deacidification processes and through microfilming of selected works. Despite the wide prevalence of this aspect of preservation (the deterioration of paper), it is one area in which the average special librarian finds little he or she can do. It tends to fall to the larger public, academic, and government-sponsored libraries to engage in processes that would save original publications or make archival copies of them. Securing the cooperation of publishers in using only permanent paper is also more of a national problem than one for individual special libraries to face.

Areas of Concern

There are several aspects of preservation, however, in which special librarians can and should take an active interest. It is generally agreed that there are three major aspects of the broad topic of the care and preservation of materials in which all librarians should be involved. As a book by Mount points out, these categories are as follows:

- Environmental factors
- Security factors
- Physical treatment of materials[1]

Environmental factors include temperature, humidity, and dirt. Security is an obvious category, involving protection against theft, fire, floods, and similar harmful incidents. Physical treatment refers to binding of serials, shelving materials properly, and conversion to microforms when deemed appropriate.

Topics as far-reaching as these require more lengthy treatment than can be given here; the reader should consider longer works on these topics, such as the book by Morrow.[2] She covers the major aspects of preservation, including real-life examples. In addition, the book by Swartzburg is recommended since it addresses the areas of concern mentioned above, applying them to a wide range of materials, such as books, maps, and recordings.[3]

Environmental Factors

This category, as mentioned above, includes concern about atmospheric conditions. An article which is aimed at the preservation problems of special libraries, written by Boomgaarden, emphasizes this particular aspect.[4] He describes the need for keeping temperatures in the range of 68-70 degrees Fahrenheit and holding humidity levels to the range of 40 to 50 percent. It is rather obvious that these factors, if not properly controlled, will have a deleterious effect on library materials. Air conditioning and well-designed heating systems can go a long way toward solving these problems. The treatment of vermin, another harmful environmental condition, often requires the services of specialized companies.

Security Factor

Security factors, as mentioned above, go beyond safeguarding collections against theft, important though that may be. Special libraries, largely limited to use by employees of sponsoring organizations, have less concern about theft than libraries open to the general public. Many special libraries are open at all hours, including nights and weekends, when they are not staffed. Losses have not been a problem in most cases.

Such libraries are not, however, immune from damage due to fires and floods. Building codes require smoke and other fire alarms in modern construction, but this should not lull special librarians into a false sense of security. Managers should be careful there are no electrical hazards, such as hot plates in staff areas or overloaded electrical circuits. Fire drills should be part of an organization's security program.

Floods, which can be caused by a variety of reasons, could be devastating for libraries unless proper actions are taken at once after a flood subsides. Freeze drying of wet books, when properly carried out, can save a high percentage of books. An article by Brady and Guido describes a flood at Washington State University in 1985.[5] Although the number of books involved was small, the main value of the article is in its discussion of the need for a disaster plan in all libraries so that mistakes would not be made during the confusion of an emergency.

Physical Treatment of Materials

Periodicals.   One problem which virtually all special libraries/information centers have is that of handling periodical issues. Such issues are indispensable because of their current information and specific treatment of topics, but at the same time they are more trouble to handle than books. Decisions must be made about how to treat each title, since what may be appropriate for one periodical might not be suitable for another.

Some of the main options for treating periodicals are:

- *Commercial Binding.*   This is the most expensive treatment, yet for titles receiving heavy use over the years, or titles on very important topics, the expense is well worth it. Some types of binding are more expensive than others; by giving careful specifications to the binder, cheaper methods may be used on journals not receiving as much use as others.
- *Local Binding.*   This refers to the use of stiff cardboard pieces which can be held to loose issues by heavy cord threaded through drilled holes. This is not recommended or any but the most ephemeral journals. This method does not allow for frequent use, and it ruins the issues for conventional binding.
- *Boxed Issues.*   If a title is not worth binding, it is viable to use commercial boxes to hold loose issues for as long as they are needed before being discarded. These containers are available in a variety of sizes and weights; they protect issues from becoming damaged or torn, and are more attractive than loose issues sprawling on the shelves.
- *Microforms.*   In many instances, it is more appropriate to rely on a microform copy of a journal than a full-size version. The most common formats are reels or cartridges of microfilm. There are obvious savings of shelf space and possible savings over binding costs, depending upon whether or not a title has already been filmed commercially. On the other hand, most users prefer full-size copies for greater readability, so it is not advisable to replace heavily used titles with a microfilm copy except perhaps as a backup copy for long-term retention. Microfilm can also be used as a replacement for copies printed on such poor quality paper that they would soon be unusable. Newspapers are particularly good examples of this.

Many libraries are relying more and more on microfiche versions of serials, as an alternative to microfilm reels. Needless to say, when a library has microfilm and/or microfiche, it is essential to have a reliable reader-printer so that clients can make copies for themselves of selected pages as needed.

A major concern of most libraries is that of binding important periodicals, titles needed for referral for years. Good procedures, proper standards that binderies are expected to meet, and careful management of the binding process are all part of the operation of well-run libraries. An article by Montori discusses these and other factors.[6]

No matter how carefully binding shipments are planned there will always come a time when an urgently needed volume will be at the binder. One solution is to know in advance where certain major serials can be obtained and/or copied during binding operations.

Shelving for books and journals should be carefully selected. This is covered in greater detail in Chapter 23. There is no doubt that having clean, available shelving will do a great deal in avoiding overcrowding, which is often the cause of damage to books. Vertical files are indispensable for shelving small items too small or too floppy for upright shelving.

A number of libraries collect informational materials other than the traditional books and journals. Special treatment must be given to such materials, as described in the following sections.

Photographs.   Photographs are very delicate objects, less resistant to indifferent storage and inadequate care than printed materials. An article by Kerns discusses a project at George Mason University involving old photographs.[7] They had a large collection of 50-year-old, deteriorating photographs in urgent need of preservation. A private contractor brought in the necessary equipment and maintained quality control measures at all times. Results were said to be excellent. The final product was copied in reel and in microfiche format, both positive and negative.

Maps.   Maps deserve special attention because of their size, which makes them awkward to handle and store, and because of their fragile nature. Quite a bit has been written on this subject; the paper by Kidd emphasizes ways to prevent wear and tear on map collections.[8] She discusses proper map storage containers, ways of displaying maps, and problems in making photocopies of maps. Atlases and globes are also covered in regard to these points.

Fiber Optic Cables.   As time passes, more and more libraries may be replacing conventional cables with fiber optic cables, which possess many superior qualities over traditional types. A paper by Pepplar discusses ways of caring for these newer cables.[9] He describes some of their good features, such as greater capacity for handling data, their small size, and the long distances over which they can operate. He warns users not to look directly into the end of the cable because of the concentrated light they contain; he also points out the need to avoid using right angles in laying out lengths of cable, which damages them.

Newspaper Clippings.   Those libraries that must retain newspaper clippings have long been aware of the difficulties involved because of the fragile nature of such materials as well as the relatively short life of newsprint. An article by Crowley describes a solution that may appeal to many others.[10] She used scanners to convert clippings to digital form for storage on optical disks; one disk was found to store the equivalent of over a dozen file drawers.

Computers.   Aside from keeping computers and their accessories protected from dust or dirt, there are not many requirements for caring for them. Avoidance of fluids getting into computers, protection of power supplies against power surges, keeping them under dust covers when not in use, and reasonable care in using them are the chief points in caring for computers. Having a minimum of moving parts eliminates many maintenance problems. However, computers are complicated enough so that most libraries use trained maintenance workers to maintain and repair them, whether with in-house employees or by contractual arrangements with outside firms.

References

1. Mount, Ellis. *University science and engineering libraries.* 2d ed. Westport, CT: Greenwood Press; 1985; Chapter 10.

    Describes three basic areas that affect the care of library collections—environmental factors, physical treatment, and security measures. Gives examples of how concern about each of these topics can be adapted as part of routine library operations.

2. Morrow, Carolyn Clark. *The preservation challenge: a guide to conserving library materials.* Written with Gay Walker. White Plains, NY: Knowledge Industries Publications; 1983. 232 p.

    A basic text that covers deterioration problems and how to protect materials. Case studies are included.

3. Schwartzburg, Susan, ed. *Conservation in the library: a handbook of use and care of traditional and nontraditional materials.* Westport, CT: Greenwood Press; 1983. 234 p.

    Discusses the care of a variety of materials, including both print and nonprint formats. Chapters are devoted to books, maps, photographs, slides, microforms, motion pictures, videotapes, sound recordings, videodiscs, and computer diskettes. Also deals with standards; has a glossary.

4. Boomgaarden, Wesley L. Preservation planning for the small special library. *Special Libraries.* 76(3): 204-211; 1985 Autumn.

    Presents a summary of steps that should be taken in small special libraries to prolong the useful life of library materials, including proper environmental conditions, recommended conservation operations, and factors to consider in replacing books no longer usable despite careful handling. A useful survey for the inexperienced librarian.

5. Brady, Eileen E.; Guido, John F. When is a disaster not a disaster? *Library & Archival Security.* 8(3/4): 11-23; 1988 Fall/Winter.

    Relates the actions taken after a flood threatened books in an academic library. Shows how prompt action kept damage to a minimum.

6. Montori, Carla J. Managing the library's commercial library binding program. *Technical Services Quarterly.* 5(3): 21-25; 1988.

    Points out the need for determining what standards a commercial bindery should meet, along with requiring that a sample volume be submitted during selection of a binder. Notes that prices vary a great deal, requiring careful selection to get the best source. Many other factors are covered.

7. Kerns, Ruth B. A positive approach to negatives: preserving photographs via microfilm technology. *American Archivist.* 51(1/2): 111-114; 1988 Winter & Spring.

    Describes the conversion of old photographs to microfilm, for which the results were considered excellent. Both reels of film and microfiche were created.

8.   Kidd, Betty. Prevention conservation for map collections. *Special Libraries*. 71(12): 529-538; 1980 Dec.

Covers storage, displays, and photocopying of maps. Atlases are also discussed.

9.   Pepplar, Mike. Fibre optic cables: dos and don'ts for personal computers and terminal users. *The Electronic Library*. 6(6): 140-142; 1988 Dec.

Gives instructions on how to handle fiber optic cables, including safety measures and care of the cables.

10. Crowley, Mary Jo. Optical digital disk storage: an application for news libraries. *Special Libraries*. 79(1): 34-42; 1988 Winter.

Reports on the use of optical disks for storage of newspaper clippings in a newspaper library. She compares the method to the use of microfilm. Scanners are used to convert documents to digital form; one twelve-inch disk holds the equivalent of sixteen legal-size file drawers.

Part 5

Collections

In recent years there have been developments in technology and in organizational cooperation which have diminished the need for each library to have an extensive collection in all subjects of possible interest. Improved arrangements for networks, for shared collection responsibilities, and for full-text versions of materials available on computers are some of the alternatives to building ever-larger collections in a given library. Nevertheless there are certain materials that each library must possess in order to satisfy their clients needing immediate access. Building such collections is still important.

The purpose of this section is to discuss some of the ways in which collections can be built, some of the types of materials needed in libraries, and ways to eliminate unwanted materials. Chapter 19 is devoted to types of library materials, while Chapter 20 covers the general techniques of collection development. Chapter 21 deals with weeding collections, while Chapter 22 discusses the nature of archives and records.

Chapter 19

Types of Library Materials

Special libraries/information centers collectively are interested in every type of information source, from prosaic books and journals to items less commonly found in libraries, such as engineering drawings of aircraft, correspondence files of bank executives, playbills from century-old performances, or recordings of live jazz concerts. One special library devoted to maritime subjects even collects and catalogs models of sailing ships.

This chapter will provide a brief description of the main characteristics of the various materials involved. Each type has its special value and its drawbacks, some of which will be summarized here.

Monographs

While not every special library/information center collects books heavily, it would be a rare unit which did not include at least a few in its collection. Books are usually classified as being either textbooks or monographs. A monographs can be defined simply as a book devoted to a rather specific topic, not designed for use as a general textbook and not aimed at the neophyte.

Because most special libraries serve people who are experienced in their field, basic textbooks per se have little value for such libraries, except perhaps for a few titles in a field related to the main subject concentration of the library. For example, a library serving a bank might have one good textbook on the principles of accounting. For the most part, basic textbooks add little or nothing to what has been published in more advanced works on a given topic.

One feature of special libraries is the fact that a major treatise may be so heavily used that many copies may be required. If so, the library is expected to acquire enough copies to handle the demand for it. There also might be an excellent monograph of interest to only one or two people that still might be worth acquiring for the collection.

Other Monographic Works

Other published materials which appear in monographic forms and represent useful works of a research nature are:

- *Dissertations and Master's Essays.* Such works appeal chiefly to those wanting research materials on a narrow topic. They can pertain to any discipline.
- *Conference Proceedings.* These publications often represent the first form in which research materials are published, and thus present relatively new data, depending upon publication schedules. They can pertain to any discipline.

Periodicals

If there is one single type of publication which could be generally regarded as the most important one for special libraries/information centers, it would have to be periodicals (or journals). The reason is two-fold—first, they tend to be much more up to date than books, and secondly, there are so many different types of journals that one can usually find a specific article on almost any topic desired.

While a typical special library may not have thousands of subscriptions in its collection, it may have all the major ones devoted to a particular subject field. A library serving an insurance company, for example, may have only 200 journal subscriptions but still have all of the important titles in that field.

While American special libraries do not seek foreign language books to any great extent, certain foreign language journals might be necessary to have. Many of them do have extra contents pages in English, and a few have abstracts of the articles in English as well as in the original language.

Other Serials

A wide variety of publications are issued in serial format, with a publishing schedule ranging from annually and biennially to once a day. Each type has its value and place in certain collections.

- *Newspapers.* They are invaluable for detailed accounts of certain events. Some are quite specialized in scope, such as those devoted to business, or chemicals, or health care.
- *Newsletters.* Newsletters are reliable sources (in most cases) of current, detailed information of a very narrow scope, such as a particular metal or a particular financial topic.
- *Review Series.* These publications are often issued annually, presenting a summary of important developments in narrow disciplines during the past year. They can be found in any discipline.
- *Yearbooks.* Such books commonly consist of statistical data for the past year, often in tabular form. They too can pertain to any discipline.

Reference Tools

It is important that carefully selected reference tools be readily available. The need for quick answers for inquiries requires that there be enough reference works available covering likely fields of interest. However, since no collection can be adequate for all inquiries, the reference staff should have enough alternate sources to avoid lengthy delays in finding answers.

Some of the major types of alternate sources are cited below:

- *Abstracting and Indexing Services.* Because of the importance of journals to special libraries, it is essential that they have adequate means of locating articles of interest. Multiple indexes are needed since no single indexing service will suffice. The advent of computerized databases has provided a valuable alternative to printed indexes, although many libraries prefer to have both. Sometimes simple questions can be answered more quickly using a printed index than getting online for that one query; also, many databases cover only a few recent years at this stage of development, making reliance on printed indexes necessary for older material. Some of these indexes and databases concentrate on technical reports or government documents, some are restricted to periodical articles, and others cover a mix of formats, including monographs and conference proceedings. Their cost is not low, but they are indispensable when they cover the fields of greatest interest in a library. Many are now also available in CD-ROM format.
- *Other Reference Tools.* It would be beyond the scope of this book to describe the nature of all types of reference works—handbooks, encyclopedias, dictionaries, bibliographies, directories, and guides to the literature, to cite a few examples. A wise choice of reference tools is imperative if a reference staff is to function adequately.

Unpublished Printed Materials

This category consists of materials which are less apt to be prepared and marketed by publishing firms. Most are from sources which issue these materials to provide information, not to generate profits. Many types are severely limited as to the sort of libraries which would want to collect them.

- *Patents.* Generally patents are of interest only to technical libraries concerned with the current state of the art. Special commercial indexes and/or abstracts also are available; the best ones are online.
- *Technical Reports.* These reports can be concerned with technical matters as well as with issues in the social sciences. They largely are aimed at those well versed in a particular subject. Some require restricted access, due either to commercial or military regulations.

- *Trade Catalogs*. Catalogs promote the sales of commercial products. Readers should be wary about their accuracy, but they do provide detailed information not easily found elsewhere.
- *Standards*. Published standards consist of specific descriptions of prescribed ways of preparing a product or carrying out a certain process. They are chiefly of interest to sci-tech libraries.
- *Government Publications*. These documents cover a very wide range of topics including the social sciences, humanities, and technical disciplines. They are have a wide appeal; in format they range from statistics to research topics.
- *Laboratory Notebooks*. These records recount the activities and findings of individual scientists. They are of interest only to sci-tech libraries.
- *Translations*. They can be prepared for individual clients or as part of cover-to-cover translations of journals. They can pertain to any discipline.
- *Maps*. Maps serve a wide range of interests, including technical, historical, economic, geographic, and artistic. They also can be in atlas form.
- *Field Trip Guidebooks*. Guides are mainly of interest to earth scientists for use in examining the geological features of particular regions, although other types of field guides are useful, particularly in the life sciences.

Nonprint Materials

Included in this category are any nonprint materials which have informational value, whether commercially prepared or not.

- *Graphic Forms*. The form includes pictures, photographs, motion pictures, video tapes, film strips, slides, drawings, video disks, and related types of materials. They appeal to many types of libraries, depending upon their content and purpose. They can pertain to any discipline.
- *Audio Forms*. These materials include audio cassettes, phonorecords, soundtracks of films, and other types. They have a wide appeal, depending upon their content and purpose. They can pertain to any discipline.

Archival Materials

While almost any of the above categories could be part of an archives, archival items are more apt to consist of business correspondence, business records, statistical data, personal correspondence, diaries, and similar items. They have legal, financial, and historical value. They can pertain to any discipline. See Chapter 22 for a discussion of archives and records.

Guides to the Literature

This section lists more than a dozen guides to the literature for major subject areas. The titles cited are only a fraction of those which deal with the topic of library materials; it is a *representative* selection. Some of the examples are more thorough and more carefully prepared than others, but each should be useful in its particular field.

Types of Library Materials

General Interest Guides

1. Sheehy, Eugene (and others). *Guide to reference books*. 10th ed. Chicago: American Library Association; 1986. 1,560 p.

    A comprehensive, well-edited, and well-selected annotated listing of thousands of reference books, covering all disciplines. A very useful tool. Updated by supplements; published irregularly.

2. Walford, Albert John. *Guide to reference materials*. 4th-5th ed. London: Library Association; 1980-1990.

    Covers all subject fields; all items are annotated. Volume 1 deals with science and technology, while volume 2 covers social sciences and history. Volume 3 deals with generalia, languages, literature, and the arts. A well-known source.

Arts and Humanities

General

3. Blazek, Ron; Aversa, Elizabeth. *The humanities: a selective guide to information sources*. 3d ed. Englewood, CO: Libraries Unlimited; 1988. 382 p.

    Presents sources of information pertaining to the humanities in general as well as to more specific disciplines, such as philosophy, religion, visual arts, performing arts, language, and literature. Devotes a chapter to each of these fields, listing major reference books as well as the role of computers and major organizations in each field. All items are annotated. Has a subject index and an author/title index.

Art

4. Arntzen, Etta Mae; Rainwater, Robert. *Guide to the literature of art history*. Chicago: American Library Association; 1980. 616 p.

    Indexes over 4,000 titles, arranged under headings such as general reference, particular fields of art, and art serials. All items are annotated. Has a subject index and an author-title index.

Music

5. Duckles, Vincent H.; Keller, Michael, A. *Music reference and research materials: an annotated bibliography.* 4th ed. New York: Schirmer Books; 1986. 714 p.

A selected list of published reference materials connected with musical topics. Arranged by format of materials, with other chapters dealing with specific fields, such as jazz, opera, or symphony orchestras. Has three indexes: names, subjects, and titles.

Science and Technology

General

6. Hurt, C. D. *Information sources in science and technology.* Englewood, CO: Libraries Unlimited; 1988. 362 p.

Cites and annotates more than 2,000 titles primarily of a reference nature, all English-language works. Following one chapter on multidisciplinary sources of information, the other chapters are each devoted to one format, such as dictionaries or encyclopedias. Has indexes for authors/titles and subjects.

7. *Science and Technology Annual Reference Review.* Edited by H. Robert Malinowsky. Phoenix, AZ: Oryx Press; 1989- . Annual.

A comprehensive listing of books in all areas of science and technology, each with an extensive annotation. Has indexes by author, title, subject, and type of library for which recommended. Arranged by type of publication, such as dictionaries or handbooks.

Earth Sciences

8. Hardy, Joan; Wood, D. N.; Harvey, A. P. *Information sources in the earth sciences.* 2d ed. New York: Saur; 1989. 520 p.

Besides books and journals the book covers reports, theses, maps, and conference proceedings. Disciplines included are paleontology, mineralogy, and crystallography.

Electrical Engineering

9. Ardis, Susan B.; edited by Jean M. Poland. *A guide to the literature of electrical and electronics engineering.* Englewood, CO: Libraries Unlimited; 1987. 190 p.

Covers standard English-language reference tools as well as more specialized sources, such as trade literature, patents, and standards. Has indexes for authors/titles and subjects.

Physics

10. Shaw, Dennis F., ed. *Information sources in physics.* London: Butterworths; 1985. 456 p.

Consists of 20 chapters which describe information sources dealing with various aspects of physics, including atomic physics, crystallography or electricity. Each chapter includes general reference materials on topics in each field at the level of superconductors or dynamics. The book is written in prose form, with informal citations of references rather than using formal entries. Appendixes include a list of key physics journals as well as a list of acronyms and initialisms. Has a subject index as well as an author/title index.

Social Sciences

General

11. Webb, William H., and Associates. *Sources of information in the social sciences.* 3rd ed. Chicago: American Library Association; 1986. 777 p.

A comprehensive review of the the the literature. Has articles which discuss and/or identify in informal fashion the important titles on the topic. Also often discusses the nature or meaning of the topics. Includes the general area of social sciences as well as sections devoted to history, geography, psychology, and education. Has a large index of titles, authors, and subjects.

Business

12. Lavin, Michael R. *Business information: how to find it, how to use it.* Phoenix, AZ: Oryx Press; 1987. 299 p.

Combines discussions about printed and computerized sources of information with a description of how and when to use such sources. A prose style is used, in which citations of the items being discussed are given in an informal format. The book consists of four parts which discuss basic sources, information about companies, statistical information sources, and special topics, such as marketing and tax law. Has a title index and a subject index. Provides a great deal of background information to aid one in using the best sources.

13. Strauss, Diane Wheeler. *Handbook of business information: a guide for librarians, students and researchers.* Englewood, CO: Libraries Unlimited; 1988. 537 p.

Part I is arranged by the format of information sources (such as directories, newsletters, dictionaries), while Part 2 is divided into types of business information (such as marketing, accounting, banking). In this section the author describes the nature of the subject field as well as the characteristics of the reference tools. Appendixes cover a variety of subjects, such as regional federal depository libraries or addresses of commodity exchanges. Has an author-title-subject index.

Political Science

14. Englefield, Dermot; Drewry, Gavin, eds. *Information sources in politics and political science: a survey worldwide.* Boston: Butterworths; 1984. 509 p.

Uses a prose style which describes and briefly cites important titles. Part 1 discusses major topics such as political parties or international politics, while Part 2 is arranged by countries or areas of the world, citing titles which pertain to those areas. Has a brief subject index.

Psychology

15. Borchardt, D. H. Francis, R. D. *How to find out in psychology: a guide to the literature and methods of research*. New York: Pergamon; 1984. 189 p.

Describes the nature of the various fields of psychology, then cites informally the major titles in each field. Chapters deal with historical works, reference sources, indexes and computer-based sources. Includes information on the use of the catalog and ways to present information. Has a brief subject index.

Sociology

16. Aby, Stephen H. *Sociology: a guide to reference and information sources*. Littleton, CO: Libraries Unlimited; 1987. 231 p.

Chapters in the first section list information sources on the general areas of sociology; the next section presents guides to the literature of various disciplines, such as education, psychology, and history. The largest section of the book describes the literature of various aspects of sociology, including gerontology, political sociology, sociology of religion, and similar topics. Has a subject index as well as an author/title index. All items are annotated.

Chapter 20

Collection Development

Building a well-balanced, useful collection of materials for a special library/information center is a responsibility of major importance. This chapter will discuss the main elements of collection development (sometimes called collection management)—selection principles, levels of collections, and collection development policies. The cost of developing a collection is also discussed. The book by Magrill and Corbon, while emphasizing public libraries, can serve as a good source for additional reading on basic aspects of this topic.[1]

Collection Development Policies

It is sometimes said that one cannot plan the building of a collection in special libraries because interests change too often and because urgent, last-minute demands for items cannot be fitted into a set policy. These conditions *do* exist in many special libraries, but that does not mean it is impossible to systematically build a collection. A collection development policy should be flexible enough to allow for incorporating new fields and dropping old ones, as well as for accommodating the inevitable need for acquiring miscellaneous items on a rush basis. Unless numerous items are being ordered daily on an emergency basis, such last-minute purchases should not be considered as important as building a collection following some guidelines. It is true that there are times in many sponsoring organizations when changes in goals result in days, even weeks, of crisis or upheaval, forcing the libraries to obtain materials on a rush basis. Fortunately, these crises do not occur so often that libraries should plan their collection policies around them.

Therefore, it is recommended that policies for building a collection be established (and recorded) and that accepted principles governing selection be followed. Occasional emergency purchases of odds and ends that may or may not fit the policies should not affect the building of a good collection.

Selection Principles

There are several basic principles that enter into decisions about what to add to a collection. Some of the major ones are:

- *Subject Matter.* This is probably the most important consideration for the average library. The contents must match the fields of interest of the library's sponsor.
- *Audience for Which Material is Written.* Books are written at various levels of difficulty. An excellent textbook for freshman chemistry would have no appeal for a library serving only experienced chemists.
- *Language in Which Material is Written.* Clients who are fluent in foreign languages can profit from foreign language materials. Journals published in foreign languages are often more useful than monographs because of translated contents pages and abstracts of articles.
- *Duplication of Other Works.* Some excellent books and journals might be passed by simply because they duplicate similar materials already in the collection. Libraries may have an intense need to purchase every work on a particular subject, but in most libraries, funds are not usually spent for more than occasional duplications of other works.
- *Status of the Author or Publisher.* There are famous authors whose works are so sought after that each of their books is worth acquiring; the same is true for certain publishers. Their record in producing high-quality works may be so good that libraries tend to add a new title if it is at least close to the interests of the library. Publications sponsored by important societies and institutions also fall into this class—their sponsorship may ensure that certain libraries automatically subscribe to or purchase a work.
- *Date of Publication.* The age of a monograph often has a great deal to do with its appeal. In an engineering library, for example, a book limited to the technology in use twenty years ago would normally be of no interest, unless it happened to be a classic work. However, in an art library a twenty-year-old book might still be the most useful work on the subject; if it were hundreds of years old, it might be even more important. Those special libraries/information centers which maintain collections of the history of a topic would find older works of interest, but most units cannot afford the cost, space, and staff time for such a collection.
- *Format.* Physical characteristics, such as the quality of photographs or maps, can influence a decision to buy. Likewise, whether an item is in traditional printed form or is in such formats as slides, audio or video cassettes, or motion pictures, would undoubtedly affect its reception in libraries. Some libraries have little interest in nonprint formats while others may be interested only in nonprint items. Most libraries lie somewhere between these two extremes.
- *Bibliographic Control.* In the case of serials, one important consideration is the print or online indexing services in which they are covered.

Levels of Collections

Another important aspect of collection development is the determination of the level required in a particular subject. Each special library/information center probably has several levels of interest, depending upon the topic. Some traditional levels of collections can be described as follows:

- *Exhaustive Level.* This pertains to a collection in which literally every item of a serious nature on a given topic is sought. It could, of course, be limited to certain languages or certain time periods.
- *Research Level.* This would be a collection with enough material to support independent research on the topic. Normally books, journals, special materials, and reference tools would be on hand in considerable depth.
- *Working Level.* This would consist of selected works on a subject, including books and a few key journals, that would cover current activities and major developments in a field.
- *Browsing Level.* This would apply to material in which only a few individuals had any interest and which would be used chiefly for refresher or updating purposes.

Collection Development Policy Statements

A neglected phase of collection development is the creation of written policy statements to serve as a guide to those making selections. Most libraries do not have written statements, which means that those engaged in selection must rely on their experience, their discussions with other selectors, and perhaps their intuition in making decisions. If an experienced selector were to leave such a library, much of the expertise and judgment used in the past would depart with that person.

As previously mentioned, one reason for the reluctance of those in special libraries/ information centers to write policy statements is the feeling that the subject interests of their clients change quickly, making written statements obsolete. If preparation of a policy statement were a long, tedious job, there might be some validity to the objection. But there are many ways to prepare written statements, the simplest of which need not take more than a few hours if the writer is acquainted with the collection and how it is being developed.

This section will describe some of the ways in which the policies governing the development of a collection can be recorded. The size of an organization, the number of professional librarians involved, and the complexity of the interests of the sponsor all affect what would be a desirable method of recording collection policies.

Prose Statements. This would typically consist of short paragraphs describing the collection goals, first from an overall viewpoint, then in terms of specific subject fields.

A sample of a prose statement for a library maintained by a company which manufactures jet engines might read as follows:

AJAX AIRCRAFT COMPANY LIBRARY

The collection will consist of monographs, journals, technical reports, and trade catalogs on the subjects of metallurgy, metal working, and welding, with particular emphasis on modern English language materials. Related subjects, such as plant layout and general business subjects, will also be represented. Printed and online indexing services will be provided plus other reference tools. More specific guidelines are as follows:

Metallurgy. A research-level collection will be maintained, stressing the properties and structure of ferrous and nonferrous alloys.

Metal working. A research-level collection will be maintained with emphasis on castings and sheet metal forming.

Welding. A research-level collection will be maintained on electric arc welding methods and theory.

General business subjects. A browsing-level collection will be maintained on topics of general interest, essentially confined to periodicals and loose-leaf services.

Plant layout. A browsing-level collection will be maintained on plant layout, primarily in the form of handbooks and texts plus a few key periodicals.

Such a brief statement could be prepared rather quickly, yet as conditions and needs change, it could be easily updated or amended.

Classified System. This system would be made up of classes selected from the classification scheme in which the book collection of the library is organized, such as the Dewey or Library of Congress systems. It would thus allow for as much or as little specificity of classes as desired. The designation for the class plus its English description would be used, such as *621.38 Electronics.*

As a refinement, the class coding shown above could be used in conjunction with codes indicating the level of the collection, such as 1 = Exhaustive Level, 2 = Research Level, etc. A further refinement might be desirable for any library which regularly purchased materials in foreign languages, using letter codes for languages, such as E = English language, F = Major European languages, O = Oriental languages. Special notes could be shown by a few words at the end. To designate the policy listing for a research-level collection of electronics, including English and Oriental languages but excluding television, the entry would appear as follows:

621.38 Electronics 2 E O Excludes Television.

This brief entry indicates the broad subject (electronics) excluding television, to be collected at the research level (level 2) in English and Oriental language materials.

A library using this system could precede it with a brief prose statement, if needed, particularly if there were special strengths that were difficult to show in terms of individual classes. For example, an engineering library with thousands of patents on chemistry and electronics would find it difficult to indicate that strength by the above method, so in a prose statement about the overall collection this feature could be mentioned. The printed listing of the data for each topic could be arranged by the class designation (621.38) or by the alphabetical description (electronics) or both.

A classified system can be produced either manually or by computer. The example provided shows a system arranged in two ways, one by the classification designations and the other by the alphabetical description. It is based on the Dewey Decimal System, but it could just as easily have been created using any other suitable system.

Classed Listing

623.6	Radio	3 EF
.61	Radio propagation phenomena	3 EF
.612	Tropospheric propagation	3 EF
.614	Scatter propagation	3 EFO
623.62	Radio apparatus	2 E
.622	Mobile radio	2 E
.624	Marine radio	2 E
.625	Aviation radio	1 E
.63	Radio transmitters	2 E
.64	Radio receivers	2 E

Alphabetical Listing

Aviation Radio	623.625	1 E
Marine radio	623.624	2 E
Mobile radio	623.622	2 E
Radio	623.6	3 EF
Radio apparatus	623.62	2 E
Radio propagation	623.61	3 EF
Radio receivers	623.64	2 E
Radio transmitters	623.63	2 E
Receivers, radio	623.64	2 E
Scatter propagation	623.614	3 EFO
Transmitters, radio	623.63	2 E
Tropospheric propagation	623.612	3 EF

Computerized Classified System. This method of policy statement is a variation of the classified system that involves the use of computers. The main advantage is the subsequent ease of updating the data as well as the ease of printing the list in more than one form. An example would be the preparation of one list by class designations (621.38) and one arranged by the alphabetical descriptors (electronic). Librarians sometimes find that an arrangement by class designations facilitates work with a small list, whereas the average client would usually prefer an alphabetical approach. An article by Yavarkovsky et al. describes such a computerized version.[2] Although this system was designed for a large university library, it would also be suitable for small collections. A computerized system devised for use at Bell Laboratories is explained in an article by Spaulding and Stanton.[3]

Cost of Collections

The manager of a special library/information center should be familiar with trends in current costs for different types of materials. This is a major aspect of preparing the annual budget for the unit. Continued increases in costs are also a major factor in the creation and growth of networks and other cooperative practices. Sharing costs with other libraries has become an attempt to aid tight budgets, but this is only a partial answer to rising costs.

Monographs. It is generally agreed that the best statistics on the number and cost of books published each year, covering general books as well as those devoted to specific disciplines, is found in *Publishers Weekly*, usually in the fall. The article by Grannis, published in 1989,[4] provides a wealth of information as to trends of costs and comparisons among the different subject categories. Costs have increased steadily over the years, as the following table shows.

Hardcover Average Per-Volume Prices

	1980	1989	% Increase
Overall Averages	$23.57	$39.00	65%
Art	26.64	39.96	50%
Business	22.54	37.51	66%
Law	31.63	50.85	61%
Science	35.13	66.91	90%
Technology	32.08	65.26	103%

It is clear that the prices charged for scientific and technical books are increasing more rapidly than costs of books in other disciplines; note that the percentage of increase in 10 years was 90 percent for science and over 100 percent for technology, considerably higher than was the case for non-technical books.

Journals. In a high percentage of special libraries, journals, or periodicals, are more important than books. Consequently the costs of such literature are of great concern to managers trying to keep close control of expenditures. In many cases managers with tight budgets have had to cut back on the purchase of books to be able to keep journal subscriptions intact. Often even this regrettable technique is not enough to avoid cancellations of certain subscriptions.

An excellent source of information on the costs of journal subscriptions is the annual article in *Library Journal* that normally appears in the spring or summer. An analysis of prices for 1990, written by Young and Carpenter, presents data on several aspects of journal subscriptions, such as a list of the average cost of subscriptions to journals arranged by disciplines as well as an analysis of the costs for the past several years.[5] The following list of a few subject categories shows the higher prices for sci-tech disciplines, just as was the case in the analysis of monographs.

Average Subscription Costs for Journals

	1980	1990	% of Increase
Overall average	$34.54	$93.45	171%
Business & Economics	25.42	63.25	149%
Chemistry & Physics	137.45	412.66	200%
Engineering	49.15	138.84	182%
Law	23.00	50.32	119%

A related article in the same issue with the Young-Carpenter paper shows costs for U.S. serial services (essentially abstracting/indexing services) for the past several years. This article, by Mary Elizabeth Clack, shows that the cost of a subscription to the average serial service increased 94 percent since 1980.[6] As might be expected, average costs for science and technology services were higher than those for some disciplines but were, surprisingly, somewhat less than business services.

Average Subscription Costs for Serial Services

	1980	1989	% of Increase
Overall average	$194.21	$377.24	94%
Business	294.00	523.79	78%
Law	184.38	390.98	12%
Science & technology	191.35	443.36	132%

The large increases in sci-tech costs in the past decade are very evident to librarians working in those disciplines.

It should be noted that averages such as are shown in the above tables can be misleading because the very high prices for certain important publications are far greater than the averages would lead one to think. For example, it is not unusual for some vital abstracting/indexing services to cost more than $8,000 per year, and many key journals charge over $2,000 per year for subscriptions. Similarly, monographs of major importance to special libraries can frequently cost more than $100 or $200 apiece, unlike the relatively low cost shown for averages.

Another complicating factor is the need to reconsider the value of retaining printed indexing services in disciplines where excellent online databases exist. The features of the latter sources need no explanation here, but many libraries have been more or less obliged to cancel subscriptions to printed indexes that are available online now. While there are instances where certain simple searches, such as for a particular author, can be done more quickly with a printed index than by getting online, in the long run the versatility and convenience of online databases outshine the printed indexes for most searches.

Government Publications.   For many years government reports and serials sold at relatively bargain rates. Then a new policy was instituted, requiring each publication to be self-supporting, including serials. After that, prices began to increase sharply, to the consternation of those librarians who depended heavily on documents. While no nationally known review of costs of government documents exists, the *Library Journal* article previously cited includes the average costs for indexing services covering federal documents.

References

1.   Magrill, Rose Mary; Corbin, John. *Acquisitions management and collection development in libraries.* 2d ed. Chicago: American Library Association; 1989. 285 p.

Covers a wide range of topics, including collection development policies and practices, acquisitions work, purchasing practices, and gifts and exchanges.

2.   Yavarkovsky, Jerome; Mount, Ellis; Kordish, Heika. Computer-based collection development statements for a university library. *ASIS Proceedings.* 10:240-241; 1973.

Describes a computer-based collection development system used at Columbia University Libraries for recording collection strengths and foreign language interests. Sample printouts are illustrated.

3.   Spaulding, F. H.; Stanton, R. O. Computer-aided selection in a library network. *Journal of the American Society for Information Science.* 27(5): 269-280; 1976 Sept.

A computerized system provides a record of those Dewey Decimal System classes of interest to any of the libraries at Bell Laboratories. Printouts are arranged by class numbers and by class descriptors; sample copies of printouts are shown.

4.   Grannis, Chandler B. Titles and prices, 1988; final figures. *Publishers Weekly.* 236(13): 24-27; 1989 Sept. 29.

Provides data on the costs of hardcover and paperback books published in the United States in 1988, showing also the number of books in various subject categories. Provides data for more than 20 subjects, such as art, history, and science.

5.   Young, Peter R.; Carpenter, Kathryn Hammell. Price index for 1990: U.S. periodicals. *Library Journal.* 115(7): 50-56; 1990 April 15.

Presents data on subscriptions costs for nearly 4,000 journals in several different ways, such as a list of the most expensive titles, arranged by subject category. Considered to be a reliable source of data for trends in journal costs.

6. Clack, Mary Elizabeth. U.S. periodicals; U.S. serial services. *Library Journal*. 115(7): 57; 1990 April 15.

Lists the average costs during the past ten or so years for U.S. serial services (generally meaning abstracting/indexing services) for eight categories (business, law, science/technology, etc.) Shows dollar costs as well as percentages of increases.

Chapter 21

Weeding of Materials

In most special libraries/information centers there are several reasons why weeding the collection is necessary. This chapter will discuss the reasons for weeding, the types of materials normally weeded, and some of the techniques by which weeding can be accomplished.

Weeding requires experience and good judgment. It can be fraught with pitfalls; library clients can be terribly upset if the wrong items, as they view it, are weeded. Once materials are disposed of, there is little chance of retrieving them. Replacing items previously weeded can be both embarrassing and expensive.

Reasons for Weeding

There are several factors which make weeding a collection necessary.

- *Space Requirements.* Most special libraries/information centers are quite restricted in their allotments of space, particularly in units sponsored by private companies. The demand for space is so great in such cases that there is keen competition within organizations for more room. Consequently, most libraries in these organizations must make do for many years with the same amount of space. The only solution is to keep the collection weeded regularly so that it continues to fit the space allotted. Public and academic libraries also have problems along this line, but it is not nearly as troublesome a situation as that facing units in private organizations.
- *Changing Fields of Interest.* In some libraries, fields of interest can change very quickly. Topics that were once important can lose all significance and are consequently not worth the space devoted to them.
- *Outdated Materials.* In many special libraries, the greatest need is for current information; older material is rarely used. In such units, older materials can be weeded with little fear that there will be many requests for them.
- *Physical Condition.* When materials deteriorate through age or use, the choice is to weed them or to replace them with usable copies.

There are some general principles that govern the process of weeding. Some materials may have no interest to a given special library/information center, yet may have a relatively high intrinsic value. Where regulations permit, this sort of material should be disposed of through reliable dealers or at least placed in libraries collecting such items. Simply to discard valuable items would be negligent.

If there is any possibility that materials can be of value to the organization, it is advisable to seek the opinion of one or more knowledgeable persons before removing them. Weeding requires a good understanding of the needs and interests of the sponsor and of the subject matter involved, a proficiency that may require several years of experience to acquire.

When locally prepared materials are considered for weeding, such as reports, drawings, and plans, extra care should be taken for the items may be unique. Many organizations are notoriously careless about preserving vital records of their own creation.

A general rule in regard to weeding is to retain material when there is a doubt of its value or usefulness. It is far better to delay weeding while seeking a second or third opinion than to discard material which should have been kept.

Weeding of Monographic Works.   Major factors that should be considered in weeding monographs are:

- *Subject Matter.* As previously mentioned, changes in the interests of the sponsor affect the need for given subjects. The best book in the world on a subject no longer of interest should be considered for weeding.
- *Age.* In some fields, age has little or no effect on the value of an item. However, more likely than not, older materials tend to be superseded by more up-to-date publications. Thus they should be considered in weeding.
- *Duplicate Coverage.* It is common to weed some of the less valuable titles on a given topic and keep only the best works. The number of duplicates can also be reduced. Newer works sometimes include older data, such as a cumulative set of statistics, covered previously in separate volumes. Only the new cumulation would then be needed; the other material can be discarded.
- *Alternative Sources.* When interest is waning in a particular subject, a special library/ information center might be able to rely on public or other special libraries which collect in that field to provide material when it is requested. The rising importance of networks, in which shared responsibilities for collections are stressed, makes it much more likely that alternative sources for topics outside a library's main field of interest can be found.
- *Physical Condition.* A book that is badly torn, has crumbling paper, or is otherwise in poor physical condition may have to be weeded because it is no longer usable. The question then is whether or not it should be replaced by a newer copy or by another format, such as microfilm. There are dealers which specialize in selling either microfilm copies of worthwhile books or inexpensive enlargements made from the microfilm version.
- *Level of Treatment.* Some books are more suitable for weeding than others because of the type of treatment they present. In general, a work that discusses a topic from a

broad, long-range standpoint has more lasting value than one written in the "how-to-do-it" format. The latter can become outdated more quickly due to changing equipment and procedures in a given field, whereas treatises on basic principles are of more lasting value.

- *Importance of the Author.* The more prominent the author of a specific book, the more likely it is that it should be kept. However, if its subject dictates it should be removed, extra care should be taken in finding a useful place for disposing of it.
- *Language in Which Published.* Monographs published in a foreign language receive less use than their English language counterparts and are consequently more likely candidates for weeding.

Weeding of Serials. Serials are affected by most of the factors listed for monographs, such as subjects, duplicate coverage, and alternative sources. Other factors to be considered are:

- *Publisher.* Some serials have a higher value to users simply because they may be published by major societies having great influence and importance in a given field. Such serials usually should be kept on file in the library instead of those serials issued by a less prestigious publisher if space is short.
- *Indexing Coverage.* A serial which is regularly covered by an indexing and/or abstracting service (printed or online) would normally have more value than one not so covered; its contents would be more accessible. The smaller the collection, the more important it is to get the most from every title retained.
- *Alternate Versions.* More and more serials are also available in a microform version, such as microfilm (reels or cartridges) or microfiche. The great space savings possible with microforms is important to many libraries. The poor quality of paper used in newspapers makes them almost worthless for long-term retention and consequently makes a microform version essential.
- *Age.* While serials are often disposed of because of their age, they are not usually weeded as individual items, as are monographs. No one would be apt to weed, say, only volumes 5, 10, 37, and 39 of a given series. The normal procedure is to retain complete runs of a serial for a given time period, such as the complete set of an annual serial, or all the volumes of a quarterly serial issued during the past decade. This sort of formula process requires giving individual attention to each title to determine what issues would be suitable for retention.
- *Language in Which Published.* Serials published in a foreign language frequently have more value than foreign language monographs because it is common now to find English language used for contents pages, abstracts, or even articles, whereas monographs usually do not contain any information in English. However, even such use of English may not be of enough value to warrant keeping such serials as long as those entirely in English.

In recent years there has been a great increase in the number of publicly available databases which contain the full text of materials indexed, not just bibliographic citations and abstracts of the materials. While it is more expensive to print out copies for clients from the databases than to make photocopies of the original versions, many libraries find the space savings offered by full-text databases more important than reproduction costs.

Weeding is not an easy task, and a new librarian or information center employee should not start weeding without due consideration of the problems involved. Certainly one or more people outside the library should be asked for comments once the weeding process begins. It should be done at a reasonable pace; mistakes in judgment seem to multiply if there is a rush to finish a task.

An account of the steps taken to keep a technical report collection weeded to achieve zero growth may be found in an article by Newman.[1]

Disposing of Weeded Items

Some of the options for disposing of weeded items may be unavailable to those employed in certain types of organizations, such as government sponsored libraries/information centers, where regulations may prohibit the sale and/or gift of materials. In such cases, alternative solutions may be necessary.

- *Discards.* This is the most practical means of disposing of ephemeral or defective materials, such as worn-out copies of books, trade literature, pamphlets, reports, or anything having no monetary or educational value.
- *Sale.* In some instances, the material may be worth selling. In the case of individual valuable monographs, it may be worthwhile to get bids from dealers, but this applies in a very small number of cases. Most monographs have no resale value. Periodicals, on the other hand, often can be sold to dealers who specialize in used periodicals. Certain titles are so common they have no value, but serious, high-grade journals can almost always be sold. Librarians should obtain catalogs from the leading used periodical dealers in order to become acquainted with the type of items they sell. Even if there is not a great profit made, the periodicals will be kept available for other libraries when sold to dealers. Certain items, like old reports or government publications, have little or no resale value.
- *Exchange.* A few special libraries, such as those in scholarly or academic institutions, may be able to exchange duplicates with other institutions, particularly in cases where the sponsoring organization has publications it created available for exchanges. This is rare in other types of libraries.
- *Gifts.* Any library not prohibited by its regulations may wish to make gifts of unwanted materials to nearby public or academic libraries, or perhaps to libraries in underdeveloped countries. In the past there have been organizations that collected materials to send to needy libraries, particularly in Third World countries. Locally, materials often can be offered at no cost to employees but not to individuals or libraries outside the organization. Employees sometimes appreciate having an opportunity to browse through materials before they are discarded.

- *Classified Documents.* It is almost always necessary to follow military or company regulations when disposing of materials marked as military classified or company classified. In many cases burning or shredding is required. Great care must be taken in dealing with such materials to avoid serious consequences for improper disposal.

A thorough review of the literature and principles of the process of weeding, including both traditional and newer concepts, may be found in the book by Slote.[2] He includes an analysis of the various methods along with examples from several libraries. A collection of papers edited by Mount includes discussions of the weeding in corporate versus academic libraries as well as the problems of weeding periodicals.[3]

References

1. Newman, Wilda. Managing a report collection for zero growth. *Special Libraries.* 71(5/6): 276-282; 1980 May/June.

Describes the policies governing the technical report collection of the Johns Hopkins University, Applied Physics Laboratory Library. Includes a review of the steps that led to the zero-growth plan for the collection and resulting benefits. Weeding techniques are also discussed.

2. Slote, Stanley J. *Weeding library collections: library weeding methods.* 3d ed. Englewood, CO: Libraries Unlimited; 1989. 284 p.

Reviews the literature on the subject, then discusses various methods of weeding. Provides examples from over 40 libraries.

3. Mount, Ellis, ed. *Weeding of collections in sci-tech libraries.* New York: Haworth Press; 1986. 164 p. (Also published as v.6 no.3 of *Science & Technology Libraries,* 1986 Spring.)

Contains 5 papers devoted to weeding of monographs and serials. Although sci-tech materials are stressed, has application to other disciplines as well.

Chapter 22

Archives and Records

Managers of special libraries/information centers are often given responsibility for the archives and/or the records of sponsoring organizations. Because these materials are so unlike traditional library materials, this chapter will provide a brief description of the characteristics and handling of archival items and organizational records.

Nature of Records and Archives

There is no simple definition of records, but an article by Russell included the following types of materials in its description of records: correspondence, forms, reports, drawings, specifications, maps, and photographs; they may appear in such formats as paper, microfilm, and magnetic tape.[1] They include all types of materials normally associated with the operation of a business or running an organization, and they are not confined to traditional paper formats.

Archival materials can include all the items listed above as records, and they also can include items not normally associated with operating a business, such as personal diaries, artifacts, etc. They may be considered as materials having historical significance—a feature which distinguishes them from records.

Records need to be retained for legal or financial reasons. Many items must be retained for a specific period of time established by law to substantiate the position of an organization with regard to its taxes, payroll procedures, or other such matters. Other important papers must be kept indefinitely, such as records of bank loans, mortgages, and deeds to property.

There are many items in the average organization for which there is no legal requirement for retention, yet they are of such great value to the sponsor that they must be kept for carefully determined time periods. For example, a company's sales records, production schedules, or correspondence may not be required by law to be retained, yet they are quite important to the operation of the company.

Another reason for retaining items is their historical value. Photography from the early years of an organization, the diary of an organization's founder, copies of the internal house organ or newsletter, even the first model of a product made by a company would often find a place in the archives. Such items are rich sources for future historians as well as of considerable interest to many employees. While there are no legal or financial pressures to maintain archives, many organizations have enough foresight to establish them and keep them up to date. A description of archival materials is given in the article by Kadooka-Mardfin.[2]

Those interested in the management of both archives and records should examine the book by Cook.[3] He explains their similarities and their differences, then discusses management, retrieval, and computerization of records.

Records Management

The management of the records of an organization is a separate profession, with collegiate training available for those aspiring to this sort of work. Some of the highlights of this profession are given in the article by Russell previously cited in note 1. She mentions some of the different problems that arise in controlling forms, reports, or correspondence. She also points out the advisability of using microfilm for certain types of records, the need for setting up retention schedules for different kinds of materials, and the protection that must be given to vital records needed to continue operations after a natural disaster.

Russell also describes a way to establish a records management program, including conducting a preliminary inventory to determine what records exist, establishing decisions about what to retain and for how long, locating storage areas, and selecting suitable storage materials or devices. Her article points out that good records managers can save on storage space, the number of containers required, and employee time in retrieving needed materials.

Principles of records management are stressed in the book edited by Peace, who also discusses techniques.[4]

Choosing the types of indexes and finding tools for records is a specialty in itself, since suitable means of retrieval must be selected or created according to the nature of each kind of record being considered. Rarely will a blanket solution be appropriate for all kinds of materials.

Archives Management

A description of the basic aspects of managing archives is given in the article by Kadooka-Mardfin, previously cited in note 2. The overlapping of the nature and purposes of archives and records is seen in her definitions and descriptions, yet she seems to favor the position that archives have more historical than legal and commercial importance. She points out many of the special problems of the archivist, such as the delicate condition of many types of materials. For example, the need for temperature and humidity controls is described in terms of archival management. She also discusses the establishment of an archival program at the Honolulu Municipal Reference & Records Center, covering its purpose, staffing, rate of growth, and materials collected.

As in the case of records management, the archivist must decide which types of finding tools to use. Those desiring acquaintance with the techniques traditionally used by archivists should find the book by Schellenberg helpful.[5] He also discusses various plans for arranging materials, such as chronological, geographical, or classified methods, as well as a system based on provenance (place or organization of origin). Another book to be considered is the collection of papers edited by Clark, the theme of which is the relationship of libraries and archives.

Those desiring a collection of basic readings on archival theory and practices should examine the book edited by Daniels and Walch.[6]

References

1.   Russell, Dolores E. Records management: an introduction. *Special Libraries.* 65(1): 17-21; 1974 Jan.

      Describes the nature of records management, including techniques of establishing a program, ways of handling different materials, and benefits from active programs.

2.   Kadooka-Mardfin, Jean T. Archival responsibilities of the special librarian. *Special Libraries.* 67(12): 553-558; 1976 Dec.

      Stresses the ways to create an archival program in an organization. Also describes the nature of archival materials and an actual program for a municipal reference service.

3.   Cook, Michael. *The management of information from archives.* Hants, England: Gower; 1986. 234 p.

      Although written from the British viewpoint, this is a very readable, clear account of the handling of both archives and records. Besides chapters on both of these types of records the author covers acquisition and appraisal of materials, the use of data processing techniques, and information retrieval from archives.

4.   Peace, Nancy E., ed. *Archival choices: managing the historical record in an age of abundance.* Lexington, MA: Lexington Books, D.C. Heath; 1984. 164 p.

      Stresses principles rather than techniques, although the latter are included. Chapters deal with deciding what to save, appraisal of business records, appraisal of manuscripts, and deaccessioning collections.

5.   Schellenberg, T. R. *The management of archives.* New York: Columbia University Press; 1965. 383 p.

      A classic book on the subject, discussing traditional methods for arranging and retrieving archival materials.

6.   Clark, Robert L., Jr., ed. *Archival-library relations.* New York: Bowker; 1976. 218 p.

      Consists of five papers and an annotated bibliography on the relationship between librarians and archivists. Similarities and differences are fully discussed.

7.   Daniels, Maygene F.; Walch, Timothy, eds. *A modern archives reader; basic readings in archival theory and practice.* Washington: National Archives and Records Service; 1984. 357 p.

      Consists of nine themes, such as pre-archival functions, records appraisal, arrangement of archives, and reference use of archives.

Part 6

Library Facilities and Equipment

Planning library facilities is not an uncommon experience for those employed in special libraries, whether it involves creating a completely new facility or remodeling an older one. In either case, the special librarian should be familiar with the basic aspects of facility planning; such topics are covered in Chapter 23. The role of the librarian is fully discussed, along with the part played by other people taking part in facility planning. Other topics include space utilization and moving libraries.

Chapter 24 is concerned with the nature of library furnishings and special equipment, along with some guidelines for their selection and maintenance.

Chapter 23

Planning Library Facilities

For many librarians the planning of library facilities has been a rewarding, exhilarating experience, one that generates fond memories of the entire process. Unfortunately, for other librarians the planning of a library facility has been a rather frustrating chore, bringing disappointment and regrets. In order to increase the likelihood that the readers of this book who find themselves engaged in planning a facility will have a pleasant, satisfying experience, this chapter points out some of the pitfalls, as well as the rewards, of becoming involved in facility planning. There is no way to guarantee that the experience will be rewarding, but the better the reader is prepared the more certain the rewards will be. Readers are urged to read widely on the subject and to get familiar with the planning process now, before getting involved in an actual project.

There are many steps involved in planning a facility, ranging from preparing a program (indicating what the goal of the library is) to selecting a mover to transport books to the new facility. A book edited by Mount that is devoted to the planning of special library facilities discusses all the major aspects of the process.[1] He devotes several chapters to basic topics, such as preparing the library program, using space, selecting equipment/furnishings, and moving the library. The other part of the book contains chapters written by individual authors on such subjects as pre-planning activities (before the architect arrives), the role of architects and interior designers, estimating shelving needs, and incorporation of electronic devices into the plans. Examples of floor plans and descriptions of planning experiences are given for four special libraries; there is also an annotated bibliography. This is one of the few books written about facility planning that is aimed chiefly at the special librarian.

A classic book on planning libraries, written by Leighton and Weber, deserves being consulted, although it is aimed primarily at those involved with larger libraries than the special librarian is apt to encounter.[2]

Library Programs

One of the duties of a librarian participating in the creation of a new library or the remodeling of an older one is to prepare what is called the library program. It is a document that defines the type of library wanted, its goals, its expected collection size, the size of the staff, the number of reading stations required, and similar broad topics. It enables the architect to make plans that would be more likely to be satisfactory to all concerned than if he or she just began planning with no clear ideas of what sort of facility was wanted and needed.

To write the program the librarian will need several types of statistics, such as collection growth figures, outlook for growth of space for staff members, and estimates of the space needed for library users. Other information needed includes types and numbers of special devices, such as computers, fax machines, and microfiche readers.

In regard to how the space should be utilized, it is incumbent on the librarian to advise the architect of certain requirements before the planning gets under way. The architect needs to know what sort of services are rendered to users and the environment in which they should take place. For example, placing a computer terminal in the midst of a busy traffic flow would not be as suitable as using a more quiet location.

This is the sort of information that an architect is not apt to know, and it is up to the librarian to help indicate the type of environment each segment of the library requires for best results. Pointing out the need for extra space around a reference desk is another requirement to ensure that a workable floor plan is created.

Other information to bring to the attention of the architect is the weight of library equipment, such as the stack areas or unusually heavy files. This figure, called the floor loading, must be known before construction plans are made.

The librarian must be adept in dealing with the others involved in the planning and construction processes; he or she needs to know when to press hard for certain specifications or positions and when to compromise with the viewpoints of others on the team, such as the architect, interior designers, and construction engineers. It is better to win major points even if compromises have to be made on lesser matters.

Interactions with Others

There are several others with whom the manager of the special library/information center would normally be involved in the process of creating a new or remodeled library.

Almost every sponsoring organization will have a knowledgeable employee working with the librarian. This might be the plant engineer, someone with a technical background, or the chairman of the building committee, responsible for the overall planning of a new building or a remodeling project. This person would be aware of such topics as the floor loading planned for new areas and the type of heating/ventilating system being chosen. Only the technical, not professional, aspects of a proposed plan would be apt to concern such a person.

A space planner also might be involved in the project. This is often an outside consultant, whose job it is to allocate space on an overall basis, such as deciding the footage of the library and the footage for the cafeteria. Such decisions have to be made before an architect can make even rough sketches of a new building or area. The architect is a key figure in all but small remodeling jobs. The architect is responsible for the ultimate design and construction features of the new building or area. If this is the first library project for the architect, he or she should be shown two or three good texts on library planning. Librarians should speak out about good library planning practices if their ideas differ from what the architect proposes.

Still another person involved in library planning is an interior designer, who would be concerned with the esthetic aspects of the project. Color, style, and quality of furnishings are areas of responsibility for a decorator. He or she may also be new at the business of planning a library and may profit from being exposed to key publications on the subject.

Space Utilization

How space is allotted is just as important as how much space is available. Here the librarian may be the only one on the planning team who knows from experience what the best environment is for each part of the library. Keeping noisy photocopiers or computer printers away from study areas is a typical objective. Making it easy for library users to get around the bookstacks is another. Visually imagining oneself walking around a library while looking at a proposed floor plan helps the librarian to spot potential problems.

The total space to be planned consists of space for the collection, for the staff, and for clients. Guidance for estimating such areas can be found in the book edited by Mount, which cites such figures as the normal distance between stack ranges, the capacity of stacks, or the amount of space needed for people and equipment.[3] Using these guidelines in conjunction with the facts contained in the library program, it should be possible to determine the overall space requirement.

One way to broaden an outlook on library floor plans is to visit several libraries of a similar size and type; quite often one learns a lot from other librarians' successes (and their failures). Too close a concentration on the plans at hand tend to blind one to alternative solutions. It is too late after the plans are finalized to realize that mistakes were made in allocating the space.

Two books which contain numerous descriptions and floor plans of special libraries are recommended as ways to enlarge one's concepts of what to aim for in space planning.[4,5] The first of the two texts just cited includes a useful paper that gives guidelines for planning facilities, written by Howard Rovelstad, a consultant with many years of experience. One point that he makes that is often overlooked is the need to design facilities that would be available to physically handicapped people. Another bit of his advice is to pay close attention to the acoustical treatment of the library. For example, book stacks can absorb sound if they are placed strategically; it is also true that the use of carpeting can help to deaden movement noises.

Drawing Floor Plans

Although architects are responsible for preparing detailed floor plans, it is desirable for the librarian to prepare his or her own simple floor plans, showing locations of items and their relationship to each other. Using grid paper (a good size has squares that are 1/4 inch on a side, with one inch equalling one foot), a librarian can block out where bookstacks, tables, offices, and the like could be located. Using paper templates representing furniture and stack units allows one to move things around the plan until the best arrangement is found.

Moving the Library

A real test of the librarian's skill in planning is moving the library to a new site, or moving a collection within a given library. The key to success is careful calculations and attention to details. It is a mistake to assume that the crew doing the moving knows a great deal about such a move, so it is important to have the plan so well arranged that even an inexperienced crew could carry it out successfully.

One library staff member should be appointed to be in charge of the move. He or she should take the steps necessary to decide on the best date for the move, the timing of the move (over the weekend?), and the moving firm chosen (these decisions are often made at the executive level).

The librarian and the move supervisor should determine well in advance of the move whether or not extensive weeding should take place. If material is to be weeded, it should be done before the move. Knowing the amount of material to be kept facilitates planning the move.

If the move is to a new site, the supervisor must know several facts: the location and number of stack units in the new site, the number of volumes to be moved, and the proper way to allocate them in the new shelving. If there is extra room in the stacks, one plan is to leave one or more shelves empty in each stack unit in the new site (preferably the top and the bottom shelves) so that the extra space would not be as noticeable as if a large number of sections were completely empty. The latter case might make management executives feel that too much space was allotted to the library if many sections were unused.

It is imperative that careful calculations be made so that the movers know exactly where each shelf is to go. Some librarians have used carts with shelves that are long enough to hold a typical shelf of books. The shelves, fastened to the base of the cart, might be visualized as two book cases stacked back-to-back. If the cart has large enough wheels, there would be no problem moving it across a carpeted floor. One plan consists of marking each shelf with a clear label showing the shelf to which its contents must be moved in the new site. The label would go with the books.

More than one librarian has found out after the fact that movers must be carefully instructed as to how to load shelves so that the correct order is retained. Numbers that run backward are not apt to be acceptable in most libraries! Seriously, such mistakes can turn a move into a nightmare. To help avoid such problems it is wise to have one library staff member on hand every minute while books are being reshelved. An article by Roth emphasizes this point, asserting that a library staff member is needed at both the loading and unloading points.[6]

The move should be timed so as to inconvenience library users as little as possible. Some libraries have rented a spare computer to keep in use while the other terminals are being moved. This involves advance orders for telephone lines, which usually cannot be made without careful planning. A move over a weekend, if it can be arranged, has traditionally been more desirable than one made on a weekday, even if it may involve overtime pay for the movers.

To prepare for the move a number of steps should be taken to ensure a smooth transition, especially with organizations with which the library deals. Examples include ordering new rubber stamps, notifying vendors of the new address, tagging shelves and furniture for new locations, and coordinating telephone/computer moves. A list of such steps, along with the amount of time ahead of the move that is required, is found in a book edited by Mount.[7]

A different sort of move involves rearranging books within a given library. The larger the collection, the more involved such a move could be. In recent years a number of articles have appeared which describe the use of spreadsheets for making the many calculations essential to the success of such a move. A paper by Judith Ellis explains the use of a spreadsheet in determining where to place books in the re-shelving of a large library.[8] Although her move is much larger than most special librarians would ever encounter, the principle of her methods would be worth considering.

A similar article involves the use of formulas for relocating volumes of abstracting and indexing services. The paper, written by Seiler and Robar, shows how the calculations enabled some 7,000 volumes to be rearranged in less than four days.[9] An unusual device that enables a library staff to raise and move a range of loaded bookshelves is described in a paper written by Meinke.[10]

The choice of equipment and furnishings for the library is covered in Chapter 24; this includes furniture as well as special equipment. Appendix 2 contains a description and floor plan for a modern library located at the Merrill Lynch Company in New York City. The account includes a description of the highlights of the planning process.

References

1.   Mount, Ellis, ed. *Creative planning of special library facilities*. New York: Haworth Press; 1988. 197 p.

      Has five chapters dealing with basic topics, such as the early planning stages and moving the library; then follow chapters written by an architect, a space planner, and special librarians who describe the design features of their libraries. Includes a 25-page, annotated bibliography

2.   Metcalf, Keyes D. Leighton, Philip D.; Weber, David C., eds. *Planning academic and research library buildings*. 2d ed. Chicago: American Library Association; 1986. 630 p.

      An updated version of a classic book, emphasizing the planning of academic and research libraries, including the buildings to house them. Covers a wide range of topics, going from the construction process to lighting, housing of collections, and interior design.

3.   Mount, Ellis. *op. cit*. Chap. 3, 9.

4. Mount, Ellis, ed. *Planning facilities for sci-tech libraries*. New York: Haworth Press; 1983. 183 p. (Also published as *Science & Technology Libraries*, v. 3 no. 4, 1983 Summer.)

    Provides floor plans and descriptions of nine special libraries located in industry, government, and academic settings. Also includes a paper on guidelines for planning facilities.

5. Mount, Ellis. *Innovations in planning facilities for sci-tech libraries*. New York: Haworth Press; 1986. 158 p. (Also appeared as vol. 7, no. 1 of *Science & Technology Libraries*, 1986 Fall.)

    Contains floor plans and descriptions of planning five special libraries at academic, government, and industrial installations.

6. Roth, Britain G. Moving a medical center library. *Special Libraries*. 76(1): 31-34; 1985 Winter.

    Covers all aspects of moving a 30,000 volume medical library with a minimum of disruption of service. Four 14-hour days were required for the move.

7. Mount. *Creative planning*, p. 40.

8. Ellis, Judith Compton. Planning and executing a major book shift/move using an electronic spreadsheet. *C&RL News*. 49(5): 282-287; 1988 May.

    Describes the use of a spreadsheet in planning the move of a large collection. Illustrations show the spreadsheet data and plans for the order in which the shelves would be filled. The necessary formulas for making the calculations are included.

9. Seiler, Susan L.; Robar, Terri J. Reference service vs. work crews: meeting the needs of both during a collection shift. *Reference Librarian*. No. 19: 327-339; 1987.

    Explains how to create a set of cards which indicate the location of bound volumes in a rearrangement of a collection of abstracts by call number. By virtue of the precise moves identified in advance, the whole process took a total of only about 40 man-hours.

10. Meinke, Darrel M. Pulling the rug out from under the stacks (revisited). *C&RL News*. 49(5): 288-289; 1988 May.

    Explains the construction and use of a device that makes it possible to raise and move loaded bookstacks. Soon to be marketed, the device easily raised a 30-foot range of double-faced shelving so it could be moved to a different location.

Chapter 24

Furnishings and Special Equipment for Libraries

For a library facility to be both functional and attractive its furnishings and special equipment need to be carefully selected and then located in a suitable environment. Placing an expensive computer in the wrong part of the library can diminish the value of that equipment, whereas a more logical location for it would undoubtedly improve the quality of its operation. This chapter is concerned with both traditional furniture as well as with what might be called high-tech equipment. The difficulties of making selections, a common problem for those charged with this responsibility, will be addressed as well as some considerations about the location of equipment.

Furniture

Attractive, well-made furniture adds a great deal of beauty and effectiveness to a special library. The average library user reacts very positively to a well-designed library which is furnished with carefully chosen items. Comfortable chairs, well-built tables, and thoughtfully designed work stations are important to library users. However it is not easy to find furniture that meets all the standards an organization might establish. Besides being comfortable, furniture needs to be durable so as to avoid expensive replacements too soon after it is purchased.

Many times librarians are aware of pitfalls in selecting furniture that may not be apparent to non-librarians. For example, a librarian who has seen readers tilting a chair back on its hind legs, leading perhaps to damaged chairs, would undoubtedly select new chairs whose design makes it impossible to tilt them backward. Similarly, avoiding the selection of chairs whose arms are too high to allow them to slide under a reading table would certainly be one of the responsibilities of a librarian matching selections of new chairs and new tables. Still another example is that of being aware that library users generally prefer using individual study carrels rather than large tables which seat several readers. Aside from the need to provide seating for occasional group study sessions, or the need for a large table on which to study maps or oversize books, most librarians would make sure a new library had enough small, individual carrels to suit the preferences of the majority of readers.

There is no substitute for seeing samples of furniture before it is selected, not always a simple thing to arrange.

This is one service a good interior designer could provide to save the librarian's time. Before decisions are made, librarians should study appropriate literature on the subject. One of the few books devoted entirely to furnishing libraries was written by Pierce.[1] He deals with all aspects of selecting furniture and equipment, how it is manufactured, and features to look for in making selections. There is an appendix that shows sample specifications for use in getting bids on shelving and seating. His book offers a very thorough treatment of the subject. Another book on this topic appeared recently, written by Brown.[2] She covers the characteristics of all types of furniture, the evaluation and bidding processes, and commercial sources. It includes an abundance of illustrations. The book by Mount includes a bibliography on library furniture and equipment, both selection and sources.[3] Other chapters deal with shelving and with the special problems involved in creating work stations for electronic equipment, the latter chapter written by Lorraine Schulte.

Most librarians expect to use carpeting in libraries because of its ability to reduce noise, its relative ease of maintenance, and its attractiveness. Sometimes the wrong kind of carpet is selected, however, and replacement becomes necessary. For example, a carpet which has no pattern and is a light color would be a poor choice. It would show every bit of soil and bits of paper, and would soon look shabby. A darker color, particularly one having a pattern, would be far easier to keep looking attractive. Consideration should also be given to selecting carpeting that is constructed so as to reduce static electricity, which can be troublesome around computers.

One of the most expensive items in a library is its shelving. Choices have to be made between metal or wood shelving as well as between fixed and movable shelving. A detailed analysis of the relative merits of various kinds of materials and designs of shelving is given in a chapter on the subject, written by Stankus and Rosseel in the book edited by Mount.[4] They cover both fixed and movable types, as well as alternative ways to allow for aisles in laying out stack areas.

Equipment

Libraries, especially special libraries, have come a long way in the past twenty years in their adaptation and use of what could be simply called special equipment. Many librarians can remember when a photocopier and a microform reader-printer were the only special equipment needed for what were then considered modern libraries. Now we need computers, computer printers, facsimile machines, scanners, optical disks, and electronic mail memberships to keep up with the times.

It is not possible in a short treatment to do justice to any one of these devices with regard to their features and their selection, but general guidelines follow on the subject of selecting equipment.

Selection of Special Equipment

Managers of special libraries and information centers are often faced with a multitude of advertisements for new equipment, as well as for newer models of older equipment. In each case, there are probably bewildering numbers of trade catalogs from manufacturers, jobbers, and multipurpose equipment sales firms. It is not easy to keep a broad perspective about the new devices, some of which appear to perform better than earlier models, or to offer some feature never before available in a commercial firm's product. A few general guidelines for making selections may be helpful to those investigating new equipment.

- *Operation*
  1. What features does the product offer compared to other makes and models?
  2. Is its design such that it would be simple both to operate and teach others to operate?
  3. Would there be difficulties in getting spare parts and finding suitable maintenance service?
  4. Is there a warranty available? For how long? What is covered?
  5. When was the model first put on sale? Is a new model imminent?
- *Finances*
  1. Is the price reasonable?
  2. Is a lease available as well as outright purchase? Can rental or leasing fees be applied to subsequent purchase?
  3. How much does the service contract for maintenance cost? What is covered and what would cost extra?
  4. Are there special discounts if the library is operated by a not-for-profit organization?
- *General*
  1. What has been the record of the firm in making reputable products?
  2. Is the salesperson helpful in arranging for current models of the equipment to be examined?
  3. What delivery date can be guaranteed?
  4. Does the salesperson use high-pressure or scare tactics?

While awareness of these guidelines is no guarantee of a satisfactory purchase, some obvious pitfalls can be avoided by following them. In general, it is counterproductive to let price be the deciding factor; one could easily end up with an inferior product. However, price must be a consideration, because some equipment is often overpriced. While brochures and specification sheets often provide a certain amount of factual data about a product, there is no substitute for making an investigation of the company and of the product.

As for selecting computers, the following questions might well lead a librarian to the selection of a more suitable model than if no consideration was given to these topics:

1. What tasks are being contemplated for computerization? Will a given model be able to handle all of them?

2. How much memory is needed? What is available?
3. What speed printer is available? Is the noise level excessive?
4. What kinds of programs are available?
5. Will the manufacturer or vendor provide support and training?

Sources of Information.   One of the best sources of information about new equipment is the bimonthly publication entitled *Library Technology Reports.*[5] It analyses in great detail the relative merits and weaknesses of many types of equipment. In recent years topics have included the following:

1987: Microform reader-printers: Automated systems; Optical media; Photocopiers
1988: Computer printers; Facsimile equipment; Work stations
1989: Hard disk technology; Automated cataloging support

The variety of topics is apparent from this list. The unbiased nature of the analyses makes this an invaluable source for those considering purchasing equipment.

References

1.   Pierce, William S. *Furnishing the library interior.* New York: Dekker; 1980. 288 p.

Has chapters on planning interiors, furniture design and selection, care of nonprint media, and evaluation and purchase of furniture and equipment. Has a wealth of information on these subjects.

2.   Brown, Carol R. *Selecting library furniture; a guide for librarians, designers, and architects.* Phoenix, AZ: Oryx Press; 1989. 112 p.

She uses more than 90 photographs and illustrations to enhance her description of the evaluation and selection of furniture. Chapters cover such topics as determination of what is needed, features of different types of furniture, the bid process, and the furniture market.

3.   Mount, Ellis, ed. *Creative planning of special library facilities.* New York: Haworth Press; 1988. 197 p. Chap. 3, 9, 11, 12.

Besides general comments on the selection of furniture there are chapters dealing specifically with this topic, including the design and selection of shelving as well as furniture adapted to the wiring needed for electronic devices. A bibliography includes references to furniture/equipment selection.

4.   Stankus, Tony; Rosseel, Kevin. Estimation of shelving needs: selection of equipment. *In:* Mount. *Op cit.*

Describes the relative merits of metal versus wood shelving as to appearance, construction, and durability. Also covers movable shelving of various types. Layout of stack areas in relation to aisles is discussed.

5.   *Library Technology Reports.* Chicago: American Library Association; 1965- . Bimonthly.

Provides results of analyses of commercial equipment by impartial investigators, with reports showing features of the equipment (good and bad) and costs. Each issue is devoted to just one or two products, allowing for in-depth reports. Highly recommended.

Part 7
Professional Activities

One of the traditions of librarianship has been the general support given by librarians to the concept of cooperation with their colleagues in other libraries. Cooperative activities among librarians have existed almost as long as libraries have been in existence, and, thanks to improved technology, have become more varied and effective. Chapter 25 is concerned with a description of such activities, including the more recent development of networks and their relationship to special libraries.

Chapter 26 discusses the many types of organizations that serve the professional needs of librarians; current practices, publications, and other benefits to members are described.

In Chapter 27 there is a discussion of the various ways in which employment in special libraries can be obtained. The roles of associations, library schools, and agencies are reviewed.

Chapter 25

Cooperative Activities and Networks

There is evidence that informal cooperative projects involving libraries have existed almost as long as libraries have existed. However, formal arrangements are much more recent. In recent years, formal cooperative projects, particularly those known as networks, have now achieved an importance that could not be imagined even twenty years ago.

The main reason for the growth of cooperation among libraries and information centers has been self-interest—the acknowledgment that no one library can accomplish as much by itself as it can by working with others. A desire to provide wider service also has been a major factor in cooperative efforts, but the benefits derived from these projects has undoubtedly been an even stronger incentive.

Several trends in the past decade or so have increased the growth pace of cooperative projects. One has been the economic factors that have tightened library budgets while causing steady increases in the cost of labor and materials. Another important cause of the growth of such projects has been the development of equipment and systems that can support cooperative online databases readily available to users over wide geographic areas at an affordable cost.

Most special libraries and information centers have been involved in some sort of cooperative projects for years, resulting in savings of time and money as well as in greater access to information resources. However, certain cooperative projects have been less attractive or more difficult to set up because of restrictions set by the sponsoring organizations. Top management in private companies might understandably see less value in cooperating with other libraries (perhaps including those sponsored by rival companies) than would a high official in an academic or public library. Nevertheless, special libraries and information centers continue to discover ways in which they can take part in cooperative projects and networks.

The following are examples of some of the types of cooperative projects, including networks, which have been developed.

Shared Collection Responsibilities

As far back as the turn of the century, if not before, there were agreements made among several libraries to avoid unnecessary duplications and to ensure adequate coverage of major topics. An example of such agreements was the well-known plan developed in Chicago among the Chicago Public Library, the John Crerar Library, and the Newberry Library. The arrangement grew from the creation of the Crerar Library in 1894 as a public library seeking an appropriate field. Its directors held meetings with their counterparts from the Newberry and the Public Library to decide upon a division of subjects. Crerar was to concentrate on collecting science, technology, and certain social sciences; the Public Library was to collect materials of a general nature; while the Newberry Library was to emphasize music, medicine, and history. In succeeding years, Crerar took over medicine from Newberry and relinquished the social sciences, while the Newberry Library expanded its interest in the arts and humanities. Nevertheless, it was a good example of cooperation among three major libraries at a time when such cooperation was far from commonplace.

A project which involved many libraries was the Farmington Plan, developed in 1948. Its goal was to ensure that at least one copy of each publication of research value from foreign sources would be available in a library in the United States. Participating libraries agreed to collect certain types of materials from assigned countries. The plan ceased operation in 1972, due to the accumulated problems of budgets, poor quality of service by dealers, and the withdrawal of important libraries.

A similar plan was developed in the 1960s (operating under Public Law 480) for the acquisition of materials from certain foreign countries in return for wartime assistance in World War II. In lieu of cash payments, these countries would make publications available to participating libraries in this country.

Special libraries have also been involved in cooperative projects of this sort. Those libraries devoted to a given type of collection (for example, museum libraries) often seek to reduce unnecessary duplication. At first such agreements were rather general; not until the development of networks did more specific plans arise.

More and more informal agreements are being reached by special libraries with public and academic libraries. In return for the use of larger libraries, the special libraries make available their specialized collections. A real spirit of interdependence has developed between many public libraries and their colleagues in special libraries.

The Research Libraries Group (RLG) has implemented shared collection agreements among its members, a number of whom are special libraries.

Interlibrary Loans

As a natural consequence of cooperative collection agreements, countless libraries have been involved in interlibrary loan arrangements for many decades. Some arrangements were restricted to certain libraries in a given area or organization, while others were never limited in any way. All have been entirely voluntary, and for many years the only charges levied were those the borrowing library would bear for the postage or express charges plus insurance. As time went on, more and more of the larger libraries found they were borrowing very little from other libraries but loaning quite a bit. When budgets became tights, it became necessary to recoup some of the labor costs involved in providing many interlibrary loans by charging a per volume cost for each loan.

Among special libraries, the need for access to materials not in their collections made them frequent borrowers of public and academic libraries. Besides paying charges for loans, special libraries make occasional cash donations to libraries from whom they borrow heavily. Among special libraries it is almost unheard of for one to charge the other, although payments for postage are common.

Most libraries will not loan reference materials, rare books, or fragile items. However, on rare occasions, one special library having very good relations with another special library might loan a reference work for a few hours in an emergency.

The borrowing library is expected to have done everything possible to verify the bibliographic citation for the item being requested, to make identification simpler for the loaning library. It cannot be done in all cases, but it is often quite simple to make a verification, using conventional indexes of certain databases like OCLC. A considerate librarian will attempt to spread requests for loans among several libraries rather than rely on a particular source.

An elaborate interlibrary loan system in New York State, which uses a number of special libraries and public libraries as resource centers, is described in the paper by Cabeen[1] Inquiries from libraries in New York go through channels to the state library, which can turn to the resource centers if necessary. Since that paper was written, the New York State Education Department, of which the New York State Library is a part, has sponsored the development of a new network known as NYSERNET. It is being designed with the goal of providing even better access to the state's database, which contains over 54 million records, with an eventual total of 180 million volumes.[2] It is clear that networking is a dynamic process, with changes made at frequent intervals as time and funding permit.

Directories and Union Lists

A common form of cooperation among libraries and information centers is that of producing directories of libraries and union lists of their holdings, particularly holdings of serials.

These publications may be produced on an infrequent basis or might be issued annually. Examples of directories or union lists include those produced by:

- Special libraries in a given state, city, or region of the country.
- Special libraries having the same kind of sponsor.
- Special libraries in a given corporation.
- Special libraries as well as other types of libraries having holdings of a particular kind of publication.

Directories produced by cooperative action may range from simple listings of basic information (address, head librarian, phone number, etc.) to longer entries including descriptions which indicate the main subject fields collected. Union lists usually are confined to serials and include such data as titles, years, volumes held, policies on photocopying, and similar data. Because these publications are usually produced on an informal basis, there is often no regular schedule for preparing new editions, particularly for union lists (because of the greater detail required for compiling the necessary data compared to the more simple contents of directories). Special Libraries Association chapters have been active for many years in publishing directories of their members' libraries and/or their holdings.

The usual format of a printed list is now occasionally replaced by the use of COM equipment to produce microfiche sets. Online versions are no longer restricted to those produced in large corporations or government agencies, because of the easy access to private online files available from database vendors and other commercial sources.

Networks

There are many ways of defining a network. Very simply, a library network is a formal organization of libraries formed for cooperative purposes, usually including telecommunication facilities or access for the processing of the network members' cooperative records. There are many cooperative groups and consortia which use the term *networks* that do not have telecommunication facilities; technically, they are not networks.

Even though special libraries were not the primary users intended in the creation of the largest networks, they have been members of almost every prominent network. One of the largest is OCLC (originally called the Ohio College Library Center but later changed to Online Computer Library Center). Although it began in 1967 as a cooperative activity for 54 college and university libraries in Ohio, it soon broadened its goals and membership requirements and allowed special libraries to join. By 1989 it had 20 million records in its database and was handling 15 million interlibrary loans per year. Its database can be used for preparing catalog cards (for libraries still using cards) and as a source of electronic data for downloading into local databases. It is available on commercial databases and has become a major force on the national scene.

A network consisting of many university and research libraries is the Research Libraries Group (RLG); many of its libraries include special libraries devoted to such topics as the sciences, business, and architecture. RLG has its own database, known as RLIN (Research Libraries Information Network), which allows for online shared cataloging. RLG has also spent a great deal of effort on cooperative collection development, including the agreement by members to be responsible for prescribed areas of collection. By 1979 RLIN had a total of 19 million book records; it also had other files for particular formats, such as a file of master microfilm masters in the amount of 68,000 titles. RLIN has proved itself to be a valuable resource, with its membership and its databases growing steadily.

An elaborate network of health sciences libraries is maintained by the National Library of Medicine (NLM). It provides for several online databases, each with a special area of concentration. One of them, MEDLINE, consists of thoroughly indexed articles and books on medical topics. These databases allow for online searches as well as for shared cataloging. NLM was one of the pioneers in the establishment of networks.

Special Libraries in Networks

Special libraries have a lengthy history of participation in cooperative activities and later in networks. A paper by Strable, which traces the growth of special library participation in cooperative movements and in networks, shows that as far back as 1909, the year that the Special Libraries Association was formed, a talk at its first annual conference by George Lee mentioned the value of cooperation in compiling union lists while another speaker discussed the general feature of cooperation.[3] The Strable paper also notes that in 1910 Lee described a Boston information bureau run by SLA members for the benefit of inquirers. The paper also cites an ALA study showing that there were 125 articles written about special library involvement in cooperative activities during the period 1940-1968.

Strable points out that in recent years networks were being formed to replace less formal cooperative arrangements. He differentiates between networks and cooperation by stating that networks are more formal in nature, they have better funding, they tend to include several types of libraries (special along with public and academic, for example), and, lastly, they make use of modern technology, particularly computers.

The book containing the Strable paper includes a number of valuable papers describing how special libraries have taken part in networks.[4] They deal with such topics as networks within large corporations, special library experience with OCLC, the National Library of Medicine's Regional Medical Library Network, and networks in Canadian corporate circles. This compilation of papers provides an excellent view of network participation by special libraries.

A more recent source of information on this subject is the Spring 1989 issue of *Special Libraries*.[5] The entire issue deals with networks involving special libraries, ranging from Pat Molholt's paper on the relationship between technology and networking to Beth Paskoff's summary of how and why special librarians should participate in networks. An earlier issue of *Special Libraries* that was devoted to networks appeared in 1982.[6] It centered on interlibrary loans and circulation activities.

Should the reader be curious about the omission of local area networks (LANs) from this chapter, the explanation is that, despite their name, they are essentially systems that operate within the confines of one organization, sometimes just within one room or one building. This scale of operations is quite different from the systems discussed in this chapter, which operate on a much larger base. Local area networks are covered in Chapter 11, which deals with the applications of new technology in libraries.

References

1.   Cabeen, S. K. The Engineering Societies Library and the New York Interlibrary Loan Program. *Science & Technology Libraries.* 1(2): 23-25; 1980 Winter.

Discusses the role of this library as one of a few selected resource centers for the NYSILL interlibrary loan system, which handles about 140,000 requests per year from libraries in that state. Several special libraries take part.

2. Shubert, Joseph F.; Porter, Donald. Libraries and library pilot projects on NYSERNET. *In: Connecting the networks.* Proceedings of the joint Library of Congress Network Advisory Committee and EDUCOM Meeting held Dec. 5-7, 1988. Washington: Library of Congress, Network Development and MARC Standards Office; 1989: p.45-59. (Network Planning Paper No. 18)

Describes the plans of New York state officials for creating improved networks that would link universities, research facilities, medical centers, libraries, and industrial research centers throughout New York State.

3. Strable, Edward G. The way it was. *In:* Gibson, Robert W., ed. *The special library role in networks: a conference held at the General Motors Research Laboratories, Warren, Michigan, May 5-6, 1980.* New York: Special Libraries Association; 1980: p. 1-16. 296 p.

Provides a history of special library participation in cooperative projects and in networks. It also includes comments on the definition of networks and on the benefits they offer.

4. Gibson. *Op. cit.*

5. Paskoff, Beth, ed. Networks. *Special Libraries.* 80(2): 1989 Spring.

Consists of 8 papers devoted to some aspect of networks involving special libraries. Serves as a valuable survey of the subject.

6. The growth of library networks. *Special Libraries.* 73(1): 1982 January.

Contains several articles dealing with the effects of network membership on interlibrary loans, circulation activity, and multitype cooperative groups.

Chapter 26

Professional Organizations and Continuing Education

There are many avenues open to special librarians and information center personnel for improving their skills, their understanding of their profession, and their status in the field. This chapter will discuss the role played by professional organizations in aiding such individuals and will list some of those groups apt to be of greatest value to the reader. It will also point out the agencies and organizations active in professional education.

Those employed in special libraries and information centers may work for sponsors involved in such areas as the law, engineering, accounting, or a host of other disciplines. They may therefore be interested in the professional organizations which exist for those specialties, but organizations designed for librarians and information professionals undoubtedly are going to be more important to them. A representative list of some of these groups follows later in the chapter.

Benefits of Membership in Professional Organizations

Probably the main advantage provided by membership in professional organizations is the information that can be gained about new developments, such as new techniques, new equipment, new materials, new publications, or even new personnel, at libraries and information centers. A professional who does not keep abreast will eventually suffer from this lack of knowledge, perhaps at a very inopportune moment. The learning process offered by organizations may be informal, such as through papers read at meetings, panel discussions held at conferences, or articles in periodicals sponsored by the organizations. Formal workshops and courses are also sponsored by them.

Another benefit is the opportunity to participate in worthwhile projects, or even to propose and manage such projects. Activities sponsored by organizations, or their local chapters, have included union lists, surveys, duplicate exchanges, and other publications (including dictionaries, guides to the literature, and directories). Most of these projects would never have been proposed and carried out if there had not been professional organizations to sponsor them.

Membership also affords members opportunities to learn about job openings, whether through the formal placement services operated at the organizations' annual conferences or, in some cases, through telephone "hot lines." Advertisements in official journals also help. More than one member has learned of new openings from fellow members, sometimes even in advance of formal postings. Membership and participation in professional organizations invariably lead a member to contacts with nearby libraries or those people with similar interests. These contacts can be invaluable in establishing good relations between libraries, such as interlibrary loans or other cooperative practices. Acquaintances met through organizations also can lead, in many cases, to lifelong friendships, based on having common professional interests.

As an aid to helping members communicate with each other, most organizations issue membership directories of some sort. A few are published annually, while others are less frequent. Besides the usual information (name and address) some of these directories include job titles, professional areas of interest to the member, and similar data. They are invaluable aids for keeping in touch with fellow members.

Continuing Education

While following a formal program leading to the master's degree is generally recommended as the best path for those starting a career in special libraries and information centers, it is really just the beginning of what should be a life-long pursuit of learning. The main reason for this is, of course, the need of the individual to keep abreast of new developments and to expand his or her fields of interest.

In many cases, library and information science societies offer a variety of one- or two-day workshops at their annual conferences. They also sponsor them on a regional basis in various parts of the country. They cover topics of continuing interest, such as techniques of management, legal literature, or computerized services. A few of these courses may include the awarding of Continuing Education Units (CEUs), which are a measure of non-collegiate credit courses and workshops as determined by standards set up within the profession. Most short courses or workshops, however, do not offer such units. Some organizations require that members attend a certain number of educational programs or courses in a given time period in order to retain certification; this is true of the Medical Library Association, which certifies medical librarians.

Educational programs also are sponsored by commercial firms. One well-known example is the workshops given by vendors of computerized databases, either for teaching how to use their systems or for teaching about the various databases they offer. Producers of databases also sponsor workshops to teach users the fine points of using their products. Most of these firms charge rather modest prices; a few do not charge for sessions. Some firms schedule sessions just before or just after the major conferences of associations, when many potential attendees are gathered in one city. Still other workshops are sponsored by commercial firms who hire free-lance instructors for one-day sessions, collectively covering a wide range of topics and given in key cities in various parts of the country.

Many library schools themselves offer continuing education programs, ranging from one-day workshops to multi-session courses spread over several weeks. The range of topics can vary quite a bit, depending upon the interests of students and teachers available. Another source of education is that offered within networks under the direction of network directors and their staffs. Both formal and informal courses are involved.

Library schools are the best source for those wanting formal courses, which ordinarily offer more substance than the shorter, less formal educational sessions. Graduates may want to return and take a single course to complete their preparation or to expand their fields of expertise. In some cases, graduates may be interested in acquiring a certificate, given after completing a number of courses, as evidence to their employers of their efforts at self-improvement. Those deciding upon a career of research or teaching in either librarianship or information science may opt for doctoral programs, which would probably require a year or so of course work, followed by several years spent on a dissertation.

A useful analysis of education for special librarians in the United States is found in an issue of *Special Libraries* that was devoted to that topic.[1] It includes the history of education, an analysis of its worth, and the outlook for future needs.

No matter what kind of program individuals decide upon, it is necessary to take part in activities of this sort on a regular basis. Keeping abreast of the times is a must for those employed in special libraries/information centers.

Attention is now being given to the educational needs of graduates with the M.L.S. who desire alternative careers to special libraries and information centers. Some examples are database management, training of database searchers (working for database owners or vendors), editorial work for publishers, and managing library sales departments for publishers. Still others are translating, indexing, abstracting, planning of library facilities, and systems analysis.

Selected Professional Organizations

There is no lack of organizations aimed at aiding the professional development of those interested in special libraries and information centers. The following list includes many which are quite well known in this field; however, omission of any organization from this list does not imply that it is not worthy of inclusion but is merely due to the selectiveness of this section. A useful source of data about organizations such as those listed here is the *Bowker Annual: Library and Book Trade Almanac*.

Special Libraries Association.   SLA was established in 1909 to aid those librarians who were interested in special libraries; there were relatively few at the time. Today there are more than 13,000 members, making it the third largest library association in the world, and the second largest in the United States. Its members work for special libraries, information centers, publishers, database owners, and a variety of related employers. SLA's annual conference (usually held in June) includes conference papers and continuing education courses on a number of topical subjects.

SLA consists of more than fifty local chapters, located chiefly in the United States and Canada, designed to bring together all members or interested people in a particular region or city. Each chapter meets several times per year. Some of the larger chapters have subject groups within them so that those with special interests also can meet separately. SLA is also made up of divisions, devoted to such subject areas as science-technology, business and finance, and publishing. There are approximately thirty of these divisions, whose members issue newsletters, sponsor programs at the annual conference, and take part in other projects during the year.

The main organ of SLA is *Special Libraries,* which is issued quarterly and consists of such features as papers, book reviews, reports on the association, and advertisements for jobs and products. A monthly newsletter, the *Specialist,* provides a forum for news items of a more ephemeral nature. SLA also publishes monographs on topics of interest to its members and issues a directory of members entitled *Who's Who in Special Libraries.*

In recent years SLA has made extensive enlargements in its continuing education programs. Besides courses given at the time of its annual meeting in June there are others offered during SLA's mid-winter meeting, a program which began in 1985. The latter meeting is the scene of the five-unit Middle Management Institute; its purpose is to provide attendees with courses which serve as a foundation for professional growth and development. Other courses are offered at the relatively new Executive Development Academy, which began in 1988. It is said to be the only executive management program designed specifically for information professionals. Instructors are chosen from faculty members at the Carnegie-Mellon Graduate School of Industrial Administration. The curriculum deals with corporate objectives, operational plans, strategic alternatives, financial management, and leadership; only twenty-five participants are accepted each year. Still another event is the State-of-the-Art conference held annually since 1986 in the Fall; each is centered on a theme of current interest, one being the outlook for intelligent systems and another the use of government information.

To meet the educational needs of those who are unable to attend the annual conferences, regional continuing education courses are offered at various sites around the U.S., given by experts selected by SLA headquarters. Two other means for reaching members are audio cassettes and videotapes; these may consist of talks given at previous conferences or institutes. A recent service instituted by SLA was the creation of self-study programs. An example of the latter is a kit, available in workbook format or on a computer diskette, dealing with the management of time. The kits include exercises and case studies; other topics include networking, reentry into the work force, and expert systems. Thus there are numerous opportunities for special librarians to update their skills or acquire new ones.

To aid those seeking employment, SLA has for years maintained a service at its annual conference at which job-seekers as well as employers having positions to fill can meet for interviews. To aid employment during the course of the year there was recently established a referral service at SLA Headquarters which compares the characteristics and skills of librarians registered with the service with the needs of participating employers with vacancies to fill. This computerized service is available on a fee basis to all those interested.

American Society for Information Science. This organization was originally named the American Documentation Institute. It was founded in 1937 as a group whose members were representatives of organizations interested in the handling of information. In 1952 it began to admit individual members and became the American Society for Information Science

(ASIS) in 1968. It now has approximately 3,700 members, located mostly in the United States. ASIS members work in a variety of organizations, often in positions similar to those held by members of SLA. Its annual conference (usually held in October) offers papers and panel discussions as well as selected continuing education courses.

There are currently approximately twenty-five local chapters of ASIS in the United States. There are more than twenty groups devoted to special topics, called Subject Interest Groups (or SIGs). These groups are concerned with such areas as library automation, education, and automated language processing.

The official organ of ASIS is the *Journal of the American Society for Information Science* (JASIS), where formal papers and book reviews are published bimonthly. Briefer items are found in a companion journal known as the *Bulletin of the American Society for Information Science* (BASIS), issued bimonthly. ASIS also sponsors serials and monographs, such as its *Annual Review of Information Science and Technology,* and issues an annual handbook/ directory.

Medical Library Association. This organization was founded in 1898, making it the second oldest of the professional library associations in the United States (following the American Library Association). It now has more than 5,000 individual members. Its annual conference, normally in June, is similar in format to those of others described previously. Its official organ is the *Bulletin of the Medical Library Association,* a quarterly publication. It is supplemented by the *MLA News,* a monthly journal.

American Association of Law Libraries. Another of the older organizations, the AALL was founded in 1908. Its membership total is currently approximately 4,100. Its official organ is the *Law Library Journal.*

Other Professional Organizations. In addition to the associations listed above there are several other organizations that should be noted. Some are aimed at librarians in certain types of special libraries, such as those sponsored by art museums or religious groups. Others are apt to be of interest to records managers, information specialists, or microfilm technologists. The list that follows is by no means complete; various directories should be consulted for more comprehensive listings of organizations designed for librarians and related professionals.

1. *ARMA International:* (formerly Association of Records Managers and Administrators) Established 1975. Has 8,500 members. Publishes the *Records Management Quarterly.*
2. *American Society of Indexers:* Established 1968. Has approximately 750 members. Publishes *The Indexer* (in conjunction with three other groups) and its *ASI Newsletter* (5 issues per year).
3. *American Theological Library Association:* Established 1947. Has approximately 500 individual members and 170 institutional members. Publishes the *Proceedings of the American Theological Library Association,* issued quarterly.
4. *Art Libraries Society of North America (ARLIS/NA):* Established 1972. Has approximately 1,200 members. Publishes the ARLIS/NA *Update,* issued quarterly, and *Art Documentation,* issued monthly.

5. *Association for Information and Image Management (AIIM)* (formerly the National Micrographics Association): Established 1943. Has approximately 10,000 members. Publishes *Inform*, issued monthly, and *FYI*, issued monthly.
6. *Association of Christian Librarians:* Established 1956. Has 300 members and publishes *The Christian Librarian*, issued quarterly.
7. *Association of Jewish Libraries:* Established 1965. Has 890 members. Publishes the *AJL Bulletin*, issued biennially.
8. *Canadian Association for Information Science:* Established ca. 1973. Publishes *Canadian Journal of Information Science*, issued quarterly.
9. *Catholic Library Association:* Established 1921. Has approximately 3,300 members. Publishes *Catholic Library World*, issued 10 times per year.
10. *Church and Synagogue Library Association:* Established 1967. Has approximately 1,300 members. Publishes *Lutheran Libraries*, issued quarterly.
11. *Music Library Association:* Established 1931. Has approximately 1,800 members. Publishes the *MLA Newsletter*, issued quarterly, and *Music Cataloging Bulletin*, issued monthly.
12. *Society of American Archivists:* Established 1936. Has approximately 4,300 members. Publishes *The American Archivist*, issued quarterly.
13. *Theatre Library Association:* Established 1937. Has approximately 500 members. Publishes *Broadside*, issued quarterly.

In addition to the organizations listed there are numerous others at the international, state (provincial), or regional level which may interest those involved with special libraries and information centers.

References

1. Library education in the U.S.—100 years; SLA salutes the first 100 years. *Special Libraries*. 77(4): 1986 Fall.

Marking the end of 100 years since Dewey inaugurated library education in the U.S., this issue contains a number of articles on the education of special librarians. They include a survey of special librarians, an analysis of what corporate librarians will need to know in the future, a history of education, and a look at accreditation of library schools.

Chapter 27

Employment in Special Libraries and Information Centers

Up to now this book has concentrated on the nature of special libraries and information centers—what sort of services they perform, what is expected of them by their clients, and the nature of their collections and their facilities. The book would be incomplete, however, without discussing the ways in which readers can find employment in such organizations. This chapter aims at describing some of the ways in which readers may learn about employment opportunities, some recommended ways to get job offers, some of the factors that would govern the acceptance of a particular position, and some of the long-range aspects of employment in these agencies.

A useful book that discusses the nature of the work of information professionals, including sources of information about jobs, use of resumes, and preparing for interviews, has been written by Heim and Sullivan.[1] Although it is written in terms of all types of libraries, there are many parts of interest to special librarians.

Awareness of Job Openings

There are many ways in which job openings are made known to those seeking employment, whether it be a first job after finishing one's education, or a change of jobs during one's career. It is advisable to consider all of these avenues when seeking a job, although each source of job information has its advantages and disadvantages. Sometimes a person may use only one method and find a job quickly. Other people may discover that they need to try several methods to find the right position.

Hot Lines.   A number of chapters of the Special Libraries Association have operated telephone hot lines for years, freely available to all those interested, whether SLA members or not. The service consists of recorded telephone messages which list available jobs. Perhaps only the name and phone number of the organization having the open positions are given, along with a brief description of the type of work (reference, cataloging, etc.). Depending upon the chapter's plan of operations, the listings might be updated as frequently as once a week. The brief announcements are no substitute for full information about the jobs, but they serve to alert the job hunter to what is currently available.

Advertisements.   These may be found in periodicals, newspapers, or newsletters/bulletins issued by library groups. On a broad scale the listings in SLA's newsletter, *The SpeciaList,* and other library-oriented periodicals offer the widest geographic scope of printed advertisements; they cover positions open all over the United States and Canada. Other associations, such as the American Society for Information Science, issue a separate listing of job openings rather than including them in a periodical; they also represent a wide range of geographic locations. Local newspapers often carry advertisements, primarily in a certain city or metropolitan area.

Library Schools. Many employers list positions with library schools in their area. The schools usually maintain folders containing letters from employers describing positions. Bulletin boards in the schools frequently list jobs also. Most schools attempt to aid their graduates to find jobs; some do more than others along this line.

Conference Employment Services. Conferences sponsored by library associations generally include a service whereby eligible persons, usually members of the sponsoring associations, can list their resumes as well as make appointments to meet employers having openings. SLA has done this for years, and members are generally pleased with the quality of the service.

Interviewing Teams. Large organizations have been known to advertise in library schools for potential employees, following this up with pre-arranged interviews at the various schools. Although this is not widely done, it does represent a convenient way for students to learn about job openings and get interviews.

Association Rosters. In the past few years SLA has begun a service for members seeking employment. By sending in data about themselves and their job interests, their resumes are maintained in a roster at SLA Headquarters, open to prospective employers. This computerized service is available for a fee to interested librarians and employers.

Employment Agencies. Many people rely on employment agencies for finding a job. Agencies often are aware of many jobs that may not be advertised publicly, and they often know quite a bit about the nature of the jobs that are open. Thus they might be able to fit the applicant to jobs that would best suit the person. In some cases they might know the maximum salary a particular applicant might reasonably expect in a given job.

Word of Mouth. One of the quickest ways to learn about job openings is by word of mouth. One's friends and acquaintances collectively know a lot about what is going on in regard to job openings, sometimes on a national basis. While exact details may not be known, quite often just the fact of knowing that a particular job is open is the most important bit of information to learn. Getting more details is usually a simple matter of calling the organizations involved. The process of "networking" is often valuable—this involves getting help from colleagues in the way of introductions to people who have hiring authority.

Success in Job Hunting

There are many reasons why a particular person may or may not be offered a position he or she applied for. Quite often the employer may not pick the person best suited for a particular job. Most librarians have had the experience of not being offered a job for which they believed they were the best candidate. One learns not to get discouraged; it's best to look ahead to the next opportunity.

Some applicants are able to present themselves in a very favorable manner, while others do not do justice to themselves. There are some general guidelines that may aid the job hunter in making the best impression possible:

- *Resumes.* Resumes are often the first contact applicants have with the employer. Needless to say, a resume should be carefully prepared. It should be neat, not too long, and designed to fit the job opening being applied for. It should be printed in an attractive manner. If an applicant doesn't have access to word processing or computer equipment that can print professional-looking resumes, it would be false economy to avoid going to a commercial printer and trying to get by with a resume that is less than adequate in appearance.

  A cover letter accompanying the resume is also very important. It gives the applicant the opportunity to mention special qualifications for a particular job that might not be apparent from a formal resume. Highlighting one's accomplishments related to the job is appropriate in these letters. If an interview has not been offered at this point, the letter could end by asking politely if one could be arranged in the near future.

  Several excellent books have been written about the preparation of resumes. One that many readers have highly praised is by Bostwick.[2] In view of the importance of a good resume (note that "resume" is spelled either with two accents or none at all), it would be only prudent for an applicant to devote considerable thought to the matter.

- *Interviews.* A personal interview is often the turning point at which an applicant can either make such a favorable impression that he or she is put into the list of "finalists" (if not the winner) or else not come across well and be no longer considered. The wise applicant does sufficient homework in advance, knowing at least the general nature of the organization involved, such as what it does or what it makes and what kind of library it has (gleaned from directories, if no other source is available). An applicant should be well-organized and able to state his or her qualifications in an appropriate manner. It is best to avoid the extremes of being boastful or unduly modest about one's qualifications. Asking intelligent questions about the nature of the work shows interest in the job, but questions about benefits, such as vacations and bonuses, might give the wrong impression. Salaries might not be mentioned by the employer at a first interview; however, it is not wrong to ask what the range is, deferring that topic till later in the interview. The applicant should be prepared to state what would be an acceptable salary, if the interviewer were to ask that question.

  Needless to say, the applicant should dress appropriately and neatly. Wearing jeans and sandals is a good way to spoil any chance of getting the job, and extremes of fashion should also be avoided. Being prompt for any interview is taken for granted, and a thank-you note should be sent afterward for having been granted an interview.

  The applicant should act natural and realize that he or she has a lot to offer; it is not helpful to feel that one must get a particular job at the risk of ruining one's life if it doesn't come about. It is better to have the attitude that doing one's best in an interview is all that could be expected of anyone.

Be patient about the time it takes for a decision to be made. Some organizations are notoriously slow, often taking many weeks to make up their collective minds. The applicant may want to go to interviews for several jobs, rather than counting on just one to lead to success. If a later interview leads to a job offer from another organization that is accepted, it would be only common courtesy to call or write the other places and notify them of withdrawal of an application.

• *Consideration of Job Offers.*   Once an offer of a job has been made, the applicant should give serious thought before accepting it. By the time an offer has been made, the applicant should know enough about the nature of the work to know if it would be the type of activity that he or she would enjoy. Working in an environment that is completely outside one's range of interests, or even contrary to one's standards, could be an unfortunate experience. If a person happened to feel that he or she had absolutely no interest in a particular product or service that was the prime feature of a particular organization, the job might soon become unacceptable to the person. For example, if a job hunter were trained as an artist, and had no interest whatsoever in business or technology, the person would have to decide in advance of taking a job in those fields whether or not he or she could develop an interest in such subjects. Financial needs may dictate trying the job in spite of its nature, but taking a job should mean that the applicant is willing to stay at least one year, to be fair to the organization. A day can be quite long if one isn't interested in the work. Attractive salaries do not necessarily make a job really rewarding if a person is in the wrong kind of an organization.

Some other factors should also be considered before accepting a position: for example, what is the financial soundness of the organization—is it in the midst of a takeover, or does it have a reputation of being on shaky grounds financially? The applicant should also consider the entire benefits package offered. Sometimes an excellent pension plan can be more advantageous than a higher monthly salary. Still another point to analyze as much as possible is the life style at the organization—for example, some are more formal than others, which may or may not matter to the applicant.

Entry-level jobs may not be the kinds one would wish to stay in for many years; often applicants might realize this and would take as their first job the one that comes closest to the ideal position. Later on, after a year or more of experience, it may be possible to find a more suitable job. But, as stated above, even the first job should provide a reasonable amount of interest to the applicant.

Those who have several years of experience often find that their promotions to better jobs come with leaving one organization and going to another. One reason for this is that most special libraries do not have large numbers of professionals, and waiting in one organization for a promotion up the ladder might take years to come about. On the other hand, there are people who are content to stay at one organization and wait for promotions to come about. This is usually the case when the nature of the work and other considerations, such as salaries, location of the organization, and the general environment of the organization, make the job particularly rewarding to them.

- *Alternative Careers.* Many graduates of library schools are interested in non-library careers. These include such activities as indexing, abstracting, database management, editing, or translating, to name a few choices. The above guidelines apply to them, although there would be other publications and other organizations that might be involved in announcing job openings in such fields. Some people seek such jobs after working in libraries for a while, and still others leave such jobs and go to library service. Fortunately each person can make up his or her own mind about the best career path to take.

A book edited by Mount provides discussions of the nature of alternative careers in sci-tech fields.[3] It contains descriptions of seven types of information services related to sci-tech information, such as information brokering, translating, and indexing.

References

1. Heim, Kathleen; Sullivan, Peggy. *Opportunities in library and information science.* Lincolnwood, IL: VGM Career Horizons; 1986. 150 p.

   Describes the type of work available to information professionals, the techniques of applying for positions, and long-range decisions about employment.

2. Bostwick, Burdette. *Resume writing: a comprehensive how-to-do-it guide.* 3d ed. New York: Wiley; 1985. 323 p.

   Discusses all aspects of the process of writing resumes. Contains excellent advice for this process.

3. Mount, Ellis, ed. *Alternative careers in sci-tech information service.* New York: Haworth Press; 1987. 154 p. (Also printed as: *Science & Technology Libraries.* 7(4): 1987 Summer.)

   Contains papers on careers involving these aspects of sci-tech information service: information broker, translator, acquisitions editor, information resources manager, research scientist in information science, database manager, and abstracting/indexing.

Appendix 1

Descriptions of Selected Special Libraries and Information Centers

No matter how well one tries to depict the nature of typical special libraries and information centers, it is likely the average reader will feel a need for more details on such topics as what services these organizations provide, what the size of their staffs are, to whom do library managers report in their organizations, and how large are their collections. In order to provide such information this appendix consists of descriptions of more than a dozen outstanding special libraries and information centers. Each description, written by the manager of the unit, explains the characteristics of library services, collections, and facilities offered clients of the unit.

The organizations listed here were chosen in order to represent several subject disciplines as well different sizes of staffs and collections. Geographically they include both Canada and several regions of the United States. Both for-profit and not-for-profit organizations are included. They are arranged into the following categories:

- Associations as sponsors
- Not-for-profit organizations
- For-profit organizations

Within these categories they are divided by subject fields.

Associations as Sponsors

It is not generally known, even among librarians, that many fine special libraries are sponsored by associations. These associations usually serve members of a particular profession, such as accounting or engineering. Members of the association are usually individuals, but in the example which follows the actual members are advertising agencies, whose employees are eligible to use the services of the library.

Some association-sponsored libraries have potential clients whose totals are in the tens of thousands, scattered over the entire United States in many instances. The services and collections available to the clients are made known to them through association-sponsored periodicals and brochures. Books are typically mailed to requestors, and telephone/facsimile communications are often used for the submission and the answering of requests.

The number of people served could be as few as 2,000 members, as is the case with the Council on Foreign Relations, and as many as over 400,000, as is the case with the Engineering Societies Library, which is sponsored by a number of engineering societies.

American Association of Advertising Agencies, Inc.
Member Information Service

[Advertising]

Marsha C. Appel

The American Association of Advertising Agencies Member Information Service (MIS), was founded to serve the information needs of members and staff of this national association. More than 750 member advertising agencies located all over the country have unlimited access to this customized secondary research service.

User needs focus primarily on the following topics (and the collection has been developed accordingly):

1. Advertising agency management and trends in the agency business
2. Advertising and marketing topics, procedures, and concepts
3. Products, markets, industries, and services—data to help agencies better serve their clients.

Most of the 21,000 requests handled each year arrive by phone, but about 2,500 visitors come in to use the facility on-site.

In order to accommodate the large number of projects with short deadlines, the resources are organized for quick retrieval of current data. The backbone of the collection is a network of 5,000 subject files continuously updated with information culled from the more than 200 journals that are scanned each month. That material is supplemented by indexes, handbooks, directories, and annual statistical publications. Depending on the nature of the request, other research steps taken may include telephoning experts for additional information, and online searching through Dialog, Nexis, and Datatimes.

The PC on each information specialist's desk is connected through a local area network to an online catalog and an internal database that contains details of every project handled by the department. This database is used for tracking the status of projects, obtaining detailed reports of each member's usage, and generating statistical reports of the department's work.

Technical services have been computerized with an integrated software package that handles acquisitions, cataloging, serial check-in and routing, and circulation.

The information service also handles the records management function for the entire association, including historical documents and records of its current activities. There is an ongoing program of microfilming critical AAAA documents.

Statistics

Sponsor: American Association of Advertising Agencies
Name of Unit: Member Information Service
Year established: 1935
Location: 666 Third Avenue, New York, NY 10017
Head of unit: Marsha C. Appel
Title of head of unit: Vice–President
Title of supervisor of head of unit: Senior Vice–President
Staff size: 11 professionals; 7 non-professionals
Main subjects collected: Advertising; Marketing
Collection Size:
        Books: 2,000
        Current subscriptions: 300
        Pamphlets & reports: 5,000
        Microfilm: 13 periodical titles
Number of professional users: Over 750 advertising agencies,
                           69,000 potential users

Area of unit: 3,600 sq. ft.
Number of seats for users: 7

Not-For-Profit Organizations

Many prestigious special libraries are sponsored by organizations which are in the not-for-profit category. This includes philanthropic groups, museums, educational and religious organizations, and government agencies. The libraries they sponsor may not differ a great deal from those serving for-profit groups as far as services and collections are concerned, but such factors as budgets, sources of income, and charges for services are clearly different.

Columbia University, Biological Sciences Library
[Biological Research]
Kathleen Kehoe
The Biology Library is one of eight science libraries at Columbia University. It was established in 1827 when the Zoology Department allocated $20,000 to furnish a reading room which would contain all of the available life sciences literature. Ninety-two years later, space and budget constraints precluded such comprehensive collecting. The library has now focused its scope to emphasize the literature areas which are relevant to the faculty's research interests, and which support the curriculum. The major collection areas are: biochemistry, cell biology, developmental biology, molecular biology, neurobiology, and physical anthropology. To a lesser extent the library collects materials on evolutionary biology, population biology, plant physiology, and general biology. With rare exceptions, we buy research-level English language material. Eighty percent of the budget is allocated to serials. We keep a

large number of the backruns of journals in microfilm in order to accommodate the library's space constraints. Older print materials are stored in open stacks in another location.

The library serves all Columbia University, Teacher's College, Barnard College, and Union Theological Seminary affiliates. The primary users are a much smaller group—the Biology faculty, students, and staff—about 300 people. In addition, interdisciplinary researchers from psychology, chemistry, and physical anthropology frequently use the library.

Because the number of regular users is limited, patrons receive a high level of service. Daily "journals received" lists are posted to facilitate use of the current journals area. Faculty members receive selected "tables of contents" of current journals. We compile a monthly acquisitions list which we mail to all faculty, students, and staff.

In addition, we distribute a quarterly newsletter which includes notices on staff changes, new services, new serials started, changes in software and online systems, and the like.

We provide free ready-reference searches to all patrons. In addition, we provide users with access to bibliographic and non-bibliographic databases that patrons can search at no cost. The library subscribes to "Intelligenetics Suite," a compendium of molecular biology databases which is housed on the department computer. This package gives researchers laboratory access to the nucleic acid and protein sequence databases. We also provide a 24-year collection of "Compact Cambridge Medline" (on CD-ROM), and "Current Contents Life Sciences" (on floppy disk), which are loaded on an IBM-XT in the library.

Finally, we provide extensive document delivery support for our users. In addition to interlibrary loan networks, we use commercial document delivery services to acquire materials expeditiously. Urgent requests are ordered by fax. There is no charge for any of the document delivery services.

The library is open seventy-five hours a week during the academic semester. Faculty members have complete access to the collection as they have keys to the library. We provide formal "reference hours" during the afternoons three to five hours daily.

Statistics

Sponsor: Columbia University
Name of unit: Biological Sciences Library
Year established: 1897
Location: 601 Fairchild Hall, Columbia University, New York, NY 10027
Name of head of unit: Kathleen Kehoe
Title of head of unit: Reference/Collection Development Librarian, Science & Engineering Division
Title of supervisor of head of unit: Head of Reference & Collection Development, Science & Engineering Division
Staff size: 1 professional, 1 non-professional, 3 FTE student employees
Main subjects collected: Developmental biology; Genetics; Molecular biology; Neurobiology

Collection Size:

       Books: 9,000
       Current subscriptions: 380
       Bound journal volumes: 37,000
Number of professional users: 220
Area of unit: 4,747 sq. feet
Number of seats for users: 56

The University Club Library
[Private Club]
Andrew J. Berner

The University Club is unique among New York's private social clubs in that its specific purpose, as spelled out in its 1865 charter, is "the promotion of literature and art, by establishing and maintaining a library, reading-room, and gallery of art." Since its founding, the University Club Library has developed into the world's largest and most comprehensive private club library. Housed in a landmark turn-of-the-century building, the library has been described as "one of the most beautiful examples of interior architecture in this country."

The general collection, though including materials in all subjects, is strongest in the humanities, and largely represents the late-nineteenth and early-twentieth century "ideal" of what an educated person should know, as well as what they should have available to them to expand that knowledge. The same is true of the rare book collection (which numbers approximately 2,000 volumes) and other special collections (an additional 4,000 volumes), which in addition to reflecting the overall subject strengths of the collection as a whole, include extensive works relating to such specific subjects as antebellum southern history, fine printing and illustrated books, George Cruikshank (with numerous original drawings), Californiana, the American Civil War, and the First and Second World Wars. The library is available to the members of the University Club, their families, and their guests. Scholars may apply to use the rare book and special collections on a research basis by contacting the library director.

The library offers numerous services such as current periodicals, a recreational reading collection, telephone reference, and interlibrary loan. A full-time position is devoted to the conservation and preservation of library materials. In addition, the library staff prepares regular exhibitions, and supports an active publications program. It also supports a series of monthly programs relating to books, book-collecting, literature, and libraries, presented under the auspices of the library's "friends" group, the University Club Library Associates. The library staff is also responsible for the conservation, care, and maintenance of the club's extensive art collection.

Cataloging and circulation are now automated for post-1980 acquisitions, while earlier titles continue to be represented in the card catalog. User access to the post-1980 titles is through author, title, and subject printouts, although the Library hopes soon to offer an end-user online catalog for these materials.

The founders of the University Club Library hoped that it would be a collection "which any member can consult with a reasonable chance of finding any information he may need."

While no library can truly be that complete, particularly a privately funded library, the University Club Library strives, even today, to come as close to that ideal as it can.

Statistics

Sponsor: The University Club
Name of unit: The University Club Library
Year established: 1865
Location: One West Fifty-Fourth Street, New York, NY 10019
Name of head of unit: Andrew J. Berner
Title of head of unit: Library Director
Title of supervisor of head of unit: General Manager
Staff size: 3 professionals, 2 non-professionals
Main subjects collected: Literature (belles-lettres); Biography; American & European history; Art & architecture
Collection Size:
    Books: 90,000
    Current subscriptions: 125
    Bound journal volumes: 3,500
    Microfilm: 2,800 reels
Number of professional users (potential):   10,000
Area of unit: 12,000 sq. ft. (approximate)

Whitney Museum Library
[Art Museum]
May Castleberry

The library of the Whitney Museum of American Art originated as the personal collection of Gertrude Vanderbilt Whitney, who founded the Whitney Museum in 1930. Since its inauguration, the library has emerged as a unique and important resource for the study of American art; it houses archives and a collection of over 10,000 books and catalogs.

The library began as a reading room available to the staff and artists associated with the Whitney Studio Club and Whitney Studio Galleries. These precursors of the museum, supported by Mrs. Whitney, exhibited and contributed valuable support to American art from 1918 to 1930. One form of this commitment to artists was the provision of a library offering materials for art research as well as a study area of relative comfort for artists. When the Whitney Museum opened its doors in 1931, the library had absorbed a wide range of monographic and serial publications on American art, many of which were financed by Mrs. Whitney.

Major impetus for the expansion of the library came in 1942, under the auspices of the American Art Research Council. This agency, proposed and administered by the Whitney Museum, accumulated documentation and authentication of American art by thirty museums and college art departments. The library now serves as a repository for the American Art

Research Council publications and records issued between 1942 and 1948. Since 1948, the library has grown steadily, augmented by generous gifts from staff, trustees, and other patrons, and reflects the diverse activities of the museum.

The library is a non-circulating reference collection serving all departments of the museum. Its focus corresponds with that of the museum, emphasizing Twentieth-century American painting, sculpture, drawing, and graphics. In addition, the library contains material on Colonial and Nineteenth-century American art, folk art, and photography. Excluded from this catalog, though encompassed by the library, are vertical file materials on artists and other archival matter.

The catalog conforms in general to ALA and Library of Congress principles. Certain modifications are made to suit the needs of the museum staff; for instance, additional subject headings are made for artists in group shows, while original descriptive cataloging is somewhat more abbreviated than in standard Library of Congress practice.

The reference nature of the collection necessarily restricts interlibrary loan services. The library is, however, open by appointment to researchers with advanced projects in American art.

Statistics

Sponsor: Whitney Museum of American Art
Name of Unit: Whitney Museum of American Art Library
Year established: 1930
Location: 945 Madison Avenue, New York, NY 10021
Head of Unit: May Castleberry
Title of Head: Librarian
Supervisor of Head of Unit: Associate Director of the Museum
Staff Size: 2 professionals (full-time), 1 professional (part-time), 1 non-professional (full-time), 2-4 non-professionals (part-time)
Main subjects collected: Twentieth-century American art (Painting, Sculpture, Drawing, Printmaking)
Collection Size:
        Books: 20,000 volumes
        Current subscriptions: 200
        Bound journal volumes: 4,000
        Vertical files: 200 drawers on artists
Number of professional users: 50
Area of Unit: 2,000 sq. ft.
Number of seats for users: 5

Wisconsin Regional Primate Research Center
[Zoological Research]
Lawrence Jacobsen

The library of the Wisconsin Regional Primate Research Center is one of many special libraries on the decentralized campus of the University of Wisconsin-Madison. Because the nonhuman primate is a model for studying many of man's maladies—from psychological to physiological—Center research reaches across many departments and disciplines. Included in the library's primary clientele are faculty, visiting scientists, and post-graduate and graduate students of the center and the UW Psychology Department's Harlow Primate Laboratory. The Center is also home to many affiliate scientists from various departments and schools (including psychology, zoology, veterinary science, and medicine) whose research involves using center animals and facilities. Students and faculty from the Neuroscience Training Program use the library and their book collection is integrated with the Center's.

The library collects exhaustively in the area of primatology—including monographs, journals, newsletters, audiovisual programs, primate data stored on videotape and audiotape, and rare books not already in the UW campus collection. Broad reference materials are maintained in the health, behavioral, and related life sciences. Monographs are purchased which relate to the core research program of the center—neuroscience, reproductive physiology, veterinary medicine, ethology, and conservation—but other campus libraries are heavily relied on for symposia proceedings, and more costly conference reports. Close to 90 percent of Center allocated collection funds support journals; the other 10 percent are applied to monographic and audiovisual purchases.

The principal database used is Medline, but Psych Abstracts and Biology Abstracts are accessed through BRS. The library also has recent years of the Primate Information Center (Seattle, WA) database on hard disk. This database, which is updated monthly from a search of ten different databases for primate citations, is the most comprehensive data source for primatology. In addition to outside databases, the center library has created two in-house data files—one governing its 12,000-item reprint file and searchable on the Center's UNIX system, and the other for the audiovisual collection which is managed through Knowledge Man and AskSam. The library is a contributing member in the UW NLS (Network Library System) On-Line Catalog, which provides access to materials housed in twenty-six of the major campus libraries.

In 1974, a document delivery service was established for Center staff. A graduate student from the UW library school was hired to manage the activity, which has consistently produced 4,000 requests per year from a fairly small core staff. The program has evolved so that staff can call up a document delivery form on their office terminals and send requests to the library. They are filled on a twenty-four-hour turn-around time, photocopied, and delivered to staff mail boxes.

In keeping with the regional role of the Primate Center and the charge of the National Institutes of Health Primate Centers Program, the library is playing an active role in the dissemination of information to people outside the boundaries of the campus and the state. In addition to participating in WILS (Wisconsin Interlibrary Services) and OCLC, the library publishes the newsletters *Primate Library Report: Print Acquisitions* (bimonthly) and *Primate Library Report: Audiovisual Acquisitions* (biannually), which are widely distributed and account for a major source of loans to individuals in the U.S. and abroad. The development of an audiovisual collection of 5,000 slides and videotapes relating to nonhuman primates has been well received. Both the newsletter and a newly published catalog of collection holdings have resulted in increasingly heavy use of these materials. This activity has allowed the library to pay a critical role in collecting and preserving the audiovisual record of endangered nonhuman primates whose existence is threatened by human incursion and destruction of habitat.

Statistics

Sponsor: Wisconsin Regional Primate Research Center, University of Wisconsin-Madison
Name: Primate Center Library
Year established: 1973
Location: 1220 Capitol Court, Madison, WI 53715-1299
Name of head of unit: Lawrence Jacobsen
Title of head of unit: Library Director
Title of supervisor of head of unit: Center Director
Staff size: 2.5 FTE professionals; 1.25 FTE non-professionals (total persons: 7)
Main subjects covered: Primatology; Ethology; Reproductive physiology; Neuroscience
Collection Size:
       Books: 6,000 volumes
       Bound journal volumes: 10,000
       Current subscriptions: 342
       Audiovisual: 4,500 slides, 300 videotapes, 200 audiotapes
       Reprints: 12,000
Number of professional users: 1,000 plus
Area of unit: 3,000 sq. ft.
Number of seats: 25

For-Profit Organizations

Corporations and other types of business firms have long been active in sponsoring libraries and information centers. Some firms sponsor a whole network of corporate libraries, so vital have they become to the business world. The range of services and sizes of collections offered by these units are very closely related to the success of the sponsoring firms. A variety of ways of funding is a feature of the libraries in this category, depending upon the type of businesses involved, since they include law firms, research laboratories, and publishing companies, to name but a few.

AT&T Bell Laboratories Libraries and Information Systems Center

[Scientific Research]

Joseph A. Canose

The Libraries and Information Systems Center directs the operations of the AT&T Library Network, a resource-sharing association across AT&T entity companies, linking libraries and information service groups at several AT&T sites. This network links together thirty-eight facilities and twenty specialized information service groups.

AT&T's 100,000 professional employees in over 4,000 sites nationwide are the customers of the information services provided by this network. AT&T Bell Laboratories, the research and development arm of AT&T, is the primary consumer of the network's scientific and technical information services and collections. The sales and marketing organizations within AT&T use the network's business and marketplace information services, although other parts of the company are becoming increasingly dependent on these resources.

The primary mission of the AT&T Library Network is to provide information services needed by individuals and groups within AT&T at competitive cost. Information delivery is a critical component of this mission for such a large, geographically dispersed organization. As an essential approach to minimizing the distances and costs in meeting its mission, the network provides an "electronic window" to the vast array of internal and external information services, thereby assuring that the underlying resources are managed as strategic assets providing a competitive advantage to AT&T.

Information access stations are used to maintain onsite service facilities at some sites, without the large costs of a traditional library. In order to optimize space, these access stations occupy small areas utilizing compact electronic, optical, and microform storage technology. In addition to small journal and reference book collections, these access stations are staffed by a skilled information service employee.

Another extensive aspect of our service–delivery architecture is the provision of the LINUS menu of electronic databases. This system, resident on a mainframe computer, is accessible from professional employee office terminals and work stations anywhere in AT&T. Databases on the system range from books and journals to personal information, photographs, internal documentation, and jobs, to name a few. Delivering full-text databases to employee offices is a long-term goal beginning to be realized with some internal databases on this system. The other electronic interface to the network services is a remote ordering system built around an electronic mail facade, which provides employees with access to these services via their own local computers.

Many specialized and centralized information service groups exist within the network. Examples of these groups are centralized acquisitions and cataloging, internal and external information alerting publications, in-depth business and technical searching, centralized document supply, corporate archives, and systems design and programming.

Managing the network as a customer-driven operation reflects the style of AT&T's corporate culture. Products are organized by product lines and operate on a chargeback rather than an overhead basis. Annual business plans are utilized in order to project demand and unit cost. Strategic planning is employed for future development. Other manifestations of the business orientation of operations are a centralized marketing organization and the production of an annual report, including a cash flow statement.

Although book, journal, and internal or external document supply remain the core business of the network, value–added services, that condense, announce, and analyze information in customized formats, are experiencing significant growth. A strong customer focus, with measurable quality objectives, and demonstrated value to the corporation, are key components of the network's strategy. Simple, yet effective programs, such as one-stop-information-service, take advantage of networked operations from a customer viewpoint and are driving a customer focus throughout the network.

Managing a network representing most of AT&T's major technical and business information resources involves a significant commitment of resources and is indicative of AT&T management's recognition of the value of access to strategic information assets.

Statistics

Sponsor: AT&T Bell Laboratories
Name of unit: Libraries and Information Systems Center
Year established: 1925
Location: 600 Mountain Avenue, Murray Hill, NJ 07974-2070
Name of head of unit: W. David Penniman
Title of head of unit: Libraries and Information Systems Director
Title of supervisor of head of unit: Executive Director, Technical Information Systems Division
Staff size: 85 professionals and 119 non-professionals
Main subjects collected: Telecommunications; Computing; and Business
Collection Size:
      Books: 276,000
      Current subscriptions: 12,000
      Bound journal volumes: 163,000
      Technical reports: 341,000
      Internal reports: 737,000
      Corporate archives: 867,000
Number of professional users: 100,000
Number of seats for users: Approximately 600 in 38 facilities

Booz, Allen Research Services

[Management Consultants]
Robin Blumenthal
[Note: This section was written by Richard Willner, who has since taken a position with another company.]
Booz, Allen supports Research Service units in thirteen locations worldwide. The New York unit is the largest one. Services, staffing, and resources vary with local needs and conditions.

Strong cooperation between the research units helps supply the entire firm, including smaller offices, with the best research resources available.

Together, the research centers' long-term mission is to provide assignment teams with access to all the published data relevant to the problems articulated in consulting work plans. This involves:

- Identifying all sources and data potentially relevant to a problem
- Evaluating specific source contents in relation to the problem
- Identifying any additional research steps generated by the first two

The benefits to Booz, Allen are improved client staff leveraging through cost-effective secondary research service.

The research centers have initiated cooperative information management programs to realize this mission. The first is to create firm-wide contracts for external data. This program makes basic numeric and bibliographic data available throughout the firm in a consistent format and at a reasonable cost.

We have also installed uniform library management software to facilitate firm-wide resource exchange. Additional initiatives include cooperative training and development for information specialists, research center user guides, and promotional materials.

To make the most effective use of Booz, Allen research centers, client staff are trained to contact local units early in a consulting assignment and provide key details about the client situation. That permits each unit the time to do the best possible job and also, when necessary, to contact information specialists in other offices.

Statistics

Sponsor: Booz, Allen & Hamilton Inc.
Name of Unit: Research Services
Location: 101 Park Avenue, New York, NY 10178
Year established: 1945
Name of head of unit: Robin Blumenthal
Title of head of unit: Manager of Research Services
Title of supervisor of head of unit: Vice–President in Charge of Operations & Finance
Staff size: 10 professionals / 3 support
Main subjects collected: Business; Technology
Collection Size:
        Books: 3,500
        Current subscriptions: 425
        File drawers: 625
        Report archives: 8,500 volumes
        Timesharing systems accessed: 26
        Compact disc databases: 6
Professional users: 300

Chevron Research and Technology Company

[Petroleum Engineering]

Jacqueline J. Desoer

Chevron Research and Technology Company maintains a medium-sized technical library serving the information needs of a major petroleum and petrochemical research company. The Technical Library serves 1400 scientists, engineers, and support staff working on petroleum process chemistry and engineering, catalyst research, and product development. Along with Technical Files (a records management unit which processes internal reports and correspondence) and Translation Services, it forms the company's Technical Information Center. It is one of eleven libraries within Chevron Corporation, its subsidiaries, and affiliates that make up the Chevron Library Resources Network.

The library's major functions include literature and patent searching, reference service, SDI, books and serials purchased for the collection as well as for clients, journal routing, patent procurement, and interlibrary borrowing. It is also responsible for issuing, storing, and maintaining a database of all laboratory notebooks.

The library's collection consists of books, conference proceedings, journals, government documents, patents, society publications, and published company reports. The patent collection is extensive and includes both United States and foreign patents. All significant materials are selected in analytical and organic chemistry, catalysts, petroleum refining technology, petroleum fuels and lubricants, petrochemicals, chemicals for enhanced oil recovery, industrial waste and hazardous materials minimization and management. Basic materials are also purchased in areas such as inorganic and physical chemistry, combustion processes, physics, toxicology, computers, management, and general business.

During the 1980s, the library gradually automated most of its functions. Acquisitions, cataloging, inquiry, and circulation used Sydney Development Company's integrated library software running on a Datapoint minicomputer. Serials purchasing and routing were programmed in-house and ran on the miniframe. In 1989, the library purchased a DEC MicroVAX 3600 computer and all modules were converted from Sydney to Datalib (Centel Federal Services Corporation) software. This move allowed the library to integrate all functions, automate serials check-in, and develop files for Chevron Research papers and patents, translations, and other miscellaneous data.

Staff who search the technical files have chemistry or biological science degrees. Staff with non-technical degrees specialize in searching the business, economic, and competitive intelligence files. Most have an M.L.S.

Sponsor: Chevron Research and Technology Company
Name of Unit: Technical Library
Year established: 1920
Location: 100 Chevron Way (P.O. Box 1627), Richmond, CA 94802
Head of unit: Jacqueline J. Desoer
Title of head of unit: Supervisor,   Technical Library
Title of supervisor of head of unit: Manager, Technical Information Services
Staff size: 7 information analysts; 7 library assistants

Main subjects collected: Chemistry; Petroleum refining research; Petrochemicals; Industrial waste and hazardous materials minimization, and Management.
Collection Size:

Books: 15,000

Current subscriptions: 1,350

Bound journal volumes: We no longer keep a count since we are gradually converting large numbers of older volumes to microfilm

Technical reports and pamphlets: 25,000

Patents: 2,876,000 (most on microfilm)

Number of professional users (potential): 600

Area of unit: 7,000 sq. ft.

Number of seats for users: 20

Daiwa Securities America Inc. Reference Library
[Investment Banking]
Susan M. Gormley

The purpose of establishing a library at Daiwa Securities America Inc. was to improve the productivity and capabilities of all departments located in New York City. As a fully-equipped information center, the library has greatly enhanced the ability of Daiwa America to carry out research, conduct investment banking operations, improve portfolio management, and respond quickly to worldwide requests for information.

Housed in a single location, the library is a managed collection of well-balanced general business reference materials (in English and Japanese), a collection of the most essential textbooks on financial analysis and accounting, a wide variety of business journals and periodicals (in English and Japanese), comprehensive corporate files, and the capability to carry out online database searches.

Although some of these same capabilities presently exist in various departments of Daiwa Securities, it was felt that a systematically organized reference library was important to remain competitive with other investment banking firms.

Daiwa's library is unique, in that it is the first bilingual reference library collection on Wall Street. It was generally agreed that the library's reference collection should contain 30 percent Japanese text and 70 percent in English.

There are ten major sections in the library: Annual Reports, Company Files, Industry Files, Japanese Collection, Newsletters, Newspapers, Periodicals, Quick Reference, Reference Collection and United States Government Publications.

Annual reports and company files consist of those firms in the Fortune 1,000 and include 10-Ks, 10-Qs, press releases, and interim financial statements.

Of the ten newspapers maintained in the library, eight are in English and two are in the Japanese language. Full text of English language newspapers are maintained for one year on a rolling retention basis, while the Japanese newspapers are maintained for five years. The reason for the differing lengths of retention is because of the availability of U.S. newspapers through online retrieval services.

There are approximately 120 titles in the library's periodicals collection. This collection is nicely balanced with journals geared toward general business, the securities industry, Federal Reserve materials, United States government materials, and trade journals. Departments within the firm are encouraged to contribute their journals to the library in order to share resources with all employees.

In addition, the Japanese collection consists of approximately 40 titles. As with the English language periodicals collection, some of the titles are general interest magazines, others are more focused toward the securities industry, and some are statistical in scope.

Daiwa's library subscribes to four online services; DIALOG, Nexis/Lexis, Dow Jones News/Retrieval, and Investext/Plus. These online services are utilized as a supplement to the library's print reference collection. Patrons are encouraged to retrieve articles in hard copy before requesting articles online. Online searching is mostly performed to supplement the industry files which are still in their infancy stages.

Tours of Daiwa's library are given to new employees, and color illustrations of the library are posted throughout the firm. The library publishes a bimonthly newsletter to acquaint employees with the library—its location, hours, policies, and collection. Each issue of the newsletter highlights and discusses different aspects of the collection.

Statistics

Sponsor: Daiwa Securities America Inc.
Year established: December 1988
Name of unit: Reference Library
Location: 200 Liberty Street, Tower A—24th Floor, New York, NY   10281
Name of head of unit: Susan M. Gormley
Title of head of unit: Librarian
Title of supervisor of head of unit: Assistant Director of Research
Staff size: One professional, one part-time clerical support
Main subjects collected: Securities industry; Economics; General reference works
Collection Size:
        Books: 500
        Current subscriptions: 60
        Bound journal volumes: None
        Pamphlets, reports, audiovisuals: None
Number of professional users: 150
Area of unit: 1,000 sq. ft
Number of seats for users: 7

Federal National Mortgage Association

[Real Estate Financing]

Eileen E. Rourke

Fannie Mae is the fifth largest corporation in the United States and the nation's largest investor in conventional home mortgages. Founded in 1938, Fannie Mae is now a publicly owned and privately managed corporation traded on the stock exchange. Library services are available to its 2,500 employees including five regional offices, although the major clients are the professional staff in the home office. The Corporate Library was developed to fulfill the need for a centralized resource for business and Fannie Mae information.

The mission of the Fannie Mae central library is to provide and facilitate access to information and informational materials in support of the company's programs, activities, and interests. The library is to serve as the principal research depository for published external information and as a focal point for the exchange and flow of internal information.

Besides acquiring external publications, the library serves as the official depository for most company publications and related documents, including internal historical records and files. The collection emphasizes reference materials, pertinent periodicals, newspapers, and newsletters. The library has access to all the major online databases as well as selected indexes, including CD-ROM.

Other highlights of the collection include federal census publications and statistical materials related to housing. Annual reports and SEC documents are collected on selective financial service firms.

The library provides several types of reference services, including ongoing customized database searches, monitoring of borrowing/visiting privileges with other libraries, and advice for end-user searching.

Name of unit: Corporate Library
Year established: 1989
Location: 3900 Wisconsin Ave. N.W., Washington, DC 20016
Head of unit: Eileen E. Rourke
Title of head of unit: Manager, Corporate Library Services
Title of supervisor of head of unit: Vice-President, Housing Policy Research
Main subjects collected: Housing; Real estate; Mortgage-backed securities; Banking & finance
Collection Size (in developmental stage):
          Subscriptions: 250
          Books & reports: 700
          Annual reports: 100
          Miscellaneous: Internal archives/report files
Area of unit: 1,400 sq. ft. (plus offices outside main library)
Number of seats for users: 8

Jones, Day, Reavis & Pogue

[Law Firm]

Joan E. Jarosek

Jones, Day, Reavis & Pogue is an international law firm with 17 offices in the United States and abroad. With approximately 1,000 lawyers, it is one of the largest law firms in the world. The firm is engaged in the general practice of law and is regarded as having substantial legal expertise in all areas of business activity. The ten U.S. offices of JDR&P each have their own library and librarian(s) who are responsible for meeting the information needs of their respective office. The librarians each administer their own libraries, which function as independent units. At the minimum, each library houses a core legal collection which consists of the primary sources of federal and the respective state's law, as well as secondary sources of the law representative of the particular office's practice. The librarians strive towards a cooperative arrangement in planning, collection development, and interlibrary loans. Sharing records among the libraries is extensive. The libraries subscribe to OCLC, which is utilized for cataloging and interlibrary loans. Planning has begun for a firm-wide online union catalog.

The Dallas Library's collection supports the needs of the approximately 140 resident lawyers representing several practice groups in the Dallas office: Corporate, Litigation, Tax, and Real Estate. The collection consists of the primary and secondary sources of the law. Primary sources include cases, decisions of the federal and state courts, and statutory compilations and administrative regulations of the federal and state governments. Texts and treatises comprise most of the secondary source collection and are updated by supplements, pocket parts, and revised volumes. These materials are representative of the specific practice areas, such as corporate, securities, banking, bankruptcy, tax, and labor law. A periodical collection of law reviews and trade journals and an extensive business reference collection are also part of the library's collection.

The library is responsible for providing an extensive array of services. In addition to the acquisition, cataloging, and maintenance of the collection, the librarians are regarded as the firm's information specialists. In this capacity, they are called upon to make available a wide range of reference services. These includes answering reference questions, performing research, acquiring various corporate and court documents, providing online searching on legal and non-legal databases, and a current awareness service. A newsletter, which includes the acquisitions list, database news and searching tips, and other information of interest, is produced and distributed by the library. The library also has the responsibility of coordinating database training. Desktop access to databases is available within the firm. Additionally, an attorney work product file is maintained by the library.

Statistics

Sponsor: Jones, Day, Reavis & Pogue
Name of unit: Library (Dallas Office)
Year established: 1981
Location: 2300 Trammell Crow Center, 2001 Ross Avenue, Dallas, TX 75201
Head of unit: Joan E. Jarosek
Title of head of unit: Librarian
Title of supervisor of head of unit: Office Administrator, Library Partner
Staff size: 2 professionals; 4 others
Main subjects collected: Law
Collection Size:
        Books: 30,000 volumes
        Current subscriptions: 695
        Bound journal volumes: 1,909
        Newspapers: 19
Number of professional users: 150 lawyers and 40 legal assistants
Area of unit: 8,000 sq. ft.
Number of seats for users: 40

Newsweek Editorial Library
[Periodical Publisher]
Peter Salber
[Note: This section was written by Ted Slate, who was until recently the head of the library until he was promoted to another position.]

The title—Editorial Library—is a misnomer. The library not only serves Newsweek's editorial staff in New York and its 25 bureaus in the United States and around the world, but it supports the information needs of the business departments—advertising, promotion, legal, public affairs, etc.—and the company's clients (advertisers and advertising agencies). The library's services are also available to all employees of the subsidiaries of Newsweek's parent company, the Washington Post Company. These include those on assignment in New York, the Washington Post corporate staff, the Stanley H. Kaplan Educational Centers, Post-Newsweek stations (television) and Post-Newsweek Cable.

Newsweek established the Editorial Library in 1933, the year the magazine began. The staff presently numbers twenty: eight professionals, ten full-time non-professionals, and two part-time non-professionals. They are organized into five sections: the Library Director's office (two persons), Index (two persons), Acquisitions (two persons), Reference (five librarians and a reference clerk), and Clipping, Marking and Filing (six full-time and two part-time staffers).

The Index staff provides author, title, and subject access to every story appearing in the domestic edition of the magazine, as well as in its three international editions—European, Asian, and Latin American. They also receive telephone calls and written and in-person inquiries from the general public and Newsweek staffers asking when or if a certain story or stories appeared in the magazine.

The Acquisitions section buys or borrows books, magazines of articles requested by the library or other editorial departments. It also records bibliographical information for all review books received by the magazine (any of which can be catalogued for eventual shelving in the library), catalogs all materials, and issues a "New Books List" for all domestic and foreign staffers.

The clipping, marking, and filing staff selects and preserves a wide variety of newspaper and magazine materials and files these alphabetically into one of three divisions of the files: biography, subjects/countries, and organizations. The staff also weeds unwanted clippings from the collections.

The librarians of the Reference section are assigned subject responsibilities corresponding to the departments of the magazine, e.g., national affairs, culture, medicine, sports, etc. Routinely, the library's research support consists of gathering a wide variety of background data for the research, writing, and editing staff in preparation for stories, and assisting with fact-checking after stories have been written. However, the reference staff will undertake research for any Washington Post Company staffer. Newsweek views its librarians as individuals with unique reference and research skills who should be available to all company employees for any eventuality related to the information needs of the company.

In summary, all sections of the library operate for one purpose: to support the company's reference and research needs. This objective allows for the justification of new services and the prioritization of more-established services based on budgetary or other considerations.

Sponsor: Newsweek, Inc.
Name of unit: Editorial Library
Year established: 1933
Location: 444 Madison Avenue, New York, NY 10022
Name of Head of Unit: Peter Salber
Title of Head of Unit: Library Director
Title of Supervisor of Head of Unit: Director of Research Services
Staff size: 8 professionals; 10 non-professionals
Main subjects collected: All areas of current events; Media
Collection Size:
       Books: 38,000
       Current subscriptions: 1,300
       Bound journal volumes: 1,560
       Pamphlets, reports, audio-visual units, etc.:
         4,800 reels of microfilm and microfiche
         300,000 file folders containing clippings, reports, pamphlets and journal articles
Number of professional users:
       250 in New York
       125 other editorial and advertising employees worldwide
Area of unit: 6,955 sq. ft.
Number of seats for users: 10

Royal Bank of Canada Information Resources

[International Banking]

Jane I. Dysart

Information Resources is a large special library serving a large multinational bank with many subsidiaries and affiliates. The information needs of The Royal Bank of Canada are met by four libraries: Information Resources (two locations—Montreal, Toronto), Technical Reference Centre (Toronto), Law Library (Toronto), and Law/Tax Library (Montreal). The four libraries are administratively separate but cooperate for planning, development, and interlibrary loans. The Law and Tax libraries are specialized centres serving the Law and Tax departments of the bank. The Technical Reference Centre focuses on serving the Operations and Systems areas of the bank by providing technical manuals and materials to about 3,000 staff in Toronto.

Information Resources services 1,500 bank branches across Canada and approximately 100 international sites. In 1989, Information Resources merged with the libraries of the securities firms purchased by the bank, RBC Dominion Securities, and Pemberton Securities. Services are provided to the retail, research, mergers and acquisitions, and corporate finance areas of these firms.

The majority of requests handled by Information Resources relate to company and industry information. In answering these requests, Information Resources relies on the collection described below. In addition, the department relies heavily on automation. Every person on staff has a microcomputer which is used for one or more of the following applications: word processing, spreadsheets, uploading and downloading, communications for online searching, electronic mail, periodical control (check-in, routing, subscription information), book circulation, sending facsimile transmissions. The union catalog of materials held in the two locations is online with a service bureau and accessed through communications software.

Sponsor: The Royal Bank of Canada
Name of Unit: Information Resources
Year established: 1913 in Montreal, 1972 in Toronto
Locations: Royal Bank Plaza, Toronto, Ontario, Canada, M5J 2J5
                   1 Place Ville Marie, Montreal, Quebec, Canada, H3C- 3A9
Head of Unit: Jane I. Dysart
Title: Manager of Information Resources
Supervisor of Head of Unit: Deputy Chief Economist, Economic & Corporate Affairs
Staff Size: 10 professionals; 4 support plus 1 part-time
Main subjects collected: Banking and finance; Economics;
                                         Canadian and international industries;
                                         Trade and management

Collection Size:

          Books: 30,000 volumes

          Current subscriptions: 2,200

          Bound journal volumes: 1,000

          Microfilm reels: 1,500

          Microfiche: 10,000

          Annual reports: 5,000

          Pamphlets, Clippings: 40 vertical file drawers

Special collections: Statistics (Canada on microfiche)

                         Ontario Securities Commission (filings on microfiche for 5 years)

                         Montreal Stock Exchange (filings on microfiche)

Number of potential users: 46,000

Area of units: 2,600 sq. ft. in Toronto; 3,800 in Montreal

Number of seats for users: 20

Appendix 2

Planning a Corporate Library: The Merrill Lynch Capital Markets Library

by Richard Drezen

Much can be learned by studying the steps taken in the planning of an actual library. The example chosen is that of the Merrill Lynch Capital Markets Library, located in the new World Financial Center complex in New York City. The results show the value of careful, thoughtful planning and of working closely with a team of consultants, architects, designers, and space planners.

Description of the Library

The new library contains 10,300 square feet, and, as the accompanying floor plan attests, it is a spacious facility designed for a large and active user population drawn from various Merrill Lynch divisions. The library is divided into three basic units—the reference area, the documents area, and the records center. It was felt early on in the planning that once new users entered the library it was best to introduce them to experienced staff who could answer their questions and provide assistance as needed. Consequently the reference desk was situated directly in front of the main entrance. If users need to go to the documents desk or to the records center they can be directed by the reference librarians. Reference requests are made by walk-in, telephone, fax/telecopy and electronic mail (via a local area network). Both the reference and documents desks were designed in horseshoe shapes for easy access. Designed with a shiny mahogany surface, they project an attractive and modern look.

Adjacent to the reference area is a variety of print and online services. The collection is divided into sections for books, periodicals, newspapers, government documents, and reference materials. A new electronic online catalog enables users to search book titles or authors as well as Merrill Lynch client presentations. CD-ROM products can be accessed directly by users at the reference desk. Librarians can access online systems at the reference desk or at their individual work stations, located in back of the reference desk. Photocopiers and microfilm readers are available nearby.

Many people come to the library to obtain documents. They are usually looking for some type of Securities & Exchange Commission filing on a public company. These filings or documents can be traced by using an online index at the documents desk to determine if they are available in-house or if they have to be ordered from a service bureau. If in-house, the

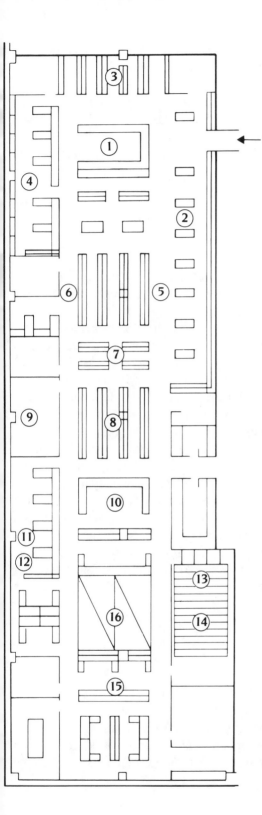

Merrill Lynch Capital Markets Library

1. Reference Desk
   • print and online sources
   • interlibrary loans

2. Books
   • reference and general circulation
   • indexes and abstracts
   • newspapers

3. Periodicals
   • magazines, journals, newsletters
   • government documents (U.S. government and multi-lateral)

4. Subject Files

5. Current Prospectuses

6. Current Annual Reports

7. International Files

8. Corporate files

9. Computer Room
   • new issues data base

10. Documents Desk
    • online indexes to SEC filings
    • laser Disclosure printer

11. Technical Services
12. • cataloging, subscriptions, routing

13. Historical Prospectuses

14. Merrill Lynch Deal Files

15. Records Center
16. • Merrill Lynch client presentations
    • microfiche collection
    • archives

documents may exist in a hard-copy format in the corporate files or may be printed from the extensive microfiche collection on a high-speed, state-of-the-art printer. A new CD-laser printer enables users to print their own documents.

The records center stores and archives internal investment banking documents using an automated file system for on-site storage. Historical documents are archived in off-site storage. The prime consideration in designing space for the records center was for space, bulk storage needs, and the ability to have close access to the system in order to maintain control over confidential records. Manual rolling files were also utilized for storing current and historical documents so that they could be accessed directly by users.

Planning the Library

The library officially opened in the new complex in the spring of 1987. The previous library had been in the old Merrill Lynch headquarters in lower Manhattan for approximately fifteen years. By the time of the planning for the move to the new building the chief librarian and her staff were confronted with the classic example of a rapidly expanding library and staff coping with a small space. Actual planning began three years prior to the move, and a library design consulting firm was contracted to assist with the design and planning of the new facility.

Planning for any new building necessitates numerous meetings, and that was the case for this library. The chief librarian met frequently with the architects, the designers, and the building planners. She used the library consultant to monitor the ensuing work, to ensure decisions that had been made were followed through on, and to act as the library's "advocate" during the entire planning process. The goal for all was a new facility that would be one of the best libraries—if not *the* best—on Wall Street and would reflect a "user-friendly" environment where users would find the information they needed as quickly as possible.

A great deal of thought was given to the library's decor. Dark wood trim and rose-colored carpeting emphasize a warm, professional look. Signs clearly identify the various sections of the library. Consideration was given to seating; five tables each accommodate four users to do work in the library. Each reference librarian has his/her own work station, thus permitting them to do research while away from the reference desk. Both the library manager and assistant manager have attractively designed offices. Toward the rear of the library is a conference room.

Moving the Library

The move into the new complex was accomplished over a weekend, and the new library was open on a Monday morning and began functioning smoothly. While there were no major problems, the chief librarian in hindsight suggested she could have used additional electrical outlets and data lines for the computers. But a thorough study of the needs of the staff and users had ensured ample space for the present and allowed flexibility for growth into the future. At the time of this writing plans are under way to further expand the library and create additional space for computer resources and direct end usage.

Statistics

Corporate Name: Merrill Lynch Capital Markets Library
Year Established: 1972
Location: Merrill Lynch World Headquarters
World Financial Center
250 Vesey Street—24th Floor
New York, NY 10281-1324
Telephone: (212) 449-3814
Hours:
Staffed: 8:30 AM-8:30 PM M-F
Open Access 24 hours—7 days a week
Manager: Eva Vanek
Assistant Manager: Susan Adinolfi
Library reports to: Director of Finance & Administration, Investment Banking
Staff size: 23 Professionals (includes 9 Librarians) 14 Others
Main subjects: Business & economics; Investments & securities; Mergers & acquisitions
Collection size: Books: 2,000 volumes
Current subscriptions: 950
Bound journal volumes: 100
Microform/Microfiche holdings: over 7,000 corporate files on domestic and international companies
Number of professional users: 700 (potential)
Area: 10,300 sq. ft.
Architects: Skidmore, Owings & Merrill
Library consultant: Designs for Information

Appendix 3

Selected Books on Special Librarianship

For readers interested in detailed information about the operation and management of special libraries/information centers that is beyond the scope of this book, there are several useful treatises that may be of help. A few of these books cover all types of special libraries, while the others are devoted to one particular type, such as health sciences or art libraries. The output is uneven, with some disciplines better represented than others. It is hoped that in due time titles dealing with topics at present neglected will appear.

This is not meant to be an exhaustive bibliography; it is very selective. Some worthwhile titles may have been overlooked in the preparation of this section. The reader should keep abreast of new titles being published as there seems to be an increase in the number of books on special librarianship appearing in recent years.

There are basically two styles used in these books: one consists of a text prepared by one or two authors, which covers the important topics in a systematic fashion. The second style is a collection of papers written by as many as seventy different authors; some articles were prepared especially for the occasion, while others were reprinted from library periodicals—a few of them have been classics of the profession.

Selected Books on Special Librarianship

General Works

1. Jackson, Eugene B., ed. *Special librarianship: a new reader*. Ann Arbor, MI: Books on Demand; 1980. 759 p.

    Although no longer a "new" source, this collection of seventy papers is still a useful compilation of articles concerned with all aspects of special librarianship, including management, public relations, reader services, technical services, and similar topics. A number of the papers are considered to be classics.

Arts and Humanities

2. Bradley, Carol June, ed. *Reader in music librarianship*. Westport, CT: Greenwood; 1983. 340 p.

Contains more than fifty articles on a wide variety of subjects, including copyright, thematic catalogs, handling of tapes and records, types of music libraries, and training for music librarianship.

3.   Bryant, E. T.; Marco, Guy A. *Music librarianship; a practical guide.* 2d ed. Metuchen, NJ: Scarecrow Press; 1985. 449 p.

Chapters deal with such topics as administration, reference books and periodicals, sound recordings, cataloging, and classification. Both the British and the U.S. practices are described.

4.   Cave, Roderick. *Rare book librarianship.* 2d rev. ed. Chicago: American Library Association; 1982. 162 p.

Discusses the nature of rare books, care and restoration of books, organizing collections, and training for the field.

5.   Jones, Lois Swan; Gibson, Sarah Scott. *Art libraries and information services: development, organization, and management.* San Diego, CA: Academic Press; 1986. 344 p.

Covers all types of art libraries, emphasizing such functions as reference services, cataloging, management, and collection development.

6.   Larsen, John C., ed. *Museum librarianship.* Hamden, CT: Shoe String Press; 1985. 136 p.

Contains nine chapters written by authorities in their respective fields, covering staffing, collection development, organizing collections, library service, and design of facilities.

Science/Technology

7.   *Handbook of medical library practice.* 4th ed. Edited by Louise Darling. Chicago: Medical Library Association; 1982-1988. 3 vols.

Volume 1 deals with public services, including lending services, reference services and research. Volume 2 concerns technical services, such as collection development, acquisition techniques, cataloging, classification, and serials control. Volume 3 centers on management topics but also includes the history of medical libraries, an account of the National Library of Medicine, and space planning.

8.   Mount, Ellis, ed. *Management of sci-tech libraries.* New York: Haworth Press; 1984. 169 p. (Also published as *Science & Technology Libraries.* 4(3/4): 1984 Spring/Summer)

Has eight papers concerned with the management techniques used in sci-tech libraries. Examples include corporate, government, and academic libraries. Planning, budgeting, and personnel management are some of the topics covered.

9.   Pruett, Nancy Jones. *Scientific and technical libraries.* San Diego, CA: Academic Press; 1986. 2 vols.

Volume 1, entitled *Functions and management,* describes a wide range of activities (reference service, collection development, document delivery, management, space planning, and library automation, among others). One chapter describes operations in three different sci-tech special libraries. Volume 2, entitled *Special formats and subject areas,* concentrates on the materials and sources used in various sci-tech libraries, such as patents, technical reports, and conference literature. The last seven chapters indicate the specific types of literature used in different sci-tech disciplines (engineering, geology, and the like).

Social Sciences

10. McMichael, Betty. *The church librarian's handbook: a complete guide for the library and resource center in Christian education.* Grand Rapids, MI: Baker Book House; 1984. 277 p.

Chapters deal with staffing, policies, technical services, selection of materials, and financing. Appendixes list a classification system as well as special subject headings appropriate for such libraries.

11. Panella, Deborah S. *Basics of law librarianship.* New York: Haworth Press; 1991. 118 p.

Aims at providing basic guidelines for the operation of any type of law library, whether corporate, government, or academic. Discusses basic operations and management, technical services, user services, and collection development. Presents an account that is suitable for the newcomer to the field.

12. *Reflections on law librarianship: a collection of interviews.* Prepared by Marjorie A. Garson, Sima Dabirashtiani, Rosalie L. Sherwin, Elmo F. Dattalo, and Susan L. Perrine. Littleton, CO: Fred B. Rothman; 1988. 262 p. Sponsored by the American Association of Law Libraries; AALL Publ. Series No. 29.

Consists of interviews of 12 law librarians representing various types of law libraries: academic, private, governmental, and court. The purpose of the book was to gain an insight into the activities of such libraries, their history, and their management. Taking a long view of the future of law libraries was another goal. Provides fascinating reading.

Special Media

13. Harrison, Helen P., ed. *Picture librarianship.* Phoenix, AZ: Oryx Press; 1981. 542 p.

Consists of three dozen articles written on all aspects of picture librarianship, ranging from processing of pictures to copyright problems. A majority of the papers describe the operation of picture libraries in the U.S. and the United Kingdom, including those in corporations, government agencies, and public libraries.

14. Larsgaard, Mary. *Map librarianship: an introduction.* 2d ed. Littleton, CO: Libraries Unlimited; 1986. 392 p.

A thorough treatment of all aspects of the topic, including acquisition, classification, care and storage of maps, reference service, and management topics.

Index

Goals
  organizational, 37-38
  written, 43
Gormley, Susan M., 204
Government publications, 139
  costs of, 151
Graphic forms, 139
Graphical displays of statistics, 81
Graphs, 81
Guides to the literature,
  selected examples of, 140-143

Hiring the staff, 63-64
History
  of information centers, 6-7
  of special libraries, 6-7
Hot lines, role of in job hunting, 186
Humanities, guides to the literature of, 140
Humidity, effects of on materials, 130
Hypertext, 89-90

Indexes, types of, 121-122
Indexing, 120-122
Indexing services, 138
Indicative abstracts, 111
Informal communication, 22-23
Information abstracts of, 25-26
  availability of, 24-25
  bibliographic citations of, 25
  costs of, 24
  definition of, 19
  nature of, 19-28
  nonverbal sources of, 22
  numerical, 21
  oral sources of, 22
  primary sources of, 22
  printed sources of, 22
  reasons for gathering, 23
  restrictions on circulation of, 24
  secondary sources of, 22
  sources of, 21-22
  types of, 21
  verbal sources of, 22
  ways of handling, 20
Information centers
  characteristics of, 3-6
  comparison with special libraries, 3, 13-14
  definition of, 2-3
  descriptions of selected examples, 191-211
  typical examples of, 14-16
Information professionals, types of, 7
Information requests, clarification of, 23-24

Information science, definition of, 19-20
Information transfer, 20-21
Informative abstracts, 111
Instructional activities, 70
Interlibrary loans, 98-99, 175-176
Interpretive information, 21
Interviewing teams, role of in job hunting, 187
Interviews
  employment, 63
  role of in job hunting, 188-189
  of users, 74, 76
Investment banking library, example and floor
  plan of, 212-215

Jacobsen, Lawrence, 197
Jarosek, Joan E., 207
Job descriptions, 57-59
  examples of, 58, 59
  role of in unionization, 66
Job hunting, techniques for, 187-190
Job offers, consideration of, 189
Job openings, awareness of, 186-187
Job titles for managers, 34
Jobbers of books, 125
Jones, Day, Reavis & Pogue Library (Dallas),
  description of, 207-208
Journals. See Periodicals.

Kehoe, Kathleen, 193

LANs. See Local area networks.
Labor unions, 65-66
Laboratory notebooks, 139
Law librarianship, books on, 218
Law library, description of, 207-208
Levels of collections, 145-146
Libraries, moving of, 165-166
Library associations, nature of, 182-185
Library bulletins, 101-102
Library committees, 73
Library facilities
  example and floor plan of
    Merrill Lynch Library, 212-215
  planning of, 162-167
Library materials, types of, 136-143
Library of Congress Classification system, 117
Library of Congress subject headings, 117
Library planning. See Facility planning; Library
  facilities; Planning.
Library schools role of,
  in continuing education, 181
  in job hunting, 187

Relations with top management, 5-6
Request for proposal (RFP), preparation of, 86 -87
Research level of collections, 146
Research Libraries Group. See RLG.
Research Libraries Information Network.
    See RLIN
Restricted circulation of information, 24
Restricted information, availability of, 107-108
Resumes, role of in job hunting, 188
Retention schedules for records, 159
Retrieval of information, 20
Retrieval services, 96-100
    comparison of manual with
    online techniques, 97-98
    online. See Online search techniques.
    techniques for, 96-97
Review series, 137
Rourke, Eileen E., 206
Royal Bank of Canada Information Resources,
    description of, 210-211

SDI. See Selective dissemination of information.
SLA. See Special Libraries Association.
Salaries
    for managers, 33-34
    in special libraries and information centers,
    surveys of, 5
Salber, Peter, 208
Sampling theory, use of in managing, 80
Science and technology,
    guides to the literature of, 141-142
Science librarianship, books on, 217-218
Science libraries
    biology, description of, 193-195
    electronics, description of, 200-201
    petroleum research, description of, 203-204
    primate research library, description of, 197-199
Searching of data. See Retrieval services.
Secondary sources of information, 22
Securities industry library, description of, 204-205
Security. See also Company security;
    Military security.
Security factors,
    effects of on care of materials, 129-130
Security of library positions,
    factors governing, 36-37
Selection principles, 144-145
Selective dissemination of information
    (SDI), 102-103
Serial services, costs of subscriptions for, 150
Serials, weeding of, factors involved, 155-156
Services offered, 4-5
    importance of in special libraries, 36

Shared collection activities, 174-175
Shelving for libraries, 169
Signs and posters, 70
Sizes
    of collections, 4
    of staffs, 4
Slate, Ted, 208
Slides, 139
    preparation of, 81
Social sciences, guides to the literature of, 142-143
Social sciences librarianship, books on, 218
Society of American Archivists, nature of, 185
Sociology, guides to the literature of, 143
Sources of information, 21-22
Sources to search, 95
Space planners for library facilities, 163
Space utilization in facilities, 164
Special librarianship
    bibliography of books on, 216-218
    collection of articles on, 216
Special libraries
    characteristics of, 3-6
    comparison with academic libraries, 8-9
    comparison with information centers, 3, 13-14
    comparison with public libraries, 8
    definition of, 2
    descriptions of selected examples, 191-211
    networks of, 178
    salary surveys of, 5
    typical examples of, 14-16
Special Libraries Association (SLA),
    nature of, 182-183
Specifications, 139
Staff positions, 54
Staffing,
    definition of, 31
Staffs
    burnout of, 67
    composition of, 57
    evaluating of, 64
    firing of, 65
    hiring of, 63-64
    organization of, 54-57
    size of, 57
    training of, 64-65
    unionization of, 65-66
Standards, 139
    for abstracts of information, 25-26
    for bibliographic citations, 25
State-of-the-art reports, 110-111
Statistical analysis, 79-80
Statistical data, collection of, 80
Statistics, nature of, 79-81

and Information Centers   **225**

Stress among staff members, 67
Subject cataloging, 117
Subject headings, 117
Subscription agents, 126
Subscriptions
    for periodicals, costs of, 149-150
    for serial services,
    costs of, 150
Supervision, 62-68
    definition of, 31
Supervisors
    attitudes of, 62-63
    qualities desired in, 62-63
Surveys of users, 74-76
    analysis of results, 76
    confidentiality of data, 75
    contents of, 75
    techniques for conducting, 75-76
    timing of, 74-75
Systems analysis, 82-84

Technical librarianship, books on, 217-218
Technical reports, 138
    indexing of, 121-122
Technical services, 115-134
Technology, role of, 79-93
Technology and science,
    guides to the literature of, 141-142
Temperatures, effects of on materials, 130
Temporary workers, 63-64
Textual data, 21
Thank-you notes, 70, 188
Theatre Library Association, nature of, 185
Thefts of materials, 130
Thesauri, 121
Time management, 44
Time schedules for data retrieval, 95-96
Timing of surveys, 74-75
Top management,
    relations of managers with 36-41
Trade catalogs, 139
Training of staff members, 64-65
Transfer of information, 20-21
Transformation of information, 20
Translating, 112
Translations, 139
    sources of, 112
Transparencies, preparation of, 81
Travel funds for managers, 33-34
Turnkey automation systems, 118-119
Turnkey systems, 86-87, 118-119

UDC. See Universal Decimal Classification.
Union lists, cooperation in producing, 176-177
Unionization of staff members, 65-66
Universal Decimal Classification (UDC), 116
University Club Library,
    description of, 195-196
Unpublished printed materials, 138-139
User services, 95-114
    examples of, 16
Users, surveys of. See Surveys of users.

Verbal sources of information, 22
Vermin, effects of on materials, 130
Video tapes, 139
    use of in orientation of employees, 71

Weeding of collections, 153-157
    disposing of weeded items, 156-157
    reasons for, 153-154
Whitney Museum of American Art Library,
    description of, 196-197
Wholesalers of books, 125
Willner, Richard, 201
Wisconsin Regional Primate Research Center
    Library, description of, 197-199
Word of mouth communication,
    role of in job hunting, 187
Work assignments, role of managers in, 66-67
Working level of collections, 146
Writing, services offered, 110-113

Yearbooks, 137

ZBB. See Zero-Based Budgeting.
Zero-Based Budgeting (ZBB), 48
Zoology library, description of 197-199

Notes

Notes

Notes

Notes

Notes

Notes